The
BASENJI

Out of Africa to You: A New Look

by Susan Coe

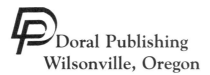

Doral Publishing
Wilsonville, Oregon

Third Printing, 1997

Published by Doral Publishing, 8560 Salish Lane #300, Wilsonville, Oregon 97070-9612.
Printed in the United States of America.

Copyedited by Luana Luther, Nancy Bridge, Robin Stark.
Book Design by Fred Christensen.
Cover Photo by Mitsuyohi Tatematsu.

Library of Congress Card Number: 94-68114
ISBN: 0-944875-42-4

Third printing

Coe, Susan.
    The basenji: out of Africa to you—a new look/ by Susan Coe.—Wilsonville, Or. :
Doral Pub., 1994.

    p. : ill. ; cm.

    Includes bibliographical references and index.
    ISBN: 0-944875-42-4

    1. Basenji. 2. Basenji—United States. I. Title.

SF429.B15C   636.7'53 dc20

CONTENTS

SECTION III—Basenji Activities

SECTION IV—Influences on the Breed

SECTION V—A Look at the Standard

SECTION VI—The Basis of Heredity

SECTION VII—Becoming A Breeder

SECTION VIII—A Look at the Standard

SECTION IX—Bibliography & Index

WHY A NEW LOOK?

Less than five years have passed since the first edition of "Out of Africa" was going to press but those few years have had a tremendous number of "firsts" for Basenjis. The most basic change was the American Kennel Club's acceptance of the newest African imports as foundation stock. Photos of all the African imports registered in 1990 have been reproduced here. The descendants of the imports have made a great splash on the show scene. Their accomplishments are recorded in this edition with photos of the dogs who have become a living part of the breed's history. America is just the right place for such a project. The great numbers of breeders and dogs in such a vast nation allow us to give these new imports a thorough chance to prove their worth to the breed while also maintaining lines free of the new imports. There have been some records set by these lines as well!

The Basenji Club of America members have voted in a new standard which was accepted by the American Kennel Club in 1990. My interpretation of the revised standard is somewhat different than the discussion of the 1954 standard.

Once I started tinkering with the book, it was hard to stop. I did manage to talk briefly about the brindle color and some of the non-standard colors which arrived with the new imports. Additionally, I tried to fine tune my remarks about obedience based on the feedback I received on the first edition and my greater understanding of the most modern training methods. New records have been set in obedience and recorded here with more coming in the next few years as one great little female closes in on her Utility Dog Excellent title... But time doesn't stand still, so this and other upcoming "firsts" will have to be covered next time!

Susan Coe, August 16, 1994

My thanks for making this book possible go to so many people it is hard to know where to start. Writing a book of this type starts with your earliest education in the breed. I must begin with the breeders of the 70's who patiently answered our questions and allowed us to see and film their dogs. They pointed us in the right direction.

Special thanks goes to Shirley Chambers who read the entire manuscript, piece by piece, making historical corrections and suggestions throughout. The scrapbooks belonging to Shirley Chambers and those of Sheila Smith were invaluable in writing the breed's history. Sally Ann Smith was wonderful in making comments on my grammar.

P. David Hill very generously allowed me to use the fruits of his late 1970's research into Basenji history.

Those who helped on specific chapters include Veronica Tudor-Williams, Maj. Al Braun, Paul van Ormer, Russell Brown, Ph.D., Linda Benson, Elizabeth White, Cecelia Wozniak, Penny Inan, and Mary Lou Kenworthy. Their essays, comments and suggestions were very helpful!

The Basenji Club of America, through the efforts of Andie Paysinger, historian, supplied stacks of early club history and newsletters as well as some photos. Marnie Lang supplied information on Canadian history and contacted Canadian breeders for me. Elspet Ford was helpful with detail questions about some early English history and photos. Thank you.

Many, many breeders have spent time searching for photos of their early dogs, and also for those special snapshots I've been able to include. They went out of their way to find photos in their possession of some of the earliest Basenjis. The photos are pretty special in this book. Thank you for entrusting me with them!

Jon Curby, Michael Work, Damara Bolte and Stan Carter deserve special thanks for keeping me up-to-date on their new African imports and for allowing me to use their photos taken in Africa during 1987 and 1988. The first chapter, especially, was greatly enhanced by these photos.

The American Kennel Club has granted permission to use copies of the slides from their slide/tape show on Basenjis.

B & E Publications has given kind permission to quote extensively from Frank Sabella and Shirlee Kalstone in their book *The Art of Handling Show Dogs*.

To the editors of *Akita World* magazine, many thanks for permission to use several parts of various issues.

To Lynn Lowy, editor and publisher of the *Great Dane Reporter*, many thanks for permission to use significant material from a number of issues.

To Joe McGinnis, of Doll/McGinnis Publications, for kind permission to use material from the "stable" of magazines they publish.

Permission has been granted by Donald Sturz, Jr., editor/publisher of the *Golden Retriever Review*, to use specific material from various issues.

To Michael Allen, editor of the *American Cocker Magazine* for permission to use the works of Dr. Alvin Grossman and others from a variety of issues.

Doral Publishing granted permission to quote extensively from *The American Cocker Spaniel* by Dr. Alvin Grossman.

Finally, my thanks to my husband, Jon Coe, who made countless suggestions and encouraged me from the beginning.

FOREWORD

Known to have been the palace dogs of the Pharaohs, and believed to have become extinct with the crumbling of the ancient Egyptian empire, the unique canine known as the Basenji, was, in the late 1800's, rediscovered by explorers who ventured into the innermost depths of the African Continent. From the favored companion of the Pharaohs, to an essential part of the lives of the African natives, the Basenji existed as an important part of both worlds. Then, in the 1900's, the Basenji was introduced to yet another world—western civilization. This world was unknown to the breed which had witnessed much of the early part of mankind's evolutionary progress. It was a world of wood and metal structures, automobiles, supermarkets, and all that which we term "modern." And yet, the innate adaptability and flexibility with which this breed is imbued, has, in less than 50 years, allowed it to become an important part of family life.

It has been dedicated breeders and fanciers which have helped the Basenji make the great transition to a world very unlike that of its origin. In my 30 years' association with the breed, I have known many such breeders whose impact upon the Basenji will be long felt. Susan Coe is, indeed, one such individual whose dedication to the betterment of the breed will leave its mark, not only through the Basenjis she has bred, but also in the invaluable information contained in her book, *The Basenji—Out of Aftica To You.*

I first came in contact with Susan some 16 years ago. She was then residing in Calgary, Canada and myself in Pennsylvania. She and her husband, Jon, were seeking stud service for a bitch who would later become the foundation of the Akuaba line of Basenjis. I realized then in speaking with her that much study and thought had preceded her search, for not only had she researched the breed in particular, but had acquired an extensive knowledge of canine structure and function, as well. It was upon this knowledge that she based her breeding program which, in the years to follow would establish Akuaba Basenjis as one of the foremost Basenji kennels in the U.S. It is with that same dedication that Susan undertook the writing of *The Basenji—Out of Africa To You* which is, in my opinion, the most complete, informative and comprehensive book written to date on the breed. The history and statistical information will become the foundation for future additions, while the information regarding selection, care and training of the Basenji, will be just as valid many years from now as it is today.

It is not easy to trace factual information on the history of the Basenji, since much of the information is varied and/or obscure, yet Susan has sifted through a myriad of letters, articles and details to arrive at the most accurate history possible. Whether one's interests in the breed lie in showing, obedience work, lure coursing, hunting, a loving companion, or all of these combined, he will find much valuable and long-needed information in this book. Susan's insight into and interpretation of the breed standard provide a mental picture of the ideal Basenji for judges and exhibitors alike. Preserved in the chapters on influential breeders and top-winning and top-producing Basenjis are the records and descriptions which often disappear into obscurity and whose values are recognized only as time passes.

The Basenji—Out of Africa To You is a most valuable asset to all who have become acquainted with or have an interest in the Basenji. Whether judge, breeder, handler, novice or one contemplating the addition of a Basenji to his life, this book represents a wealth of knowledge and information derived from Susan's research, study, experience and insight. Its publication represents a milestone in the history of the breed.

Shirley Chambers
Khajah Basenjis
Jasper, Georgia, USA

SECTION I
History

AFRICA 1987. Hunters with nets, weapons and Basenji wearing a bell. Photo courtesy of Michael Work, 1987.

CHAPTER 1

A History of the Basenji

Pariah dogs of a similar type and size to Basenjis can be found in the city streets and villages of the tropical world. They live by their wits serving as garbage clean-up, rodent control, hunting assistants and protectors. In some parts of the world they also serve as food. They must survive without protective immunizations, simple parasite control or veterinary services. Their size is neither tiny like our toy breeds nor large like our giant breeds. These dogs have evolved to a very efficient size (15 to 30 pounds) without any "breed" extravagances. Their coats are short to provide comfort in the hot climate. Their conformation is not extreme and their intelligence is very high as they must be clever and resourceful to find enough to eat.

Curly-tailed pariah dogs depicted on south wall, Ankor Watt, Cambodia.

Origins

The first records of Basenjis on the African continent appear among the first dogs ever depicted in Egyptian engravings. These little dogs are pictured near the feet of their owners or under their chairs. The Khufu dogs shown in the Great Pyramid of Khufu (Cheops) built around 2700 B.C. in the IV Dynasty are of Basenji-type. They are described by Mr. Birch in *The Transactions of the Society of Biblical Archaeology* (1875) as "Spitz-like dogs, the muzzle is short and pointed and distinctly fox-like, the ears are pointed and held erect. The tail is curled and comes close to and on the side of the back." These dogs are frequently depicted with bells tied around their necks just as European explorers found Basenjis when they were rediscovered in 19th century Africa.

Each wearing a bell, a modern champion Basenji is compared to an ancient Egyptian statue. Photo courtesy of the American Kennel Club.

Mr. Birch also describes a tablet of Pharaoh Antefaa II from 2000 B.C. showing four dogs of distinct breeds. One of the dogs is described as having a more marked stop with muzzle sharply pointed and fox-like, the ears pointed and erect with the tail curled tightly to the side of the back. Richard and Alice Fiennes in *The Natural History of the Dog* suggest it is, "the same breed as the Khufu dogs depicted on the IV Dynasty tombs some 1600 years earlier, and is probably a Basenji . . ." The Fiennes also describe two ancient skulls of Pariah dogs which reveal essential characteristics of the wild wolf stock from which all domesticated dogs are descended. They go on to say, "The little skull from the tomb of the first century B.C., at Denderah in Upper Egypt . . . is of very great interest . . . it had been buried with ceremony in a prepared grave, and although exhibiting characteristics resembling semi-wild creatures, it was more likely to have been a household dog of Basenji-type . . ."

Further south, in Libya, there are rock and cave paintings whose time frame begins much earlier at 6000 B.C. and ends in the first century A.D. There are drawings of pariah-type dogs in some of these hunting scenes. Since there are similar barkless dogs in Asia, it may be that Basenji-like pariah dogs originally came from Asia and moved on to Africa with very early migrations or were traded over many thousands of years before records were made; and they passed through northern Africa where the Basenji breed type became established.

Pygmies are among the oldest races of mankind. They are hunter-gatherers and they maintain one of the world's simplest levels of material technology. They are very slow to adopt new ideas so their maintenance and use of Basenjis could easily date back many centuries. Pygmies formerly lived in a continuous belt of rain forest that stretched across the African continent at the equator.

The Basenjis in Liberia, where our black and white Basenjis originated, would represent the western reaches of this belt. The pariah dogs of the Congo belt are described by H. Epstein in *The Origin of the Domestic Animals of Africa* as "generally fawn, yellow, red or white, more rarely variegated. The tail is commonly carried close to the ground; occasionally it is curled up. These dogs usually howl but do not bark." So we see that the general dog population of this region is rather Basenji-like and has the very specific barkless characteristic.

This native African Basenji enjoys relaxing with its family. Like our American Basenjis, it has unfurled its tail and allowed its ears to droop while it dozes. Photo courtesy of Michael Work, 1987.

The Pygmies are known to have had contact with the Egyptians through the various dynasties. Pygmies are represented in Egyptian work in a number of instances including depictions of Egyptian divinities such as Osiris and Bes. One Pygmy's name was written as Akka and he resembles the modern day Aka Pygmies of Uele. It is recorded that Prince Herkhuf of Elephantine led an expedition to the home of the semi-lengendary Pygmies in the VI Dynasty. We shall never know whether the Basenjis originally came to central Africa from Asia long before the Egyptian Dynasties and then were acquired by Egyptians from their expeditions into equatorial Africa or the reverse, with Egyptians introducing Basenjis into central Africa. The former seems more likely since the Pygmies were the more ancient group and slow to accept new things. Egyptians were expanding into new territories as well as absorbing adjacent peoples and were probably much more likely to accept Basenjis from Pygmies or even to demand them as tribute. The Egyptians had many kinds of dogs, and most appear to have been well established in type when they first appeared in ancient Egyptian art. This suggests that they may have been developed elsewhere.

A young African girl carrying a well-wrinkled puppy. Photo courtesy of Michael Work, 1987.

Each native group must have its own story about the origin of their dogs. Lona B. Kenney related this legend in her 1972 book, *Mboka, A Congo Memory*. Eventually, the conversation about the riverside people and the Ngombe turned to stories about dogs, and so were many others, although in quite a different way—they liked them roasted. Grandfather did not own a dog now, for he was still loyal to the memory of his old Basenji dog, which had given its life to save grandfather from a leopard. When one morning Molali had brought home a small Basenji puppy, probably stolen, which he planned for his evening meal, grandfather had been so angered that, forgetting that his son was an adult and the father of a family, he seized an iron rod that he kept in one corner and had tried to thrash Molali with it. Molali jumped from side to side like a little boy, trying to dodge his father's blows and begging forgiveness, but his voice only guided the blind old man in the right direction. In fact, our shared love of animals made me overlook grandfather's leopard-tooth necklace. It was not surprising, therefore, to see his animation grow now, and hear him tell one dog story after another. The last legend of the evening was the most enjoyable.

''Dogs have not always belonged to men,'' grandfather, who had become slightly hoarse, began his story. ''Before belonging to anyone, the mbwa (dogs) were free and lived in the forest in long tunnels underneath the earth where no one could follow them. Only the males came up to catch fish that they brought back to the females and the puppies, for the females were forbidden to leave the tunnels. One day, however, a female, like so many other females everywhere, disobeyed the rule and was snatched by Assa, the Spirit of Wrath, whose tongue is as long and forked as that of a snake, and from which oozes a poisonous froth. He compelled her to lead him to the dogs' tunnels, where he viciously bit them all. Poisoned by the spirit of Assa, they fought among themselves and ended up by devouring one another. Alone the little bitch that had shown Assa the way was spared. In due time, she gave birth to a litter of puppies and from that time on dogs became the slaves of Assa. Assa mistreated the dogs; he starved and abused them and finally began eating them. All those dogs that had any strength left fled to villages, seeking protection from Assa, who now, having long since finished off his remaining dogs, tries to carry away our own. These days when a dog disappears from our mboka, it is never certain whether it has been taken by a leopard or by Assa. Those who have followed their stolen dogs' bloody trails have often overheard their dying complaint and a wicked voice hissing, ''Assa, Assa!'' Sometimes a dog manages to escape the venomous claws of the Spirit of Wrath. But the animal soon develops a forked tongue dripping with slaver, and attacks his master, for he is possessed by the angry spirit of Assa.''

The grandfather sighed, and added astutely, probably for his son Molali's benefit, ''And, if the dogs should begin to fear that they might be eaten, they will return to Assa.''

But Molali did not appear to be impressed.

''Did you not say when you told this story the last time, that dogs had first belonged to birds?'' he remarked and quickly retreated out of reach of his father's walking stick.

And I couldn't stop thinking of how all these beautiful legends, transmitted orally from generation to generation were destined to change over the years, influenced by failing memories of the old, and perhaps also by the personal inspiration of creative storytellers like my grand old friend, Baloki's and Molali Moke's grandfather.

CHAPTER 2

Basenjis Rediscovered

Comments about Basenjis began appearing around 1870 in the writings of explorers in Africa. Dr. Schweinfurth, who visited Africa between 1868 and 1871, was one of the very first explorers to reach the pygmy people. He wrote of the Mangbattu and Azende (Nyam-Nyam), "[their] dogs are distinguished by small stature, straight legs, a curled tail, and short smooth coat which is red or yellow in color with the neck commonly white." He is also quoted as saying, "They are made to wear little bells around the neck so that they should not be lost in the long steppe-grass."

These two men are making a Basenji hunting bell. The bells vary in materials and design from village to village. Photo courtesy of Michael Work, 1987.

Mr. H.H. Johnston notes their barkless quality in 1882. The pariah dogs of Africa in general did not bark although they were capable of nearly all the other sounds dogs make. However, not all African barkless pariah dogs had the conformation characteristics of our Basenjis. The Nyam-Nyam (Azende), the Mangbattu (people of the Ubangi-Uele basin in eastern Congo), the Ituri Pygmies, as well as the western Bantu people of the lower Congo and southern Sudan had dogs that are described very much like our modern Basenjis. British personnel in the southern Sudan, who were the early pioneers of our breed, found the most typical and desirable specimens within the area of the southern Sudan, Zaire and equatorial Africa.

There have been a number of descriptions of Basenjis hunting with their tribes in Africa. An understanding of their abilities and hunting style may shed some light on our Basenjis' high intelligence and general personality characteristics. Jean-Pierre Hallet was assigned to various parts of the Congo by the Belgian government. He usually went native, living among local peoples, in order to get a greater insight into the customs of the people. In *Congo Kitabu*, he describes his experiences among the Bambuti Pygmies and tells of this hunt:

I watched curiously as flattened wooden bells were attached with strips of

The first Basenji to reach America was this stuffed specimen which appeared in this exhibit of a pygmy family group in 1912 at the Natural History Museum in New York. Photo courtesy of The Dept. of Library Services, American Museum of Natural History.

hide to the animals' necks. They hung on the dogs' chests, looking like castanets equipped with three or four little wooden clappers. They were an obvious necessity for tracking the game, since the dogs were completely mute apparently of the same stock which had produced the famous "barkless Basenji." Then the men formed themselves into two separate hunting parties: three men and one dog marched off into the forest together, while four men took two dogs in the opposite direction. Long after the two groups of hunters disappeared into the bush, I could still hear the incredible racket.

"Why do they make so much noise?" I asked.

"That is the only way they can keep together while they look for the game. When they really find something, they stop all the chatter. Then they make sounds like a monkey or bird to signal each other while they close in for the kill."

Some three or four hours later one of the hunter groups returned, rejoicing noisily with a mede (a fifteen-pound forest antelope), and a potto (a small primate). The other hunting party came creeping back into camp very quietly, empty handed. Their faces were drawn, their eyes were cast down and none of them spoke more than a few words. Even the animals' bells were silent; the humiliated hunters had stuffed the bells with grass to silence the mocking clip-clop sound of the hunt."

Doug Allan, in *Facing Danger in the Last Wilderness*, describes another Pygmy hunt where the courage and dedication of the Basenji is shown.

Three Pygmy hunters were moving swiftly through the forest on the trail of some animal and their dog was just a few feet from the first hunter. Suddenly a leopard sprang from a low branch upon the first Pygmy, who was quick enough to dart beyond the reach of a man-killing first blow but not quick enough to avoid the slashing of his right shoulder and arm. He flung his spear at the mad beast, but his bleeding arm was unable to guide it right. The spear missed its mark and the Pygmy managed to clamber up a small tree. The leopard might have gone after him but its attention was diverted by the charge of the second hunter. The cat-like creature swerved toward him just as he aimed his spear, so that it too missed and broke against a rock.

Luckily for the second hunter, the leopard saw number three and went for him, enabling the second to climb to temporary safety. The third hunter kept hold of his spear and tried to plunge it into the animal as it sprang. The spear merely sliced its leg a bit, serving only to make him angrier than before. Then the leopard and hunter number three battled it out, the hunter struggling to keep the beast's claws from his throat and at the same time maneuvering to get in another thrust with his spear.

He would have been slashed to ribbons if it had not been for the dog . . . rushed at the leopard from the side and from the rear, snapping at the big cat's legs and flank, then racing off as it turned away from the hunter momentarily to get rid of the pesky dog. The two hunters in the trees could do nothing to help! They had no weapons and one was badly wounded and bleeding profusely. All they could do was watch man and leopard struggle, with the dog snarling, rushing and getting in and out. Once he sank his fangs into the leopard's tail and tugged. The beast whirled, howled, and obviously decided to kill the pest once and for all.

That gave the third hunter just the chance he needed. He lunged with his spear, which pierced the leopard's side, cut into its heart and dropped it. But, this time the hunter was so badly wounded that he could hardly stand but all three men managed to get back home. As their wounds were cleaned and dressed, they all sang the praises of the dog, giving him full credit for saving their lives.

In an article written by David Wilkie and Gilda Morelli on modern life among the Efe pygmies entitled, "Pitfalls of the Pygmy Hunt," appearing in the December 1988 issue of Natural History Magazine, there is a clear and detailed description of a modern hunt that varies little from the stories written decades ago that you are reading in this chapter. Photo courtesy of Michael Work, 1987.

Felice Beliotti, in *Fabulous Congo*, also describes Basenjis used to track down a wounded leopard. She went on to describe how Basenjis are used to find a leopard who makes itself a nuisance to the Plains people. Poisoned arrows and spears are used to kill the leopard. Bellotti also notes that Basenjis are used for putting up bird, but that the dogs point in the case of hares and antelope. Alan P. Merrian, in *An African World—The Basongye Village of Lupupa Ngye*, describes the hunting process when a hunter might be following game for an entire day.

The village fundi feels that the best way of hunting is with a group of people divided into two parts, one consisting of about ten men with guns, and the other five men with dogs. Dogs are used to drive game towards the hunters. No special training is provided young dogs; but a promising animal is given meat to eat, and if it continues well, he is finally taken over as a hunting dog. This involves special magic in which the hunter-magician takes a piece of the intestine of any animal, a piece of the brain of any animal, some dirt from the track of any animal and a piece of wood of the *Kalonda mishi* tree, mixes them together with water, and puts bits of the mixture into each nostril of the dog. This keeps the dog aware of the scent of animals and may be repeated before every hunt. If the hunter wishes to pursue a specific animal, he cooks a quantity of maize with the intestines of a monkey; at the time of preparation he names the animal he wishes to capture and gives the mixture to the dog to eat, so it will pursue only the animal named. Besides driving game, the dog's work is to corner animals for the hunter to kill. Since dogs are not trained as retrievers (considered impossible because the "dogs want to eat the meat"), it is up to the hunter to be on the spot when a small animal is cornered.

Dogs are belled so that the hunter will know where they are; the special wooden bells, which are stuffed with leaves to prevent noise when stealth is needed, are called *kidibu* (plural, *bidibu*). The side-blown antelope horn is used both to encourage the dogs into attacking the animal and to call them home. In spite of the availability and established practice of using dogs, the master hunter says he does not often use them because "they make too much noise and they always want to chase the game." He does take a dog, however, when he knows an animal with young is about, for it will search out the young.

It would appear that native African Basenjis are just as "helpful" as are our present American Basenjis. These two could have much curlier tails. Photo courtesy of Michael Work, 1987.

———11———

Esther Horner spent many years in Africa working with the missions of the Presbyterian Church. She describes a typical hunt in her *Jungles Ahead!*

Njana walked over to the "talking drum" and beat out his message, "Hark! Every man his spear! Every man his spear!"

Before the dawn . . . we go to the forest . . . the hunger for meat has overcome us . . . in the morning . . . from the village of Njana, we go on a hunt . . ."

Eyene, young son of Njana, called the hunting hounds. When he took the collars with the pod-shaped iron bells from the bark wall, the dogs whined in excitement. The barkless Basenji of the central African forest, small, short-haired, quick-footed, is an ideal hunter in thick underbrush. The dull jangle of the bells is an exhilarating sound to hunting dogs; they too will eat on the morrow. Eyene tied the brace of trembling dogs with bush vine to the central pole of his mother's kitchen. The dogs lay down, protesting the hours till dawn.

The dog bells made a pleasant sound as the company filed through the damp underbrush behind the village cocoa garden into the dense growth of the forest. On signal from the leader, who was following animal tracks, the party spread out in a great circle through the forest. Nets were spread, each holding his position as planned. The drummer boys scattered behind; they began an excited rhythm.

The rhythm broke with the clatter of bells and the youths urged the dogs, "Catch, Catch!" Excitement mounted as the dogs scurried back and forth, sniffing the ground through the underbrush. A dog zigzagged past.

There was never a doubt as to when a dog routed an animal. Eyene heard the sudden flurry, a frantic scurry, the jangle and clatter of bells. Excited whines from the dogs, a crackling of brush. Then shouts of encouragement from the youths. A chant went up. Every man stood at attention in a threatening attitude like a line of driver ants, alert, vibrating with readiness. The forest echoed the wild, glad sound. Traditional hunt songs rose above the din but the men holding the nets stood quiet, not speaking a word lest the animal turn from the nets in flight.

Like a flash, an antelope brushed a net. The man nearest quickly thrust his spear in perfect aim. Eyene knew it because he heard the hunter claim in a loud voice, "To me belongs the thigh quarter." He who arrives first when an animal brushes another's net has claim to the choice portion of the meat.

Together they had an average day's catch of four large antelope, three small. The larger animals were strung on poles and borne proudly on the shoulders of the men.

In a personal letter, Colin Turnbull, author of *The Forest People*, commented on the dogs he had seen in Africa. The dogs he saw were red with very little white and his impression was that they were used more by Pygmies who were archers than the net hunters. However, every Pygmy village of from 15 to 20 families had one or two dogs. He felt they would have been embarrassed if they had none. He pointed out that individuals assumed the care of the dogs but since there is little concept of private ownership among the Pygmies, the dogs belonged to the entire group of families. Treatment of the dogs among the Pygmies he saw was not good. In fact, the dogs seemed more like wild animals living in a symbiotic relationship with the humans. The village dogs he saw away from the Pygmies, on the other hand, were more domesticated, better treated and even allowed inside the houses.

Paul Schebesta wrote in *Revisiting My Pygmy Hosts* that, "It would be almost impossible for the pygmies to track down game without the aid of these hunting dogs. For this reason these dogs are considered to be the most valuable asset to pygmy communities and are gladly accepted as payment in the matrimonial market."

Describing a 1907 expedition in *Land and Peoples of the Kasai*, Hilton Simpson recounts a Bushongo tribe's hunt.

> We numbered about 50 altogether and were accompanied by some 20 tan and white prick-eared dogs . . . the nets are very long and only about three-feet high, they are placed in line and the game driven towards them . . . the owners of the dogs were busy tying rattles round these animals. Each dog has a spherical rattle hollowed from a solid piece of wood strapped tightly round its loins, their object being to make a noise as the line of dogs and beaters advances, for the dogs themselves do not usually give tongue unless they actually get a view of their quarry . . . Soon the beaters could be heard drawing nearer, and the rattles of the dogs distinguished as these animals darted hither and thither in the dense undergrowth, occasionally, though very rarely, giving vent to a short, sharp, yelp.

The treatment and affection given to dogs in Africa by the native people varies from tribe to tribe and from village to village. Photo courtesy of Michael Work, 1987.

The Bayenzi and Bushongo, unlike some of the tribes, took very good care of their dogs. This account by Mr. Simpson expresses the Bayenzi's special feelings for their Basenjis:

We engaged two native lads, Buya, who was a Bayenzi, and Benga. The Bayenzi tribe are cannibals; the Bapende, to which Benga belonged, are not. We once overheard the following conversation on cannibalism: "You Bapende," scornfully remarked Buya, "you kill dogs to eat them." "Well," replied Benga, "you Bayenzi can't talk, you eat men." This caused an outburst of indignation on the part of the little cannibal. "It is all very well to eat your enemies when you have killed them in battle, that is a natural thing to do, but no decent person would think of eating his best friend. You Bapende are disgusting, you think nothing of eating dogs, the greatest friend of man."

CHAPTER 3

The Basenji is Exported

The first Basenjis to be exhibited at a dog event appeared at Crufts in London, England, in 1895. Unfortunately, these Basenjis died shortly thereafter from distemper. At the same time, two Basenjis were known to be in France but nothing further is known of them. A photo appeared in a 1908 issue of *Illustrated Kennel News* depicting a bitch and her daughter. The daughter had been bred at the Berlin Zoo. Again, nothing more came of these two. A stuffed specimen of a Basenji reached America, in 1912, and was exhibited as a part of an African Pygmy village at the American Museum of Natural History, New York. Several additional attempts were made to import Basenjis into Europe; but it wasn't until 1936 that Mrs. Olivia Burns' Bongo, Bereke and Bokoto of Blean successfully passed through English quarantine to begin the breed's history in Europe and America. The litter produced in quarantine, out of Bokoto and sired by Bongo, made quite an impact when exhibited at Crufts, in 1937.

Photo]   BONGO OF BLEAN.   *[Fall*
THE BLEAN BASENJIS
(The Pioneer Kennel)

One of the earliest African imports.

Mrs. Burns was able to bring in an additional three Basenjis in 1937. Among these three was the male Bakuma of Blean who was exported to the United States directly from quarantine. Bakuma traveled with two young

This old cutting is from the New York Sun, *with a written-in date of October 1937. It shows Mr. Byron Rogers with Basashi of Blean (bitch) and the native import, Bakuma of Blean (dog), later known as Phemister's Bois.*

bitches from the Blean kennel. The bitches died about a year later and the dog disappeared. The next Basenjis to come to North America came to Dr. Richmond in Toronto, Canada, in 1939, from Veronica Tudor-Williams' "of the Congo" kennel but these two died of distemper. Distemper vaccines had been improving each year and finally, Dr. Richmond successfully brought four Basenjis into Canada in 1940: two males, Kwillo and Koodoo of the Congo, and two females, Kikuyu and Kiteve of the Congo. All four of these imports were entered at the great Morris and Essex show in New Jersey in 1941, for "Exhibition Only." They created quite a stir of excitement in the U.S. dog show world at that time. Kwillo of the Congo became the first Basenji champion in the world when he won his Canadian championship in 1942.

The year 1941 saw more African Basenjis arriving in the United States. First was Congo, who was a stowaway in the hold of a ship loaded with coffee. She survived without food or water during the three-week voyage. After some time of recovery at the Society for the Prevention of Cruelty to Animals, she

Barkless Basenji puppies owned by Dr. A.R.B. Richmond of Toronto "being shown in this country for the first time at Morris and Essex today." This photo and caption appeared in the **New York Sun** *newspaper. A penciled-in date on the clipping reads May 31, 1941.*

"Congo," the stowaway.

was obtained by Al and Mary Phemister. Congo was a mostly white dog with a brindle patch on her side. Her tail had been docked. She was bred to Koodoo of the Congo, who the Phemisters had obtained from Dr. Richmond, and produced Phemister's Barrie who, in 1942, became the first Basenji to win an obedience Companion Dog title. Barrie went on to win his Companion Dog Excellent title in 1944. The Phemister's also obtained a male whose papers had been lost and named him Phemister's Bois. He is believed to be the lost Bakuma of Blean as Bakuma's pet name was Bois and photos of the two are identical.

"Barkless Basenji dogs, mute but fearless, came from Africa with the gorillas, made friends with them. The Basenjis chased the little apes around and were playfully tossed about in return." Kindu and Kasenji were among the Basenjis in this shipment. Photo by John Phillips, Life Magazine © *September 22, 1941, Time, Inc.*

Four Basenjis were shipped to New York in 1941, carried with a shipment of eight baby gorillas. These Basenjis had been collected by Phil Carroll, an employee of Henry Trefflich. Neither of these men knew of the efforts to establish the breed in England and North America but they felt such attractive and unusual dogs would appeal to U.S. dog lovers. Mr. Carroll secured eleven specimens he felt were typical but seven escaped just before they were to be shipped. Two of the remaining four were exhibited at the Westminster Kennel Club show in New York, in 1942, for "Exhibition Only" as they were not yet registered by the American Kennel Club. These two, Kindu and Kasenyi, were obtained by Mrs. Tress Taaffe, in 1943, and were the foundation of her Basenji kennel.

CHAPTER 4

American Kennel Club Recognition

The Basenji Club of America was formed in 1942. The members determined to accept the standard that had been drawn up by the Basenji Club of England in that same year. The American Kennel Club accepted the standard as official and, in 1943, the breed became eligible for registration with 59 Basenjis registered within the first few months.

Now the dogs you have just been introduced to began to make a mark in show and breeding records. Kindu, from the gorilla shipment, won 2nd in the Hound Group from Judge Derek Rayne in Vallejo, California, in July, 1945.

Kasenyi (sitting) and Kindu (standing) arrived in the 1941 gorilla shipment.

When interviewed in 1982, Mr. Rayne remembered placing Kindu in the group but did not remember the dog in detail. He did say, "that the breed was not as elegant as they are today . . . noticed improvement in gait . . . noted that the breed is often lacking in wrinkles and/or breed expression (today) . . . the earlier dogs were seldom tri-colors—mostly red with less white than today . . . that the Basenji is one of the few breeds that overall have improved since . . . [he has] been judging, 40 plus years."

Kindu and Kasenyi produced a litter of one female and four males in May, 1946. One of the males was Ch. Kingolo who won his championship in 1949.

Ch. Kingolo (1949).

He was a very important sire during his time in the States and was exported to Great Britain, in 1952, where he continued to produce champions. He is said to have produced at least one champion in every litter he sired. Kindu and Kasenyi themselves went to Hawaii where they produced a litter in January, 1947. A male from that litter, Akamai of Koko Crater, was the great-grandsire of the first American Kennel Club all-breed Best in Show Basenji; Philo's Blaze of Koko Crater was Best in Show in Hawaii in October, 1956. The show had an entry of 80 dogs.

Phemister's Bois was also an important early sire. He produced the first American champion, Ch. Phemister's Melengo (title completed in 1945), from a litter he sired out of the English import Zinnia of the Congo. Zinnia was the daughter of an African import into England, Amatangazig of the Congo. Zinnia became a champion in 1946. You can begin to see how close our first Basenji show dogs were to African stock.

Ch. Phemister's Melengo—the first American Basenji champion.

Eng. Ch. Fern of the Congo and Eng. Ch. Brown Trout of the Congo, who were littermates, became the first English champions in February of 1947. Fern had an unusually late season shortly after and was bred to Brown Trout. In April, 1947, they produced a litter of three: one red and white, and the first two tri-color (black, tan and white) Basenjis born outside of Africa. One of these tris, Black Idol of the Congo, became the first tri in America when he was imported later that year. The first Basenji Hound Group winner in the United States was also a tri-color. In 1952, Ch. Black Mist of the Congo won a Hound Group I.

The Basenji Club of America held its first specialty show on June 11, 1950. Judge Alva Rosenberg found his Best of Breed among the 20 entrants in Mr. George Gilky's Ch. Rhosenji Beau with Best of Opposite Sex won by Ch. Rhosenji Ginger. The year 1951 saw a total of 151 Basenjis registered with the AKC. A total of 651 were registered in 1957, showing substantial growth in the breed. There were 1,546 Basenjis registered with the American Kennel Club from a total of 523 registered litters in 1987. The National Specialty held in Illinois, in September of 1987, had an entry of 217 Basenjis.

The popular movie, "Goodbye, My Lady" gave the breed a big boost in 1950. Even today, people inquiring about a Basenji sometimes mention seeing the movie and then say, "and I've wanted a Basenji ever since." The movie hasn't been shown, even on late-night television, in many years; but we are hopeful that Warner Brothers will be making a video available. After filming was completed, star Brandon de Wilde took home the starring Basenji, My Lady of the Congo. After acting as an adviser during the filming, Mrs. Sheila Anderson of Glenairley Basenjis in British Columbia, took home one of the several doubles in the film. This dog became Am./Can. Ch. Flageolet of the Congo.

The 1952 movie, "The African Queen," starring Humphrey Bogart and

Katherine Hepburn, does not feature Basenjis but you may want to watch the introductory scenes carefully. These scenes were filmed in Africa and as the camera pans the congregation, there, sitting on an African's lap, is a Basenji!

The Canadians remained active through these years with their own stock as well as English and American imports. Ch. Abakaru of Blue Nile became the first American and Canadian champion in 1953. It is reported by his owner, Mrs. Roberta Jenkins, that Basenjis were placing well in the groups during the fifties with many Best Puppy, Group Brace and Show Brace wins.

Am. & Can. Ch. Dainty Dancer of Glenairley became the first Basenji to win a Best in Show in Canada, on September 6, 1957. She was just 9 months old. Dainty Dancer's pedigree goes back to the 1952 African import into England, Wau of the Congo. In August of 1958, she became the first Basenji to win Best in Show in the continental U.S. when she was Best at the Olympic Kennel Club show in Washington state over an entry of 557. She had a total of seven Best in Show wins in the two countries. Dainty Dancer was handled by a professional handler in those days and many years later he told us that she refused to allow a judge to pass her by. If they walked by, she turned and gave them a yodel to attract their attention!

*Ch. **Dainty Dancer of Glenairley**, handled by Bob Hastings, was the first Canadian Best in Show winner.* Photo courtesy of Mrs. M. Robertson.

CHAPTER 5

Late Imports

Miss Tudor-Williams ("of the Congo" Basenjis), accompanied by Mr. Michael Hughes-Halls, Basenji fancier from Rhodesia, and Col. John Rybot, another Basenji enthusiast from England, went on an expedition to Africa in 1959. As they approached "Basenji Country" in the south Sudan, they observed many red, prick eared, curly tailed dogs which obviously had Basenji in their ancestry. Mr. Walter Philo, *AKC Gazette* columnist, reported: "To a Basenji expert, Miss Tudor-Williams wrote, it is just a dog but to the uninitiated it might resemble a bad Basenji for it is red in color, usually with white feet. It is of varying size, slim and long-backed with an almost straight tail, a somewhat domed head, little or no wrinkle and rather large erect ears."

As the expedition continued, the true Basenji-type became more common. Miss Tudor-Williams describes them:

> The majority of heads were good with little cheekiness and short muzzles. Eyes, though, were often rather large and too wide-set. Easily the most attractive were small wedge-shaped heads with small triangular ears set on top. Eyes were mostly dark; noses, black. Wrinkle was rather disappointing. It was there, but usually not nearly so defined as in most English-bred dogs, though some native specimens had beautifully fine wrinkles. Tails were generally high-set with usually a single curl, though we saw a number of wonderful tails, curled tightly in a double twist and carried closely to one side of the hip. Naturally we also saw a number of less attractive center curls. Feet were small and oval, but I was surprised to see such long nails on hunting dogs. I do not remember seeing a single cow-hocked Basenji and, contrary to what we had expected, we did not once see a dog with the "characteristic" umbilical hernia.
>
> Colors, to be sure, were of the utmost interest to us. The usual shade was a poorish chestnut, probably bleached by the sun, though a fair number were a glorious bright red. Many were bountifully marked with white—blaze, legs, and collar. I estimate that one-quarter were typical tri-colors of black, tan and white. We did find one black and white dog without any tan, proving that reports of the black and white Basenji were no rumor."
>
> Our most sensational discovery was the presence of true tiger-striped brindles and in considerable numbers—bright red with black stripes. This is a variation I had not known to exist. In fact, in one locality there were *only* tiger-striped Basenjis."

The expedition brought two Basenjis back to England. Fula of the Congo, who became an exceptionally important import, and Tiger, a tiger-striped brindle whose color was not well received in England. Tiger went back to

The tiger-striped brindle was discovered in Africa during the 1959 expedition. Here "Tiger" (later named M'Binza of Laughing Brook) is encouraged by Veronica Tudor-Williams to pose for a snapshot. Photo courtesy of Veronica Tudor-Williams.

Africa with Mr. Hughes-Halls and became Rhodesian and South African Ch. Binza of Laughing Brook. Although several of Binza's offspring came back to England, the tiger-stripe brindle color was not established. Binza's great grandson, Black M'Binza of the Congo, a tri-color, came to the United States as a young dog and one occasionally finds his name in American pedigrees. Fula of the Congo did a great deal for the breed all over the world with improvements in type and temperament in her offspring.

The first Basenji to be registered with the American Kennel Club as a black and white was Khajah's Black Fula Challenge who was born in January, 1964. Challenge came from two red and white English imports bred down from Fula of the Congo. When Challenge matured, he developed some tan hairs in his black coat but not in the typical tri-color pattern. This color has come to be known as "Fula black" and is not considered desirable. The first pure black and white champion in the world was South African Ch. Taysenji Tahzu who was part Liberian and part Anglo-American stock. Tahzu was brought to England when her owner, Mrs. Ford, returned home from Africa.

There were other efforts to bring black and whites out of Liberia including those of Gwen Stanich in the midwest. However, the most important import

Fula of the Congo was imported from Africa, to England, in 1959. Veronica Tudor-Williams reports that the majority of dogs seen during the 1959 African expedition were common village dogs. They saw very few "true" Basenjis and those few were in very remote areas. Courtesy of Veronica Tudor-Williams.

to our current Basenjis was Kiki of Cryon. Since the American Kennel Club had closed registrations to African native dogs, Kiki could not be registered in

Kiki of Cryon was a native African imported into America.

Kiki's daughter, Black Diamond of Cryon, was sired by a dog from English bloodlines, Gunn's Ramses.

the United States. Her daughter, Black Diamond of Cryon (sired by Gunn's Ramses, who was from English bloodlines) was bred to Khajah's Black Fula Challenge and two of these pups were imported into England by Cdr. and Mrs. Stringer. Mrs. Chambers of Khajah Kennels described Kiki as having particularly good proportions and a well-curled tail. Diamond, she felt, could rival anything, in any color, in the modern show ring. The dog puppy, Sheen of Horsley, became the grandfather of the first black and white bitch champion, Eng. Ch. Sircillitar of Horsley. Some Horsley black and whites returned to America after three generations of breeding in England when they could then

Sheen and Satin of Horsley were exported to England and are shown here in quarantine. They were children of Black Diamond by Khajah's Black Fula Challenge who was from two English imports.

Several generations later, Ch. Sir Datar of Horsley, shown here as a young dog, returned the black and white color to America.

be registered with the American Kennel Club. Ch. Sir Datar of Horsley came to Khajah Kennels, in 1969, and quickly became the first black and white American champion. He has been important in the development of black and whites in America.

The Cabrillo Kennel Club in California on May 19, 1973, was the setting for the first black and white Hound Group winner, Ch. Bushveld Black Shikari. No black and whites have taken a Best in Show as of this writing.

So, we find no new imports after the 1960's. Breed pioneer Veronica Tudor-Williams noted in an article printed in 1979: "In the writer's opinion, the real foundation stock, whose blood is carried by practically every Basenji in the world, consists of: Bongo, Bereke, Bokoto, Bashele and Bungwa of Blean, Amatangazig, Wau and Fula of the Congo and Kindu and Kasenyi through their son, Ch. Kingolo." I think we can add Phemister's Bois (Bakuma of Blean) to this list as being very influential in America and Kiki of Cryon can be added as an influential import, especially in the States, which brings our primary foundation to a total of 12 imported individuals.

CHAPTER 6

Continuing Efforts at Importations from Africa

Are there still "true" Basenjis in Africa? The photo on the left is of a red and white male seen in Africa in 1987. The photo on the right is of Ch. Bettina's Bronze Wing, a red and white female born in America in 1954; her parents were imported from the English "of the Congo" kennel. (L: Courtesy of Michael Work; R: A Darling photo.)

After many years with no further imports from Africa, 1987 found two American Basenji breeders, Mr. Jon Curby and Mr. Michael Work, making a trip to Africa in an effort to bring out new Basenjis. Mr. Curby was particularly interested in obtaining tiger-striped brindle Basenjis. They returned from their trip very excited with a report similar to others that the further away from "civilization" they traveled, the more typically Basenji the dogs became. Mr. Curby commented on Basenjis in Africa:

> In general, adult dogs appear to be in excellent health and condition with good treatment and feeding by their owners. All the dogs have ticks, fleas and hookworms which must do some damage. Puppies are most affected by these pests and it appears that the period between weaning and six months of age may be critical to their survival. We saw many large litters of young puppies (five to six weeks), but rarely more than two pups in litters older than nine or ten weeks . . . Of the approximately 300 dogs we saw, about one-half were brindle. The color appears to have the same degree of variation and genetics

These photos taken by Michael Work in 1987 show a typical litter of healthy, well-fed puppies before weaning (left). Jon Curby is shown on the right holding a puppy and says that most puppies seen during the 1987 and 1988 trips "were difficult to evaluate because the puppies become malnourished quickly when weaned and only recover if they are able to hunt small animals and birds on their own. Their lack of condition makes them appear to have very large heads and ears."

that we see in other AKC breeds [with brindle coloring] . . . The degree of
brindle varies. A dog could have very few black marks on one part or be red
with a covering of uniformly spaced lines. Others were predominantly black
on the dorsal area with red between the stripes on the sides and head. There
was no evidence that the brindle dogs' being part of the population had any
effect on the quality of color in red and tri dogs. Over the entire trip, we saw
only three dogs that could have been pure black and white, and two other
black and whites that had red hair scattered in the black . . . We saw several
examples of two rather unusual colors. One is a tri-color dog with a tan mask
covering the face just over the eyes creating a look similar to that of a
Malamute. The other color was what Veronica Tudor-Williams described as a
"mahogany tri," a tri-color dog with dark red replacing what is usually black.
The tan and white colors appear in the same places they usually do. We were
able to bring seven puppies back with us. Three pups were females and four
males. Of the seven puppies, there was one brindle male, one brindle female,
two tri-colored males, one red male and two red females. The two tris, the red
male and one red female are litter mates. All of the others were from separate
litters and separate geographic areas.

*Michael Work related that they saw many Basenjis and Basenji-like dogs during
the 1987 African trip. It was not unusual to find a single very typical Basenji,
such as this handsome red and white male (standing), among a group of dogs of
lesser quality who generally had low-set tails and ears, poor proportions and
muscling with poorly curled tails.* Photo courtesy of Michael Work.

The male who didn't want to move to America. He is a half-brother to the litter born during the flight home in 1988. This male had such presence and so many virtues that he could easily have become a champion. Photo courtesy of Jon Curby, 1988.

These two females are from the litter whelped in transit from Africa to America. They are about 12 weeks old in this photo. Photo courtesy of Jon Curby, 1988.

Mr. Curby, Miss Damara Bolté and Mr. Stan Carter, DVM, made an additional trip in 1988 to the northeastern corner of Zaire close to the Sudanese border. They traveled from Kinshasa, Zaire's capital, to Isoro and then up to the area of Doruma, which is populated by the Azande people. This time they returned with 14 Basenjis, including a mother and her newborn litter. They were interested in obtaining dogs that seemed to be exceptional in one or more features. They came across a quite typey adult red male, but he was not comfortable enough with them to bring back. They were, however, able to bring back his red and white dam, who was in whelp. She became Avongara N'Gondi (see photo). The red dog could be the sire of the litter, but the owner did not know. The owner assured them the birth was a week away, but the pups were born while in transit. All survived the ordeal and prospered. The Basenjis brought back in 1988 were tris, reds and brindles. Mr. Curby felt that the dogs obtained on the second trip were of better quality than those obtained on the first trip.

When the dogs were brought back from Africa there was no guarantee that the American Club would register them. After the Basenji Club of America voted to accept the new imports and the brindle color, a two-fold effort was started to convince the AKC that our breed could truly use the new genetic material and that the standard should be updated to include the brindle color. Damara Bolté, representing the BCOA Standards Committee, spent a great deal of time working, reworking and re-reworking the standard.

Avongara N'Gondi came to the U.S. from Africa in 1988. She moved from the bush into the home of Stan Carter, DVM, with impeccable manners.

Avongara Bazingbi was born in February 1987 in the Uele District of Zaire.

Her goal was to make it adhere to the format requested by the AKC without changing the intent of the 1954 standard but including the brindle and white color. The group which imported the new dogs made a presentation to the AKC and authored several articles to help people understand why these new dogs would be worth the effort. Finally everything was in place in 1990. The Basenji Club of America and the American Kennel Club had accepted both the new standard and the new imports.

A total of 21 Basenjis were imported as a result of the two trips, including the six born in transit. Of these dogs, 13 were deemed worthy of registration. This is about the same as the number of earlier imports from which all previously registered Basenjis were descended. All the 1987 and 1988 African imports used the Avongara prefix in their names. Avongara—the clan from which all Azande chiefs are chosen—has also been used as a prefix in the few African-to-African breedings which have been made.

Esenjo was imported in 1978 by a man returning from an engineering job in Africa. He had tried and failed to buy a Basenji from the pygmies in the Ituri forest. Later, during the drought season, he gave the pygmies two water buffaloes he had shot, and they gave him a Basenji puppy in appreciation. Esenjo, meaning happiness, came to the United States when she was 10 weeks old. In 1983, Esenjo's owner contacted Margaret and John Sommers because he wanted a litter from her. But they were skeptical of his story. But after he produced "papers"—actually an official veterinary certificate of export from Zaire—they were pleased to try breeding Esenjo to one of their males. Although Esenjo was no longer alive when the newer imports were registered,

Avongara Diagba was born in the Uele District of Zaire in January 1988. He is the brindle sire of the litter from Avongara M'Bliki, and their progeny are mentioned often in the text.

her progeny were and so she became the 14th import registered in 1990. (See photos of these 14 dogs.)

The Basenji Club of America has established a special committee to keep track of the new dogs and their offspring. Photos, notes and videotape are being kept so that future Basenji fanciers will have access to accurate records of the newcomers and their progeny.

The impact of the new African imports is spreading. Through early 1994,

Avongara Elly was born March 12, 1988, and is from Isiro, Zaire. Elly and M'Bliki are the only imports to win points at dog shows.

Avongara Gangura was born in December 1986 in the Uele District of Zaire. This brindle is the grandfather of the first group-winning brindle and the great-grandfather of the first best-in- show brindle.

Avongara Goldi was born in January 1987 in Zaire's Uele District and has not been used for breeding.

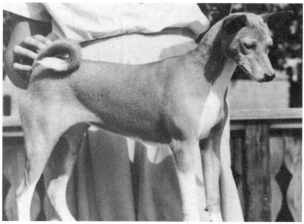

Avongara Kposi was born in January 1988 in Zaire's Uele District.

all the registered imports except Avongara Goldi, Avongara Nabodio and Avongara Wele have produced litters. Esenjo had just the one litter with six puppies. At the time of writing, Margaret Sommer in California and Nancy Sullivan in Virginia have the only descendants of Esenjo. The remaining 10 imports have produced 25 litters with a total of 132 puppies. There have been five litters from import-to-import breeding.

One of the first things learned about these new dogs was that they were not fond of the show ring. While some made appearances at shows and won a few points, none of them showed well. Apparently the showmanship we have fostered in our dogs is not an important characteristic of a hunting dog in Africa. As expected, good and bad conformation points have surfaced in the first generation. The original group produced a few champions and even breed winners. The third generation presented us with Hound Group winners. The new pedigrees also appeared in field and obedience trials.

Sally Wuornos is quite proud to be the owner of the only AKC-titled Basenji with strictly new import breeding. Her Avongara Bote, CDX, was from Damara Bolté's breeding of Avongara Diagba to Avongara M'Bliki. He earned his companion dog and companion dog excellent titles in 1990.

The first American champion half-African was Ch. Akuaba On The Wild Side (see photo), a red-and-white bitch sired by Avongara Renzi. Wily completed her title on May 9, 1992. She has also won a best in field and is the dam of champions. The first brindle half-African champion was Ch. Pendragon Kazor Shadowplay, sired by Avongara Gangura. Player finished his title on January 31, 1993. He is also the sire of champions. At this writing, two other African imports have produced champions. Avongara N'Gondi is the dam of Ch. Silvercreek's Gale Force, Ch. Akuaba's African Free-For-All, Ch. Akuaba's Freeflight to KISA and Ch. Akuaba's African Free Agent, all

Avongara M'Bliki is shown in 1994 at the age of 6 1/2. Photo by Barbara Eastwood.

red and white from two different litters. N'Gondi now becomes the only import to qualify for the Brood Bitch Honor Roll. Avongara Elly is the dam of Ch. Kibushi Prime Target, a red-and-white dog who is the first half-African male champion. Prime Target has gone on to produce champions himself. Avongara Donner, from the Diagba and M'Bliki litter, is the sire of Ch. Reveille Thyme. I'm confident the list will grow in the next few years.

The half-African Kibushi Get Sirius (see photo), owned by Michael Work, is clearly becoming the top producing half-African. Chris is a brindle and white also sired by Avongara Gangura. He is the sire of the first two brindle and white American champions, the quarter-African litter sisters, Ch. Chamga's Ashanti Sana Bukavu (see photo), who became the first brindle champion in American and the second in the world when she completed here title on July 19, 1991, and littermate Ch. Changa's Hot Damn Here I Am followed shortly thereafter. Chris is also the sire of the first brindle group one winner, Ch. Klassic's Eye of the Tiger, who took Group First at Oakland County Kennel Club in November 1992. The second brindle winner and now the first Best in Show from any of the new Africans is Ch. Changa's Dan Patch (see photo). Dan won best in show at the Del Sur Kennel Club in California on May 22, 1994. The judge was Mrs. E. L. Rotman. Dan is a grandson of Kibushi Get Sirius and is therefore one-eighth African. Not surprisingly, both these group winners have become popular stud dogs.

Another quarter-African group-one winner is the bitch Ch. Kibushi Highfalutin of Vasia (see photo). Violet had several group first wins, a specialty breed win and a group Top Ten ranking in confirmation. She is a red-and-white granddaughter of Avongara Zamee.

The top half-African lure coursing dog has been Blucrest Mfalme Mbwabubu, LCM, a brindle and white (see photo). Best-in-Field winning Vito is a son of Avongara Kweli, another from the Diagba and M'Bliki litter.

Brenda Jones-Greenberg and Karon Begeman have been experimenting with close inbreeding on the new imports in Arizona. At this writing, they have just had their third-generation litter. They started with offspring of Avongara Gangura, Avongara N'Gola, Avongara Diagba and Avongara Elly. Brenda and Karon are enjoying their research and have found the dogs different from the typical Basenji found in America. The dogs seem to have "soft" temperaments, good hunting instincts and tremendous appetites. They have begun to try lure coursing and are doing well.

Canada accepted the brindle color quickly but the European countries were slow to accept it. Two brindles were exported to England in 1992 but they have not yet been shown because of the controversy over the color change to the standard. Both Australia and England will accept any dog registered with the American Kennel Club, so their imports can be any percentage of the new foundation stock. Canada, some of the European countries and the International Federation insist on a pedigree with three generations of AKC-registered dogs. This requirement limits their imports to one-eighth

Avongara Nabodio was born March 12, 1988, and is from Isoro, Zaire. Nobodio has the open-faced or capped tricolor markings.

Esenjo was born June 19, 1978, in Zaire.

Avongara N'Gola was born in January 1988 in Zaire's Uele District.

new Africans. Thus far the impact of the new dogs has effectively been limited to North America.

This review has made it appear as though everything went very smoothly. Of course, there were problems. Some off colors which had not been seen since the earliest years of the breed appeared. Some "capped" or "open-faced"

Avongara N'Gondi was born in Zaire's Uele District, but her age is not known. Pasi is the dam of more champions than any of the other new foundation stock.

Avongara Renzi was born March 12, 1987, in Isoro, Zaire. He is the sire of the first half-African champion.

tris like Avongara Nabodio were seen. There were reds and brindles with lemon melon pips and sometimes a lemon mask. In some cases there was too much white. The saddle tricolor, like a beagle pattern, appeared. The saddle sometimes appeared on the brindles. When the brindle dogs are combined with the normal Basenji tricolor, the red on the tri can be brindled. Carol Webb coined the word "trindle" for this marking. When I heard about the color, I thought it would be muddy and unattractive. However, when I saw the dogs they turned out to be rather pleasant appearing. Our standard does not allow for any of these colors or patterns. So breeders must keep the color patterns in mind when breeding with the new imports and their descendants.

Some of the descendants of the new dogs do not have the outgoing, confident temperaments we like to see in our Basenjis. However, I have not heard of difficult, aggressive temperaments but rather dogs that are unsure. This will be a factor to be considered in breeding from the new dogs as well.

The African imports are now over six and seven years old. All except Avongara Wele, who died in an accident, are faring well. All of the imports tested HA clear. No coloboma, no PRA and minimal PPM appeared in their eyes. All the 1987 and 1988 imports had their hips x-rayed and rated as good or excellent. Esenjo was not x-rayed. So far none have shown signs of our late-onset health problems. It is much too soon, of course, to know about the long-term health of their progeny. The much older Avongara N'Gondi, who came as an adult, is spayed and retired. Esenjo was born in 1978 and was put to sleep

Avongara Wele was born in January 1988 in the Uele District of Zaire and died in an accident before he could be used for breeding.

Avongara Zamee was born in January 1987 in the Uele District of Zaire and is the grandmother of a group-winning bitch.

in 1985 when she had a herniated disk. The remaining six bitches have the potential of producing just one or two more litters each. The males should be useful for breeding a maximum of five or six years. There is some talk of saving frozen semen from the males.

Opinion is still divided on the value of the new imports. Familiarity with the new dogs has broken through the barriers with some breeders. Those of us who have been involved with the newcomers in whatever small way have enjoyed the experience. This is a fascinating time to be involved with Basenjis. The show records suggest the imports have combined well with our dogs. The overall quality and type has not been lost. If there have been health gains, the whole endeavor will have been a great success.

Ch. Akuaba on the Wild Side, the first half-African champion, was bred by Susan Coe (shown at right) and Debra Janes Blake. Here Judge James White awards Wily Best of Breed after admiring her head and small ears.

Half-African Kibushi Get Sirius has become a top-producing sire of both brindles and reds. Chris has a lovely head and good movement, and he has passed his qualities to progeny from a variety of bitches.

The quarter-African red bitch Ch. Kibushi Highfalutin of Vasia is another Group One winner descended from the new Africans. Violet was bred by J. and M. Kaufman-Sauther and is owned and handled by Vicki Curby and Brenda Cassell.

Ch. Changa Ashanti Sana Bukavu, a one-quarter
African, was the first brindle champion. She was bred
by June Young and is owned by Michael Work.

Ch. Changa's Dan Patch, whose great grandfather was born in the African
Bush in 1986, is shown taking an all-breed Best of Show in California. Dan
was bred by June Young and is owned by June and Cecily Rappe.

Brindle half-African Blucrest Mfalme Mbwabubu, TT, LCM, was the first American Sighthound Field Association Field Champion and Lure Courser of Merit. Vito, who became the association's Number One Basenji in 1993, was bred by Dorothy Ammons and is owned by Sue Campeau and John Parker. Photo by Robert Nix.

Avongara Diagba.

Avongara Gangura.

Akuaba The Red Fox at 10 months of age.

SECTION II
What Makes Up A Basenji

- *What is a Basenji?*
- *Personality*
- *Why Don't Basenjis Bark?*

Photo by Gail MacLean.

CHAPTER 7

What is a Basenji?

Sleek, short coat in dazzling red, lustrous black or tri-color, pricked ears, and curly tail are trademarks of the deer-like Basenji. "Small, lightly built, short-backed dog . . ." begins the General Appearance section of the Basenji's standard. The Basenji is a very easy size to handle. At 20 to 25 pounds, it is easily lifted, when necessary, and doesn't take up too much room in house or car. The short back and light build give it tremendous agility both in the field or bouncing about the house or yard. The coat is completely odor free, requires minimal grooming and sheds mud effortlessly as it dries. Many people who are allergic to dogs can live with a Basenji. The body type carries through the sleek look, with all parts fitting into a smoothly delineated whole.

Correct breeding is shown also in the quality of the head with its aristo-cratic, chiseled form and almond-shaped, dark, expressive eyes. Wrinkles appear on the forehead when the ears are pricked forward giving the typical curious, worried expression.

The tightly curled tail is actually straight when the pups are born. The curl soon begins to develop, and usually reaches its final curl when the pup has finished teething at six months old. Children and dog show judges seem to be endlessly fascinated with a Basenji's tail curl, and often uncurl it just to see what will happen! Care should be taken, as some Basenjis have such a tight curl that it is uncomfortable for them to have the tail unfurled. Generally, however, a Basenji's tail curl is controlled by muscles. When the dog relaxes in sleep the tail uncurls. Old Basenjis seem to lose some of the curl in their tails as their general muscle tone lessens.

8

Personality

A Basenji is more than a small, sleek, clean dog known for his barkless quality. The primary words that come to mind when thinking about them are curious, alert, smart, proud, loving and independent—all at the same time! The Basenji comes by these characteristics honestly, based on his life in Africa. He needed all these characteristics to survive as a hunting dog.

As soon as a Basenji puppy completely opens his eyes (at about three weeks old) he begins investigating his environment. At that age he already needs to know what it smells like, what it looks like and how it tastes. "It" can be his blanket, newspapers, box, mother, or anything that appears in the box.

Three-week old puppies are already learning about their world.
Photo by Jon Coe.

This alert curiosity will continue for the life of the dog. If a Basenji didn't possess this need to learn about everything, how could he have possibly learned to exist among the dangers of the African rain forest? In our modern world, this instinct means that a Basenji is going to go over his new home very thoroughly when he first arrives and will be forever curious about anything new brought home. A Basenji should not be a hyperactive dog, but he really

This puppy is sampling the flavor of fresh, green grass. Photo courtesy of Charletta Jones.

enjoys some stimulation in his life from time to time. Human company is a treat for a Basenji. There are new smells to be investigated on the person, on his coat or in her purse if it has been placed within reach. Also there is the opportunity to see how much attention can be obtained from the newcomer. The average Basenji enjoys any outing for the stimulation it gives. Even a car ride is great fun.

A Basenji is usually easy to house train as he is naturally clean. Unfortunately, the house training almost invariably regresses during the first rain storm. Basenjis simply do not like to get wet so your extra supervision is required to keep house training moving along. Every Basenji likes his comforts with warm and dry being at the top of the list. He loves to sit in a sunny window seat—warmth with a view! Your vigilance is sometimes required during the winter months as the Basenji is known to cuddle up too close to a heater or fireplace for his own safety. Some have described the Basenji as a heat-seeking missile.

Sometimes the characteristics which make the Basenji different are surprising and amusing. Recently, the Nabisco Food Company called us to inquire about using a Basenji on the packaging of one of their new pet food

Although Basenjis dislike getting wet in the rain, this girl demonstrates that snow is acceptable for quick winter games and outings. Photo courtesy of Charletta Jones.

products. When we arrived for the photo session, with dogs in hand, the photographer started talking about their short coats. Not realizing where his comments were leading, I agreed they had short hair just like they were supposed to. He went on to say that when they had Dachshunds in for photos they walked them up and down the hallway so the dogs would pant. They wanted your regular happy dog look. After I explained that Basenjis rarely pant, there was a strained silence. Well, I don't know if Basenjis will be appearing on your grocer's shelf or not because our Basenjis wouldn't pant in an air-conditioned building!

A Basenji is smart enough to learn things quickly but doesn't always choose to do what he has learned when you want him to. Probably this shows up most clearly when dealing with the command "come." You know he has heard your call, for he turned his ear in your direction to catch the sounds. He knows you want him to come and yet he continues doing whatever it is he is doing. Why? Well, he has decided whatever smells so good is more important. This is a thinking dog and therefore a more difficult dog to live with than one who obeys instantly, without question. But, for the Basenji lover, this is one of the things that makes the breed interesting. Your Basenji loves you, but there is a time for cuddling and ear scratching and a time for hunting or investigating.

No other dog that I know of will look you squarely in the eye. A Basenji has enough self-esteem to look right into your soul. Proud and alert when out meeting strangers (especially dog strangers), he is loving and silly at home

The expressive face and gestures typical of Basenjis are demonstrated by this Canadian puppy. Photo courtesy of Paul De Nardo.

with many games played with a very expressive face and gestures. Basenjis can be impossible to live with at times and impossible to live without if you are the right kind of person.

Every Basenji probably thinks his middle name must be "no" and he has wonderful ways of trying to make up when he hears that word. This is one place where a yodel, that special Basenji sound, may be used to win back your favor. The yodel's main use is as "Hello, I'm so happy to see you!" This is saved for the moment you return from an outing without him. Some Basenjis feel any visitor should also be given a big "hello" in yodel form. Some yodels are loud as a bugle blast, some very melodious, and some very quiet. The quietest Basenjis never yodel or may just have a bit of a yodel combined with a yawn. Besides the typical yodel or crow, the Basenji is quite capable of producing the common dog growl, an extraordinary coyote-like howl and, in extreme situations, almost a scream. There have been a few, a very few, Basenjis that have been capable of saying a few words. Jeremy O'Tennji comes to mind as the talker I was introduced to some years ago. Sheila Smith and her daughter would sit him up in a chair at the dining room table, bribe him with liver bits and give him cues: "What is your favorite ice cream?" "Vanilla," could easily be distinguished as the answer. "What is your favorite color?" "Yellow." And, "What do coyotes say?" brought forth a long, mournful howl.

Jeremy O'Tennji—"The Talking Basenji." Photos by Jon Coe.

CHAPTER 9

Why Don't Basenjis Bark?

I've included parts of three articles that appeared in *The Basenji* magazine, in 1983, to show some opinions regarding this characteristic.

The following illustration and write-up originally appeared as a poster prepared by Elizabeth White:

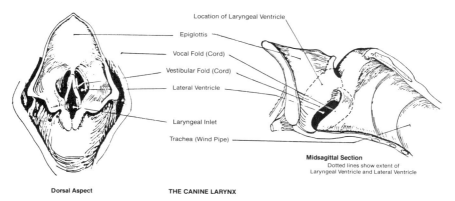

Location of Laryngeal Ventricle

Epiglottis

Vocal Fold (Cord)

Vestibular Fold (Cord)

Lateral Ventricle

Laryngeal Inlet

Trachea (Wind Pipe)

Midsagittal Section
Dotted lines show extent of
Laryngeal Ventricle and Lateral Ventricle

Dorsal Aspect   **THE CANINE LARYNX**

Figure II-1. Why are Basenjis Barkless?

The Basenji's voice box (larynx) has all the features of the canine larynx. In the Basenji, the laryngeal ventricle, which is located between the vocal and vestibular folds, is shallow compared to other domestic dogs. The shallow laryngeal ventricle apparently limits the movement of the vocal cords. This is the probable cause of barklessness in Basenjis.

"We have examined the larynx of the Basenji and compared it with a normal dog and also a cow. The vocal folds and muscles do not appear different. The ventricle has a position as usual except that it is very shallow. This prevents the vocal fold from being free on its lateral side. Apparently, this limits the vibrations of the vocal fold." Based on their finds, the Basenji does not bark due to a physical structure that differs from other dogs. (From *Basenjis, the Barkless Dogs* by Veronica Tudor-Williams, who quoted from *Basenji—Dog from the Past* by F.B. Johnson.)

This second section is excerpted by Veronica Tudor-Williams and is originally from an article that appeared in *Small Animal Journal* by Dr. R.R. Ashdown of the Royal Veterinary Hospital in Britain.

The larynxes were removed, post mortem, from two Basenjis—B1 (Fula of the Congo, born in Central Africa) and B2, a 12-year old female (Ch. Fulafab of the Congo, Fula's granddaughter) whom Mrs. Prestige was generous enough to donate shortly afterwards. Neither of these dogs had ever been known to bark. Similar material was prepared from seven dogs of both sexes ranging from a Great Dane to mongrels. The surface features were studied with special attention to the vestibular and vocal folds, the laryngeal recess and the laryngeal saccule. Muscles, nerves and folds showed no striking differences in the Basenjis. Right and left laryngeal recesses and saccules were radiographed after filling with barium sulphate. In Basenji B2, the left and right laryngeal recesses were completely filled by thick folds of mucosa and were therefore markedly shallow and less extensive than those seen in the other dogs. In Basenji B1, the same was true; also a careful search failed to reveal any sign of a laryngeal saccule leading from the right recess in B1, though in the left recess a small orifice was present through which a blunted bristle could be introduced to a depth of 7 mm. In the comparable larynx of the other dogs the width of the orifices were 16 and 17 mm, respectively. Similar values were obtained for the other dogs. In all of the "normal" dogs the saccules expanded dorsally to occupy a large space between the vestibular folds and the thyroid cartilages. In the Basenji larynxes, however, this was not so on either side; and on the radiographs of the two Basenjis and one Fox Terrier the differences are clearly indicated.

The oscillograms published in Tembrok (1964) reveal that in barking there is a sudden onset of high intensity sound and it is a possibility that a reduction in mobility in these folds might affect ability to bark. It should be stressed that Basenjis are not lacking in vocal powers; they seem unable to bark, but make their own special sound which Miss Tudor-Williams describes as "not unlike a young cockerel's first attempt at crowing."

A yodeling Basenji. *Photo courtesy of the American Kennel Club.*

The final article was written by Jon Coe and gives another side to the answer of the question, "Why Don't Basenjis Bark?" and some thoughts on why this would be a desirable trait.

Perhaps this question has been asked for as long as Basenjis have been compared to other dogs. The usual response is that they just can't. Much less often someone suggests that they could, but just won't or don't. Anatomical research . . . has been done to justify the first premise—that Basenjis can't bark. It is inconclusive ". . . the vocal folds and muscles do not appear different." Only superficial differences were found in the ventricle. Although this may produce a slightly different sound of bark, I doubt that it could account for the difference in barking *behavior* between, say, a Basenji and a Beagle or terrier. Consideration of physiological equipment (vocal folds, etc.) cannot be separated from the study of behavior and motivation. For example, a debarked dog attempts to bark just as much as he did before being debarked.

In *Genetics and the Social Behavior of the Dog* (1965), Scott and Fuller did a thorough study of barking behavior, comparing Basenjis, Beagles, Shelties, Cockers and Wirehaired Fox Terriers. The following quotes summarize their findings:

"Barklessness. One of the striking characteristics of the Basenji breed is the fact that these dogs rarely bark. We can only speculate as to why this trait developed, since it was already present in the breed when it was brought out of Africa. It is possible that barking, which is an alarm signal given by dogs whenever a strange animal or person approaches their home territories, is not conducive to survival in the African forests. Leopards are reputably fond of dog meat, and it may be that the dog which barks simply attracts attention to itself and comes to an untimely end. Although travelers have described Basenjis as being very noisy in their native African habitat, especially at night, none of the sounds produced are like barks, being variously described as 'crowing,' 'yowling,' and 'howling.' This suggests that the Basenjis may have developed sounds with unusual acoustic qualities. The barking of most dogs, as analyzed on the sonograph, consists of a succession of short, sharp, monotonous sounds which are very easy to localize. That is, barking conveys accurate information as to the location of the barking animal. On the other hand, sounds which vary in pitch, loudness, and duration are much more difficult to localize with respect to direction and distance, as anyone who has had experience with the vocalizations of coyotes will recognize. While distinctly different from coyotes, the Basenji sounds have similar qualities of variability and may serve the same adaptive and protective function. In any case, Basenjis bark very little compared to other breeds of dogs and, whenever different breeds of dogs live together, the Basenjis' relative silence is extremely noticeable. As a stranger walks by the dog runs at our laboratory, a chorus of barks arises from a group of Cocker Spaniels and from a nearby group of Shetland Sheepdogs. In a pen between, a litter of Basenjis look up without opening their mouths.

"Darwin thought that wolves do not ordinarily bark and that when they do it is because they have learned the habit from dogs. All modern observers of wolves under any conditions, whether in zoos or in the remote wilderness, agree that they bark, although not as much as many dog breeds. The barklessness of the Basenji is therefore not a primitive ancestral trait but rather a new and unusual characteristic, produced by some sort of selection.

"Obviously, Basenjis (or at least the strain which we have) are not completely barkless. When sufficiently excited, they will bark. [A table showed] that Basenjis barked during 20 percent of the opportunities given them during the dominance test, whereas the Cocker Spaniels barked during 68 percent. The Basenjis usually gave only one or two low "woofs" when they did bark, the average number being about two. At eleven weeks of age, the largest number of barks given by any Basenji during the dominance test was 20 and the next highest was 12. More than this, the sound which the Basenjis make has a different quality from that of other breeds. Thus, there are three different aspects of what looks offhand to be a simple behavior trait. One is the threshold of stimulation—very high in the Basenji and very low in the Cocker Spaniel. A second trait is the tendency to bark only a small number of times rather than to become excited and bark continuously as do many Cocker Spaniels. The maximum number of barks recorded for a Cocker in a ten-minute period was 907, or more than 90 a minute."

Jon Coe continues:

. . . through experimental breedings between Basenjis and Cocker Spaniels, Scott and Fuller determined that the trait of being easily stimulated to bark is probably controlled by a single dominant inherited gene. Their opinion seems to be that it is the high threshold of stimulation that makes Basenjis barkless. In other words, they can bark but don't, at least not very often.

Now every new owner of a Basenji is in for a number of surprises. How many times has a new owner called to say, "Hey, that puppy just barked! I thought Basenjis weren't supposed to bark." The truth is they do have a warning call like all other canids. This is the "woof" Scott and Fuller mentioned. It is part of a startle reaction and can be heard in wolves, foxes, jackals and cape hunting dogs which are all breeds that normally don't bark. This leads me to speculate on another possibility. Perhaps Basenjis don't bark simply because they *never did!* In this I disagree with Scott & Fuller's assertion above. If infrequent barking is an ancestral trait of wolves, why can't it be an ancestral trait of Basenjis as well?

The usual assumption is that the barking characteristic was established through selective breeding along with curling tails, droop ears, multiple colors and all the other features of physique and temperament that resulted in today's breeds of dogs. This assumption then assumes that Basenjis descended from an early variety of barking dogs who then lost the bark due to environmental selection against barking, such as predation by leopards. A problem with this theory is that leopards are not limited to Africa, the Basenji's ancestral home, but are found throughout the Near East and Asia as well. Leopards range from Afghanistan to Korea and from Borneo to Lake Baykal. One assumes that dogs throughout this region have been preyed upon by leopards, but they still bark. Barking may attract a leopard but is also an excellent defense, especially when it summons help. Leopards are commonly treed by smaller barking dogs.

If, on the other hand, the Basenji breed derived from domestic ancestors so ancient that the barking character had not yet been selected for, then modern Basenjis would simply never have developed this trait at all.

There are a number of dog breeds that emerged before the advent of human writing or pictorial records and whose age is therefore speculative. Yet the fact that all of these breeds are very different from their wolf ancestors shows that great periods of time and many intermediate breeds separate them from wolves. Yet of these breeds, which include Greyhounds, Salukis, Mastiffs and other dogs of antiquity, only Basenjis are confirmed to have an annual photoperiodic breeding season for both dogs and bitches, as is found in wolves. Other primitive behaviors such as production of milk and maternal care by unbred "aunts" and regurgitation of food for pups by males are occasionally found in Basenjis, but may also occur in other breeds.

The Basenji breed, which is similar to other primitive pariah breeds around the world, certainly existed long before it was recorded in Egyptian tombs of thousands of years ago. Did it or its direct antecedents trace their origins to a time and place before dogs barked?

The 1987 African expedition came across this Basenji wearing a typical bell, with a hunting party in Zaire, Africa. Photo courtesy of Michael Work.

SECTION III
Basenji Activities

- *First You Have To Live With Your Basenji*
- *The Hunting Basenji*
- *The Basenji in Lure Coursing*
- *The Basenji As A Show Dog*
- *The Basenji As An Obedience Dog*

The Basenji is a versatile dog who can perform well in many endeavors. The bond between dog and owner will be enhanced if the dog is allowed to be more than a lawn ornament or couch potato. He can excel in one field or many and have a great time doing it. The owner who involves himself in activities with his Basenji will notice an almost psychic teamwork develop between the two of them. The chapters that follow will introduce potential adventures in the hunting field, show ring, lure coursing field or obedience trial that you may enjoy looking into. Let's start at the beginning.

See that Basenji puppy look out of those newly opened eyes. He discovers his littermates; he reaches out to touch them. Soon he is able to listen to sounds and record what they mean. Rattle goes the food pan—here comes dinner. Heavy footsteps—here comes a man and some entertainment. There is a higher, gentler voice—a woman to take care of me. Laughter and rowdy voices—kids can be great fun. These are some of the early associations your puppy may already have. Whether an effort is made or not, the puppy is going to learn what sounds and sights mean. The associations between sounds and sights and the puppy's response to them can be controlled. The breeder has probably begun working on these associations to be sure they are positive; to be sure the pup is started out in the right direction.

The associations and habits the pup learns first are going to remain with the pup for life. Whether your Basenji is to be a house pet only or a show dog, a hunting dog, a lure-coursing dog, an obedience dog or all of these activities are planned, early socialization and minimal early training will be invaluable in your endeavors together. Your puppy is learning from the moment you bring him home and he might as well be learning the right habits and responses so that he will fit into your lifestyle and be prepared for a varied life with you.

CHAPTER 10

First You Have to Live With Your Basenji

The first concern is always house training. Your Basenji puppy should be partially trained already. If the pups are in a large enough pen or box, they will naturally use a particular corner or area of the pen as a toilet. Many breeders provide a large box of paper or kitty litter as a toilet and the pups learn to use it by simply being placed in it when they first wake up or after they eat. The first step is made as there is now a particular place to go.

When the pup comes home, the same technique can be used. Concentrate on house training during that first few weeks by being very vigilant about your pup's habits. Take him out when he first wakes, after he eats or after he has been playing in the house. Take him out frequently and stay with him to be sure he eliminates. Quietly tell him he's a good pup and bring him back inside. Don't scold him when he makes accidents, but rush him outside if he is found in the act. The pup does not associate the "product" with the "act" so rubbing his nose in the "product" does no good. Watch the pup carefully for behavioral clues about his bodily needs. Some Basenji owners have successfully taught their pups to ring a bell hung low at the door as a signal that they need to go out. My dogs are clued to the word "outside." When they look like they need to go out, usually shown by nervous activity or poking at me, I ask, "Do you want to go outside?" If they do, they rush to the door.

If you want the pup to use a particular part of the yard as his toilet, always take him there. If you live in snow country, a pile of straw on the snow will protect the pup from the extreme cold and he will eventually learn to use that part of the yard as his toilet. Generally, given the run of a large yard, a pup doesn't go out too far, but as he matures, he goes further and further. When the dog is all grown up he will likely be using the most distant portion of the yard and/or the part with some cover. A privacy-seeking Basenji with his head in a hedge and his behind sticking out is always good for a chuckle. Yes, there will be lapses, especially during the first bad weather, and these will require your attention again but punishment is rarely necessary.

Crate training can help house train your Basenji. The pup doesn't like to soil his own bed so the pup crated overnight will wake you when he needs to eliminate. Placing a crate for him beside your bed at night will ensure that you

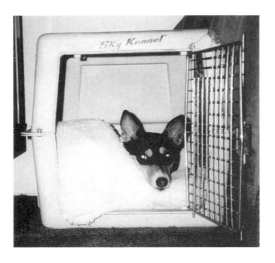

The crate will become a den for your Basenji. He'll go there when he prefers peace and quiet. It will also be a bit of home to carry along for his comfort when you travel. Photo courtesy of Jo Clopper.

hear him when he wakes and, additionally, your presence nearby will assure him he has not been abandoned. The pup should also learn to take some of his daily naps in his crate as well. Take him outside as soon as he wakes up.

Why do Basenji breeders emphasize crate training so much? It takes from one and a half to two years for your Basenji to reach dependable mature behavior. The youngster who is left to his own devices during that immature period of his life can develop many behavioral problems. Simply leaving him confined to a bathroom, laundry room or backyard can invite surprising destruction during play activities or if the pup panics at being abandoned.

Puppies left alone discover all the wrong things to do! Photo courtesy of Marilyn Leighton.

A Basenji puppy needs your time and supervision to learn what are dog toys and to learn that socks, toes, etc. are forbidden. Photo courtesy of Nancy Swanson.

Scratching at plaster board walls, chewing cabinet corners or digging countless holes in the yard are considered good clean fun if no one is there to explain what is unacceptable behavior. Chewing on electrical cords can cost your pup his life. Protect your puppy, home and possessions by crate training that Basenji from the beginning. Don't, however, use the crate as a substitute for spending time with your puppy teaching him good manners.

You will find this training useful throughout the dog's life as you can take your dog along when you travel, even on an airplane trip. You'll find motel owners and relatives are happier to see you arrive when your dog is crate trained. Start thinking about all the situations where that crate training could be priceless.

You must decide the rules for your Basenji before he comes home. Must he never get up on the furniture? Never let him on the furniture then. Make it a habit. You don't like to have your dog jumping up on yourself or visitors? Start now. It is easy at this young age to catch the pup before he jumps or even as he jumps up. Place him back on the floor in a sitting position and pet him briefly while he sits. Ask your visitors to do the same. The simple repetition of being rewarded with petting and kind words for sitting in front of a visitor or family

Puppy games are rough and tumble. Photo courtesy of Trish Davis.

member will ensure that the pup never learns to jump up on people for attention. Instead he will sit for attention. It won't make him "hand shy" or less eager to meet visitors or other strangers.

All Basenjis use their mouths to chew on one another. It is their way to play dog games. It is your job to teach them that people games are different. No, a puppy's nip is not much but that pup is going to grow up and it won't be cute anymore. Don't wait to teach your dog appropriate people games. Use either a substitute toy to give the pup whenever it tries to nip or chew or, if necessary, take it by the muzzle saying a sharp "no" before substituting a chew toy. Be firm, not mean.

Isn't it cute how he steals your sock and runs away hoping you will play chase? It won't be cute for long! It will simply be frustrating and you will soon have a dog you can't live with. That pup may start by chewing a little on your shoelaces but he may well end up chewing up the whole shoe if you don't stop him immediately. You can make use of the Basenji's dislike of water to control the naughty pup from a distance. A good method for correcting bad behavior involves using a common, old-fashioned water pistol or a spray water bottle on the "stream" setting. This can be especially useful when the pup continues his naughty behavior until you come to him for a correction when he runs off before the correction can be made. Using the word "no" as the correction is given will give the word additional meaning for the pup. If you are having trouble getting these basic ideas across, don't delay getting a book on dog training or finding a kindergarten puppy training class where you can get advice. The longer any problem behavior goes on, the more difficult it will be to change the behavior.

Be sure the puppy's early experiences are good ones. *Photo by Susan Coe.*

You should have the raw material of a basically friendly and outgoing Basenji. Be sure this pup has human visitors, and sees a variety of places, meets a variety of people ranging from adults to babies. Always be watchful to see that these early meetings are friendly, positive occasions. Instill a basic trust of the human race in your pup and you will have a friendly adult Basenji. It is wise, as well, to arrange introductions to other friendly canines so your adult Basenji will get along well in a canine environment such as might be found at a family picnic, a dog show or at a lure coursing or obedience trial.

As the Basenji matures he is rather like a human teenager, and may want to test his place. The young dog may try to challenge your position of authority at some point, often around seven to twelve months of age. This is typical behavior in a group of dogs. The youngster challenges the dominant animal to see just how much authority can be taken. You must respond firmly, and quickly as the dominant individual. It is rare for the dominant dog in such a situation to ever hurt the young dog. He usually just flips the younger dog over on his back and stands over him. You can do the same thing, keeping the young dog on his back briefly and then ignoring him for a bit after the confrontation.

A Basenji isn't a natural at obedience. The only way to make any obedience a part of your Basenji's basic personality is to start immediately. Again, he is going to be learning how to get along in this world and he might as well learn your way. Whether you are planning to go into formal obedience later or simply want a livable house pet, a few basic responses will really help. Again, start now. Since "come" is among the most difficult commands for a Basenji, start by calling the pup at random times and rewarding him with a tidbit from a supply in your pocket. Or involve another member of the family and call the pup back and forth between you. Hide from him. This is great fun which can sometimes be rewarded with a pat and kind words and other times with those wonderful tidbits. Condition your Basenji pup to come when called. It will help. Leash training, heeling or show training can start similarly. (More detail follows in each specialized section.) The most important thing to remember is that your work now will be richly rewarded in the future with an enjoyable Basenji companion.

11

The Hunting Basenji

Let's Take That Basenji Hunting!
by Paul van Ormer

I would not attempt to say why other folks own a Basenji or why some hunt with them. I can only speak for myself. I enjoy watching a Basenji work a field, muscles rippling as he gaits back and forth across that field. I also derive a lot of pleasure from observing his little idiosyncratic traits. Then again, there is a certain amount of challenge. Basenjis are often spoken of as being hard-headed, independent and aloof, yet in reality they are not. Mr. Phemister once said, "The trouble with dogs is people—the Basenji is a very intelligent animal and is clever enough to talk one out of training him." With this I heartily agree, though it seems to me that when hunting, mine try hard to please. Constantly on the move, still they frequently come in and look up at me for a word of praise and a friendly pat. Wish I could say they were perfect, never making a false point, finding and retrieving every dead bird and obeying every command but, that's just asking too much.

I write this primarily to those owners of Basenjis that have never used their favorite for hunting. To the owners with trained dogs this is more or less old stuff. We all know that the Basenji was, and is used in Africa as a hunting dog, mainly a driver, and it is truly so. He is a fast dog and likes any game that will run from him, often catching the pursued before it can reach a hole in the ground, a brush pile, or a tree. However, "The Wild Thing" has a great many virtues and hunting potential that tend to make it more popular with hunters in our own country. It adapts well and does a good job on a squirrel, rabbit, quail and pheasant. I have even toyed with the thought of training one of mine to night hunt.

Let's consider the squirrel at present, for in the fall of the year they are easy to find as they will be shucking nuts, eating some and storing some away preparatory to the coming winter snows. Even if you do not care to actually shoot any squirrel, preferring instead to merely go nut gathering, at least take

This black and white puts up a pheasant in the California grasslands. Photo courtesy of Terri Gavaletz.

your Basenji with you. Watch him as he casts about, investigating every strange scent or object. No doubt, if this is a new experience for him, you will see him shy away from many of the strange objects encountered, perhaps a corn shuck on the ground or a leaf blowing towards him. He will circle with head cocked, very alert and very cautious until he determines what kind of thing it is. As you watch you will probably notice your Basenji throw his head in the air, sniffing and listening or perhaps he will find a scent on the ground which he will follow with as much surety and a great deal faster than some of the other hounds. Should you happen to see a squirrel in a tree that your dog doesn't notice, then by all means try to show it to him. When he knows there is something up a tree he will rear up on said tree and probably moan. If he happens to actually see the game he is likely to try to climb up in the tree after it. To me, the fact that the Basenji doesn't bawl on trail or bark at treed quarry is a distinct advantage in squirrel hunting.

If you are one of the many that like to go afield after quail or pheasant, don't hesitate to take your Basenji with you for it will do a creditable job. It won't perform in the same manner as a trained Pointer or Setter, still it will be a definite help in showing you when you are getting close to game. The Basenji can be trained to point (in its own way), honor and retrieve.

Let me tell you about an outing we made the latter part of one December when we had snow and cold weather and then some warming days like we get in Missouri. On one of these warming days my number one son, Bill, came by the house and said he had been out to Ray Terril's the day before and found four covies. He asked if I didn't want to take my "African Possom Hound" (as he calls them) out that afternoon, and, of course, I was agreeable.

Now Ray's farm consists of about 300 acres of rolling, very poor land, lots of waist-high buffalo grass, briar patches and thickets. There were two fields that had been planted with milo and corn, both harvested. Most of the snow had melted, the branches were running and the cultivated fields were very, very muddy. In fact, in crossing them our feet resembled snow shoes. The 'Senji, for some reason, wanted to hunt these fields and went back and forth across them several times with head in the air. When he finally gave up (there was nothing in them) and moved out, he was a real muddy little dog but going strong.

We moved over to the grass and here the 'Senji had to work hard. The gait was gone, replaced by a jumping movement. At times he would find the going a little easier and his progress could be observed by the movement of the grass. As I hunted through the grass, I hunted into a little clear space except for the heavy growth of briars that covered it. This patch was crisscrossed with many rabbit runs and old 'Senji put his nose to the ground and from the sniffing and snorting you would have thought there was a Coonhound on the trail. He was doing a pretty good job of traveling the rabbit trails, then all at once he started to slow down and get closer to the ground, almost like a cat stalking a bird. I wondered, could it be quail or just a rabbit. It was a rabbit that broke out

Working through a harvested cornfield. *Photo courtesy of the American Kennel Club.*

about ten feet in front of him, and in hot pursuit he ran smack into a bunch of briars. "Yipe," he said, and cautiously backed out and on to trail the rabbit to a hole. I blew the whistle and he returned. Had we been hunting rabbits I could have had several as I had observed quite a few slipping back through the grass and briars as they heard the dogs working. We usually hunt rabbits with rifle and pistol, but never shoot one when quail hunting.

It looked like this hunt was going to be a zero. I was getting more and more tired and stopped often to smoke a cigarette and rest. The 'Senji was getting tired too and would come in and rest when I did. After all, he had been running all afternoon and part of the time jumping. 'Senji has an aversion to the "stik-tites" that stuck to him and at every rest period would busily remove them. Then, apparently thinking that they bothered me, would remove them from my hunting pants. One of those aforementioned characteristic idiosyncrasies that make you proud of your Basenji.

I finally decided to go to the car and told Bill so. He said that he was going to circle one of the hills and would join me. He had gotten part way down the draw when a couple of shots from the hillside put me back in the mood and I rejoined the party. Old 'Senji came to life too, and just like a fresh dog went to casting back and forth, part of the time with head up and part of the time with head down. We had found part of a covey on the south side of the hill in the grass and got three, with some good dog work. The 'Senji made a nice point, find and retrieve.

While this wasn't the most productive hunt of the season, it afforded an opportunity to observe the Basenji working under very adverse conditions and I wasn't the least bit disappointed.

One of my Basenjis that I frequently let stay in the house loves to sit at the screen door and constantly sniff the air for strange scents. He really likes to hunt and sometimes catches a bird on the wing. In common with other dogs, or with people, some of our Basenjis will be more alert and aggressive than others but I have found them all to be very proficient in their ability to hunt.

I hope I have been able to put this together with some facility and I certainly don't want to set myself up as an authority on the hunting Basenji. Rather just an old hillbilly using common sense. While it is doubtful if our Basenjis can compete with the same degree of skill shown by some of our highly-trained dog breeds specializing in one field, nevertheless they are real good all-around hunting dogs and well worth taking with you.

Training the Basenji for the Field
by Major A.L. Braun

There are several things which many people talk about but few do anything about. One of them is the hunting capability of the Basenji. Most breeders of Basenjis will expound on the fine hunting qualities of the breed, but never hunt with them. This is unfortunate, since though a well-controlled Basenji does make a wonderful pet, and a well-constructed Basenji does make a fine show animal, it is the Basenji who has been trained and who is being used as a hunter who gives the most pleasure.

As our breed is becoming better known and more popular, I am gratified that more people are becoming interested in the breed as a hunting dog. Those few of us who have hunted regularly with these dogs in this country are being asked with ever-increasing frequency by novice Basenji owners how they should go about training their dogs for the field. There has been very little written on the subject, perhaps because we who do hunt with Basenjis are having too much fun at it to take the time to write about it!

Major Al Braun at Lost Lake, Michigan with his hunting dog "Salty" and a partridge they bagged.

Because of the Basenji's distinctive traits, there are people who feel he is difficult to train, or that he should be field trained differently than other hunting dogs. While I do not agree with this feeling completely, I do agree that it takes a thorough understanding of this breed's temperament to train him to obey your commands happily. He must be made to feel that what you want is what he wants, without insulting his intelligence. It is almost impossible to train him to do your bidding through force alone. He will eventually obey, but resentfully and with reluctance. Much better results can be obtained through patient, loving firmness. He must be taught that you are the boss and he must obey, but that you do love and understand him.

Most people who have contacted me about how to field train a Basenji already have one which is six or more months old. Many old-time hunters and trainers claim that field training should begin only when a dog is mature. I agree that a mature Basenji can be trained, and have done so myself with success. But, unless the dog has had some basic training as a puppy, I feel that chances of success are slim and require a great deal more patience, knowledge and time than most of us have. It is, I am convinced, much easier and better to start with a puppy.

I also believe it is best to start with a pup selected from a litter which is the result of a mating of Basenjis who have demonstrated hunting desire and

An all-purpose hunter, this Basenji is retrieving a duck! Photo courtesy of Mr. Heck.

ability. Within that litter, there will be some pups who from infancy display more hunting tendencies than others. They will notice birds perched or flying nearby and will take an active interest in them, perhaps freezing in their tracks when they see them or they may go into the Basenji "point" with both forelegs flat to the ground and rear end up in a crouch; or they may streak toward it and flush it. These are the pups who also most enjoy chasing and retrieving a ball. If you take such a pup and train it properly, your chances of having a worthwhile hunting companion are very good.

Basic training should start at a very early age. You should buy your pup and take him home when he is seven to eight weeks old, at which time his nervous system and brain have nearly adult capacity and he can learn to respond to humans. This is the time to establish your relationship with your dog. You are taking the place of his parent, and you can begin his training as a gun-dog now by making your informal play an important part of his discipline.

From the 7th to the 12th week, you should spend as much time with your pup as possible since this is the period when he is most receptive to, and retentive of, training given. You should feed the dog yourself to build emotional security and establish rapport; give him a definite, and preferably, a separate place to sleep, and teach him to cope with the frustrations of puppyhood. Through constant repetition, the pup first learns his name; then the meaning of a firm "No!" followed by corrective action; and "Good Dog" followed by gentle fondling. With firm but loving discipline and plenty of praise, and with patience on your part, at the end of his 12th week, your pup will know and respond to his name, will be housebroken, and will be walking nicely with you on leash. Throughout this period, the pup learns the most important lesson, that you are the boss, but life can be pleasant when he pleases you. These are the things the pup must learn for him to be an enjoyable lifetime companion for you, both as a pet and as a hunting dog.

Formal hunting training starts at 12 weeks. From this time until the pup is about four months old, you concentrate on teaching him to sit, stay and come. I won't go into detail here on how to achieve this. There are entire books on the subject (the Blanche Saunders book is a good one), and you can observe the training at an obedience school, then use what you've learned to train your dog yourself at home. The reason for this is that most obedience schools will not accept a dog until he is six months old, and some obedience trainers use methods which do not work well with Basenjis. Also, the type of obedience training given in many such schools results in a stylized formal type of routine which the dog follows only when in the ring and ignores when out of it, especially on the recall (come). You must teach your dog to respond to the commands, sit, stay and come promptly and happily in a field situation, rather than in the rigid, militaristic manner taught in obedience schools. The basic training tool is voice command, and when the dog is responding to that, you teach him also to follow your directions by hand signal and whistle. The hand signal for "Sit" is given with a closed hand held up with forefinger extended, then dropping the hand and pointing the finger to the ground. The hand signal for "Stay" is the upraised hand with palm out. For "Come," you give the hand signal for stay and then drop the hand toward the ground, simultaneously giving two blasts on the whistle. Obedience to these commands is essential for further training.

Since the Basenji's natural hunting instinct is to find, flush, drive and hold game, you could use this natural instinct together with the commands he now knows and make a pretty good hunting dog out of him. Take him to a field, preferably in an isolated area away from traffic, and, of course, one where you expect to find the type of game you want him to hunt. Release him, and he should start exploring the terrain with his nose and eyes. If he takes off out of gun range, give the hand and whistle commands for come and when he returns, praise him and send him off again with the verbal command "Go on." It won't take him long to learn that you want him to course back and forth in front of you, and the limit of distance he may go. He will also learn through praise that while quartering he is encouraged to indulge his instinct to find game. When he finds it he will naturally burst in and flush it. Since he is within gun range, you have your shot. When you knock down the game, you may wish to allow your dog to nuzzle and mouth it so that he knows what he's after. Some hunters also give their dogs the game's heart, liver, etc., particularly when the hunt is over, to sharpen their hunting desire. I personally like to work in the field with a dog who is a bit hungry, never with one who has just eaten. If you take him out and work with him in this fashion with any frequency, before your Basenji is a year old, you will have a dog that you can

Basenjis are happy to hunt in any cover. *Photo courtesy of Jon Coe.*

take into the field, knowing that he will find and flush game within gun range for you.

For some hunters, however, this may not be enough; so when the dog is responding immediately and correctly to the vocal and visual signals for sit, stay and come (which should be by four months of age), you can start training him to stop in his tracks while running. You may wish to use the obedience school method known as "Drop on Recall" but I do not feel this is effective for field work. I prefer instead a method developed by a gun-dog man in which he gets the running dog to respond to the hand signal for stay while he shouts the command "Whoa." Then he gradually diminishes the use of the hand signal until the dog is responding to the verbal command. He uses the command whoa only when game is involved—to stop the dog, steady him on point, preventing him from flushing the bird and to teach him to honor the point of another dog. When he wishes to stop the dog on occasions when game is not involved, he uses the command "Sit." Once you have taught your dog to stop instantly on command in the field, you are well on your way in "high school" field training.

To familiarize your dog with the scent, feel and sight of birds, if you haven't an abundance of live game in your area, you can use a training tool made up of a fly rod with a wing attached by a piece of strong string about eight feet long. With this tool and the proper voice and hand commands, you can teach your dog not to rush in on a still bird, to stalk a moving bird, to move in easy, and to freeze (which is about as close as you'll get most Basenjis to come to a point). Using this tool in conjunction with a cap pistol, you can familiarize your dog with the noise of a gun shot while the wing is swirling around in the air above him. With the wing off the rod, you can also start his lessons on retrieving.

The ground work is now laid. You have a lot more work to do together, but from now on it's mostly in gaining experience in the field.

THE RABBIT HUNT
Catching the scent and
turning.

The rabbit is sighted.

He's got the rabbit!

Showing off his catch.

Photos courtesy of A.L. Braun

Basenji Field Trials

by Susan Coe

In the late 1970's, there was a strong group of Basenji fanciers in Minnesota who sponsored field trials for Basenjis each June. I was able to attend them several times and met Major Braun there the year he judged the trial. It was very interesting to see how really competent dogs (who may have never been off leash in the country before!) could really be in a field trial. There is a great deal of natural ability in the breed. Unfortunately, the time and effort of putting on these trials was too much for this group of enthusiasts and the field trials are no longer held. This is a report written by Earl Evans on the trial that took place on June 7 and 8, 1980.

Our judges were Mr. Roy Kollath, who breeds and hunts Weimaraners, is an officer in the Northstar Weimaraner Club, and who was one of the judges in our 1974 National Trial and one of our matches; and Mr. Charles Finman who breeds Basenjis and Rhodesian Ridgebacks and who has been very active in every field trial the Heart of Minnesota Basenji Club has ever held.

The weather both days was overcast with a fairly strong wind and also fairly high humidity. There were four pheasants placed in the bird field. For the puppy class, they were all in cages; but for the other two classes, the fourth bird was rocked to sleep and placed in a location where the gallery could watch the bird and see the dog on the find, wing and shot. Long leads were permitted in the puppy class, but as has been proven and said so often before, they hamper the dog and also have been proven to be unnecessary. This year, only two dogs left the hunting area and both were brought back by voice control. When a Basenji is given a chance to hunt, he will prefer hunting over any other thing.

All Basenjis follow the same basic hunting pattern. In the first burst of enthusiasm, they may range out much further than usual, but after a few minutes they settle down to working the terrain ahead of the hunter. The hunter should work them into the wind. Their normal hunting range is well within shot gun range. A juicy scent will bring them to full attention and there is never a doubt on the part of even the most inexperienced hunter that they are on scent, they will then move toward the game in a zigzag pattern using their nose and then jump the game. It is that simple and that beautiful, watching a Basenji do what they have been bred thousands of years to do—find game.

The major differences between the entered dogs was not really in the dogs. Once they know what they are out there for, they settle down and hunt. However, if a dog has never been in a hunting situation before it will take him some time to find out what is wanted. Once that's discovered, they are right in the thick of it, and loving every minute. The real difference is in the handlers. The person who has never hunted before, is much like the person who has never shown in the ring before. He can ruin a good dog's chance of winning. He will invariably try to over-control the dog and many times call the dog off a promising scent. This, of course, confuses the dog. A novice will also "upwind" the dog; *i.e.*, get between a bird and the source of the scent. When a human stands between a bird and the dog, the bird scent cannot be picked up by the dog. Always let the dog work ahead of you, into the wind, and stay behind him. A few hours out in the field with an experienced hunter and his dog are worth volumes.

The judges' comments on this year's trial were that the dogs were under better control and tended to work the wind and the natural cover better. Every dog was steady to wing and shot (many had never been fired over before) and pursued and located the downed birds. The distance for picking up scent ranged up to and between 15 and 20 yards, which is excellent. Judge Roy Kollath said the Basenjis had really improved over the six years since he had last judged one of our trials.

Basically, the difference this year between placing and not placing, and 4th and 1st place, was the dog and the handler having at least some experience in a hunting situation.

Ch. Akuaba's Periel d'Akili, C.D., LCM, *shown here making a fast turn on the lure,* **was the first winner of the Konde Memorial Award for top lure coursing Basenji.** *Photo courtesy of Pat Fisher.*

CHAPTER 12

The Basenji in Lure Coursing

The Race

by Jon Coe

The dogs are keen, very keen. They strain against their collars, then look back over their shoulders, urging us, "Come on—let's go! Let's go! We've waited all week, and now it's time!"

Twenty feet ahead lies the lure, an unimpressive tatter of a white plastic bag not yet brought alive by the lure operator's magic. The Basenjis, too, know it's not real, not yet alive, but deep within wells the urgent racial memory of generations without number—"There's your prey—get it!"

The starter's ready now; he signals the operator and the lure is suddenly reborn, flashing away . . . "Tally Ho!"

There they go! It's a good start. From the starting line it is hard to see who's ahead until Akua makes her move, as she always does, and cuts across the inside lane ahead of Suni, her daughter.

The day is a fine one and the grass is freshly mown. It'll be a fast race if the Basenjis don't lose the lure, but it's quickly approaching the first turn—there it is flashing away at right angles. The hounds were close and the turn caught them by surprise. There's a lot of hard braking and banking, sending grass flying as they cut after the lure. They make a good turn, but no four-footed runner can run around a pulley like a lure on a line, and the dogs have lost ground.

Akua is still in the lead, and you can bet she'll stay there. The dogs are running at right angles to the gallery now and Tembo, five yards back, is clearly distinguishable by his longer, easier stride. Suni, an equal distance behind the male, is running hard but not making up ground.

The dogs are running full out with their tails uncoiled behind them as the lure takes the second turn at the 200 yard mark. This turn was an easy 120° to the left and the Basenjis were far enough behind to adjust direction before hitting the turn and gained a bit on the rabbit. But just as they straightened out, the lure cuts back to the right and again there is fast braking and cutting.

Approaching the far corner, the lure operator slows his machine and Akua shoots forward after the lagging rabbit. She is only three yards from the lure when it hits the pulley and darts with a flash to the right at nearly 90°. Akua is caught outside and off guard and as she brakes, Tembo leaps past on the inside, driving hard. Before Akua can get up steam, Suni also passes and her mother is unexpectedly behind.

The little hounds seem infinitely far away now as the setting sun throws them into silhouette before the tall golden grass of the field beyond. Everyone is squinting and the squinting increases the other-worldly effect. The hounds seem to swim through the golden liquid radiance, their coats ember-like in straining silence.

They are tiring now, slackening the pace slightly after a quarter mile of exertion. Akua is coasting a little, anticipating the final turn. After three seasons of racing, she knows the lure will turn just before it reaches the tall grass 50 yards ahead, yet she runs true and never cuts across. She also knows the rabbit is just a piece of plastic, yet something inside generations old says, "Stay on it—it's real."

Tembo also knows the course and he, too, is coasting just a little, saving himself for the last sprint.

Suni's running hard. She must know she won't win, she never has, but like all Basenjis, she loves to run and that rabbit is bouncing and flashing before her. "There, see, it hit the corner, quickly now Tembo, get it!"

Tembo hit the corner well, timing himself to drive out of the turn. Akua has gained in the 30 yards before the pulley, anticipating the flashing lure's turn, and she too powers away leaving Suni breathless and behind, but also driving hard for the finish line 200 yards away.

Now the race is full on. None of the events of the first four turns matter as Akua pulls even with Tembo. The big male sees the little bitch and knows what her determined grimace means—she'll win or drop, but she won't lose! Tembo renews his effort. His better rear angulation and far more powerful shoulders

Dharian Fancy Dancer of Woz, C.D., F.Ch., leads her sire, Small's Fancy Lad of Woz, C.D., T.T., on the straight-away in California. Photo courtesy of S. Ann Ductor.

have brought him this far with less effort and he should run away from the stalwart little bitch now. But Akua's body is tight, and hard, and incredibly well conditioned, and she won't be left!

Coming down to the finish, the hounds are approaching the gallery and it's impossible to see who's ahead. You can hear the hard breathing now and the pounding feet. The lure operator has killed his motor. Akua has the lure. Tembo grabs the other end and Suni grabs on too.

We run to get the dogs and save the lure, but we're too late. Akua has half of it, carrying it up and down proudly before the roaring crowd, then trots off to chew her prize in private.

Tembo and Suni are still holding the other half of the lure together, running as a brace and sharing their trophy. We catch them easily and by a little coaxing with another lure, get Akua on lead also. They're happy now, but still lunging at the remnants of plastic scattered about. After 660 yards they'd gladly take another turn around the course. In two minutes they won't even be panting. After all, if the daylight holds out they might get two more turns to run tonight.

It had been a good race.

The Basenji in Lure Coursing Competition

The first weekend after Basenjis received approval to compete in American Sighthound Field Association lure coursing trials, almost seven-year-old Bubalak's Divine Bette won the breed's first Best in Field award beating all competing sighthound breeds on September 3, 1979! The Basenji had arrived with fanfare. Bette's enthusiasm did not wane and she went on to become the first Basenji field champion on November 18, 1979.

Basenji fanciers' interest in the sport of lure coursing has boomed, with from 16 to over 30 Basenjis attaining field championship each year. Ch. Betsy Ross Flags A Flyin, F.Ch., became the first dual champion in 1980. In the overall figures since 1979, approximately 45% of the field champions have also won their conformation championships. A few have also attained their obedience title which shows the flexibility of the breed and the ease with which they can switch between roles. The first Lure Courser of Merit title was completed by Dokhues Enuf Lovins, LCM, in 1981.

In 1986 a question regarding the eligibility of the Basenji to compete in lure field trials was brought before the A.S.F.A. Some members felt the Basenji should not be allowed to compete with the other sighthounds since it: 1) was not a true sighthound; and 2) was too aggressive toward other dogs on the field. Letters and articles appeared in abundance in all the appropriate magazines and a strong educational program ensued. The representatives of the member clubs at the A.S.F.A. 1987 Annual Meeting determined that Basenjis should continue to compete, as they were certainly capable as sighthounds and

Bubalak's Divine Bette, F.Ch., was the first Basenji Best in Field winner (shown here) and the first Basenji Field Champion.

they were really not excused for aggression any more than other competing breeds. A great effort went into this counter movement and many people were involved to protect this sport for Basenjis.

Training for a Field Coursing Career

Dogs cannot compete at A.S.F.A. trials until they are a year old. This rule was developed to protect the young, immature dog from seriously hurting himself. However, it does not hurt to begin early to develop some of the skills that will be required of your dog on the field. Even a two month-old pup can learn to chase after a bit of rabbit skin that you might get from a rabbit breeder (or you could use some other type of animal fur if you can find it). A tatter of cloth or a favorite toy can be used but the real skin seems to increase the desire in some dogs to chase and catch the lure. A lure on a string or a string attached to a pole can be used to play chase with the pup. Each pup should get individual turns to chase after the lure, catch it, play tug of war and develop

The Huntmaster calls "Tally Ho" and the Basenjis are released at this coursing trial near Seattle, Washington. Photo courtesy of Nancy Swanson.

confidence in himself. You do not want the pups to push one another away from the lure or learn to fight over it. The sessions should be kept short, about five minutes, and should end with an enthusiastic puppy wanting more. A piece of white plastic bag should be added to the lure fairly soon to help the dog associate the real skin with the flashing white plastic bag which is the standard lure at the field trials.

Enthusiasm and follow count for 30% of the score in competitive coursing, with agility being worth another 25%. These are the points that you can begin to develop in your dog before he is even six months old. At about six months you can seek out the coursing enthusiasts in your area and begin to take your pup for brief runs on the practice fields. This will accustom your Basenji to the lure machine, the gallery of onlookers, and the traveling required. The pup should be run alone until he is fairly experienced and is definitely on the lure. Sometimes in coursing you will see a poorly-trained dog chasing the other dogs on the field rather than the lure.

An additional 35% of the score your dog achieves at lure trials is based on the speed he runs. Desire can certainly increase speed but the construction of your dog will limit his top speed. A well-put-together dog should be the fastest dog, if he has the desire. The final item considered in your dog's score will be his endurance. The actual trials require two lengthy runs and you can certainly increase your Basenji's stamina by being sure he is in top physical condition—good health and good muscle tone. Once your dog is old enough for the actual lure field trials, begin to be aware of his condition. Unless he has many dog friends to run with in a big enclosed yard, you may want to condition him by long runs in the country, taking him along jogging or running him beside your bicycle. The average Basenji can be competitive without all this extra work but if you want to give your dog some edge over the competition, this may be the way.

Aggression or interfering with another dog on the field are cause for disqualification from lure coursing. These are serious offenses on the part of the lure coursing dog which can cause needless injury as well as spoiling a career in lure coursing for the attacked dog. It is very important to begin early with your future lure coursing Basenji in developing a friendly disposition toward other dogs. Be sure to allow your pup to meet friendly dogs of all sizes and breeds to ensure his understanding of dog personality. The trips to practices should offer an opportunity for your pup to meet well-mannered dogs of all the sighthound breeds.

If your Basenji is already over a year old when you decide to give lure coursing a try, consider his personality first. Will he be able to get along on the field? Each dog must run with two other dogs of his own breed to gain points toward his title. Will your dog get along with two strange dogs? If you think there is a good chance that he will get along with other dogs, spend a bit of time with a rabbit skin and string to see how he reacts. Is he enthusiastic about chasing it? If so, search out coursing enthusiasts in your area and get your dog onto the practice field. The American Sighthound Field Association is a group of hard-working volunteers, so ask Basenji or other sighthound breeders you meet at shows or through national magazines for information about the coursing crowd in your area. While all sighthound owners do not course their dogs, most know enough to help you locate the right people.

Yes, your Basenji will be off lead and really out of your control during a field run but the properly trained dog rarely leaves the field. His interest is totally on the lure from the time you release him until you promptly pick him up when the lure stops. Remember, train your dog by himself rather than immediately putting him on the field with other dogs. Your new coursing acquaintances will be able to explain how a trial is run, how the dogs are

Bushbabies Pippin Vinegar (front) and Cambria's Tobii Tuu demonstrate the use of muzzles in coursing. *Photo courtesy of George Gavaletz.*

released, the basic rules you'll need to know and how to enter an upcoming trial.

The A.S.F.A. has a regular newsletter entitled *FAN (Field Advisory News)* which you will want to obtain to learn more about this sport. They offer articles and tips as well as publishing trial results and new titles.

The hunting instinct is very strong in the breed, and most Basenjis love to chase anything. Lure coursing is a sport that your dog will truly enjoy. He will show you just how much fun it can be by his enthusiasm on practice or trial day. Those shining eyes speak clearly. His strength when lunging at the end of the lead while he awaits his turn will amaze you. The beauty of his coat flashing in the sun and his rippling muscles as he runs full out across the beautiful green landscape will be poetry to your eyes.

The power of lure coursing embodied in Dharian Fancy Dancer of Woz, C.D., F.Ch. *Photo courtesy of S. Ann Ductor.*

Ch. Aleika Absinthe Rajah's JR's alert, showy attitude helped him to become a Best in Show winner and Number One Basenji for two years. *Photo courtesy of the American Kennel Club.*

13

The Basenji As A Show Dog

The Basenji's striking, clean good looks and flowing, ground-covering movement have brought him into full competition in the Hound Group and Best in Show ring in the 1980's. As more and more judges have become familiar with the breed, they have come to appreciate the Basenji's qualities as an all-purpose hound, for he is neither a classic scent hound nor a classic gazehound. His talents in the hunting field include pointing, flushing, coursing and driving, so the Basenji's build must reflect his varied activities. He should be built without extremes of conformation, as described in the Basenji standard.

The quizzical, wrinkled expression of the Basenji's head is well known. Unfortunately, the judge in the show ring often gives more consideration to the wrinkle than to the actual shape of the head. Exhibitors, breeders and judges still need to familiarize themselves with this portion of the standard. The dog's expressive head and curliness of tail must be considered only a part of the total picture that makes up the Basenji.

Showing dogs is both an educational and a social event. The shows should be enjoyed for themselves as well as for the ego-boost they offer. The judging results and discussions with other dog people can broaden your understanding of the standard and prepare you for a future in breeding or may simply offer an interesting hobby within itself.

Ease of grooming and the straightforward presentation of the Basenji make him a great prospect for the owner to handle at dog shows. If you are interested in showing, before you obtain a new Basenji, you should contact breeders of top-quality show dogs about acquiring one of the best. You will be able to begin training the pup as soon as it arrives using the instructions that follow. Don't be afraid to try doing it all yourself.

Is your adult Basenji a candidate for the show ring? You should make a thorough study of the standard section of this book and then attend some dog shows to see how your Basenji compares. It takes a great deal of time to learn what the standard means and how it applies to individual dogs so you may need some advice from the breeder of your dog or a professional handler familiar with Basenjis. The section which follows about training a puppy will also apply to an adult Basenji, as patience and repetition are the primary ingredients in any training venture. Handling classes that may be

Showing should be fun. Judge Ed Gilbert and breeder/owner/handler Carol Webb have trouble controlling their laughter after Ch. Kazor's Dandy Deerstalker has some "Basenji fun" during this photo session.

offered by one of your local kennel clubs will give you and your dog invaluable experience in a show ring-like environment. Acquaintances made in class may become great future friends!

Training your dog can make the difference between a winner and an also-ran. To ensure you get words of wisdom about show training I am going to quote one of the greatest handler/trainers of modern show dogs, Frank Sabella. Mr. Sabella is now an AKC licensed judge. In his book (written with Shirlee Kalstone) *The Art of Handling Show Dogs*, published by B & E Publications, he covers all the bases in the early training of a show dog.

Introduction

Show training is so important that it becomes a part of the puppy's life. Training for the show ring should begin as soon as you purchase your puppy or from the time it is weaned, if you were its breeder. Especially with a baby puppy, your main objective is to begin establishing a pleasant, loving relationship which will become the basis of more formal training in the future.

Dogs are required to do two things in the conformation ring: to be set up or posed (and to hold that pose for an indefinite length of time during the judge's examination) and to gait (individually and in a group). While show training is not difficult, it does require time, patience, sensitivity and consistency on the part of the trainer.

Many people make the mistake of waiting for a puppy to grow up and then begin to train it. We don't mean to imply that some successful dogs did not start this way but, without a doubt, dogs that have the right kind of basic training as puppies are always the ones that stand in the ring with head and tail up, full of assurance. Just the repetition of correctly posing and leading the puppy will teach it to walk confidently on lead and to feel comfortable while being handled—and that's really what early training is for—to ensure that your puppy will grow into an adult that is confident and self assured in the show ring!

At what age should you begin training your puppy? Each dog is an individual and should be treated as such, so there are no "set" age limits as to when to begin basic or advanced show training. Generally, when you start basic training depends not only on your patience, sensitivity and consistency, but also on the puppy's capabilities and desire to accept being posed and lead trained.

Very young puppies are highly motivated by and responsive to their owners but, like babies, they have short concentration periods. Even though intelligence develops rapidly in a puppy, early training should always be started on a "fun" basis. Don't be in a hurry to start formal training too early; the first part of a puppy's life should be fun time and every dog should be allowed to enjoy its puppyhood.

Early Socialization Important

As the owner or breeder of a young puppy, you alone are responsible for its early socialization and training. Socialization can be described as the way in which a dog develops a relationship with its dam, littermates, other animals and man. Just as a youngster must receive a formal education and also learn to become a responsible member of society, so must you provide the best environment for your dog's potential to be brought out and developed completely. A young puppy is very impressionable and the socialization and training it receives at an early age sets the tone for its lifetime characteristics. If a puppy receives the proper socialization, is treated with sensitivity, patience and consistency, if it learns to be loved and respected, then it will always be happiest when pleasing you.

Earlier in this chapter, we mentioned that with a young puppy you want to begin basic training by establishing a happy and loving rapport between you and the dog. Pat and handle the puppy frequently, speaking reassuringly and using praise often. Let the puppy become accustomed to being petted and handled by strangers. A well-socialized puppy loves to make new friends and this kind of interaction between puppy and humans or other animals will be a prerequiste for the basic show training to follow. Hopefully, by the time the puppy is about 7 to 8 weeks old, it has learned a little about life. If it has been properly socialized, it is light-hearted and untroubled, because it has learned that it is loved and respected. Now it must be taught certain basics which lead eventually to more formal training for the show ring.

Here are some suggestions to consider before you begin basic training:

1. First training sessions should be given in familiar surroundings, preferably at home, and without noises or other distractions.
2. Make the first training periods short, not more than 10 minutes in length. As the sessions progress successfully, gradually lengthen each training period, but never more than 30 minutes in any single session.
3. If the puppy is restless or won't concentrate, postpone the lesson and try again the following day. Be sure, too, that you are not tired or impatient for the training sessions should always be relaxed and enjoyable for both of you.
4. Be consistent during the lessons. Use a firm tone of voice when giving commands. Some of the first words your puppy will learn in posing and lead training are "Come," "Stand," "Stay," and "No." Be sure you use the same word for the same command each time.
5. Remember that a young puppy is inexperienced, so be gentle and patient. Don't rush your puppy; give it time to understand what you expect and to learn how to respond.
6. Don't be too insistent at first. Puppies learn by repetition, correction and praise. Don't punish a puppy if it seems confused; instead, correct it until it does what you want, then offer plenty of praise. It is important that your puppy understand each training step thoroughly before going on to the next.
7. Always end each training session on a pleasant note and once again, give plenty of praise and perhaps reward the puppy with its favorite treat. A puppy can learn almost anything if given love and understanding.

Table Training

A grooming table should be one of your first investments, for it will be an indispensable help in establishing habit patterns. Most professional handlers, experienced exhibitors and breeders table train puppies at an early age because, aside from the convenience of having the animal at their working height, there is also an invaluable psychological advantage to table training (Figure III-1). Even though the puppy is off the ground and expe-

Figure III-1. A grooming table is of indispensable help in training young puppies. A portable type illustrated here is covered with a non-slip surface and has an adjustable post and loop which can be removed when not in use. Portable tables are easy to fold up, making them convenient to transport to and from matches and shows.

riencing a new situation, it is given confidence by the presence of its owner and submits to any handling or grooming, thereby establishing a rapport between the puppy and trainer.

It is easier to control a young puppy by teaching it to pose on a table . . . and recently, it is common to see judges using tables in the ring to examine other small breeds. On larger breeds, even though adult dogs are posed on the ground, early table training will be invaluable for teaching ground posing later on.

The majority of coated breeds require some type of regular grooming in addition to preparation at the show before going into the ring. Even smooth-coated breeds need regular care. Early grooming training on the table will teach the dog to learn to relax. Later on, when the coat grows longer or the dog needs special attention, it will not object if it has to spend longer periods on the table and will rest and feel totally secure while being worked on. As a part of the training you should practice posing the dog at the end of each grooming session.

The table you select should be sturdy and covered with a non-slip rubber top. There are many different types of grooming tables: portable (which fold up and are easy to carry along to matches and shows), adjustable (which move up or down) or a combination crate with grooming table top (these often have drawers between the crate and top to hold equipment). Some tables are equipped with a post and loop collar, which can be slipped around a dog's neck to hold the head up and keep it from moving or jumping off the table. If you do use a loop to give the puppy more confidence, never use one with any type of choking action. Never leave a young puppy alone with its head in a loop or standing by itself on a table unless you are sure it will stay.

Posing

You can start posing your puppy on a table as early as 6 weeks. In the beginning just stand the puppy on the table and get it used to being off the ground. Once this has been accomplished, then start positioning the legs in a show pose. Next, begin training it to be handled—feel its body, look at its teeth and let other people do the same. Experiencing all this at an early age will give the puppy confidence and make it used to being handled by strangers, which will be invaluable later on for the puppy's show career. If you persevere in the beginning you will discover that your puppy will never forget this basic training and later it will be much easier to work with.

When lifting the puppy for the first time, care should be taken not to frighten it. Don't come down too quickly on the puppy or attempt to lift it by grasping the back of the neck or picking it up by the front legs. Instead, kneel down to the puppy's level and let it come to you. Speak assuringly and pat the puppy if you can. Then using both hands to lift the puppy's front and rear, pick it up and place it on the table. Do be aware that a puppy might try to wiggle out of your arms so make sure you have a secure grip on the dog as you lift it and after you set it down on the table.

Be sure the table surface is not slippery and use the following method to pose the puppy:

Figure III-2—Grasp the puppy with your left hand between the back legs and your right hand under the chest, at the same time giving the command "stand" or "stay". When you pose the dog in the ring, in the majority of times this is the way it will be facing the judge (see Figure III-2A & 2B). If the puppy fusses and does not want to stand, keep your hands in the same position and slightly lift the front feet off the table and put them down, then lift the rear legs off the table and put them down, doing both movements in a slight rocking motion. Repeat this several times to distract the puppy and get it to settle down.

Figure III-3—Move your right hand from under the chest and place it on the neck as shown, with the weight of the head resting on the top part of your hand. Don't grasp the neck too heavily; use a light touch, just enough so that you can control the puppy from moving to either side or out of your hand.

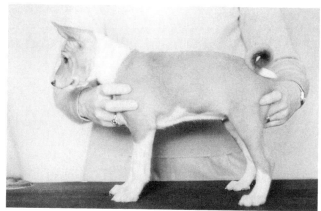

Figure III-2

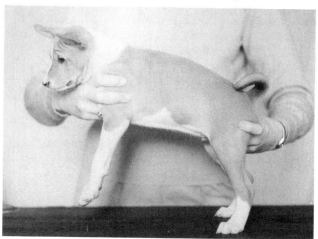

Figure III-2A

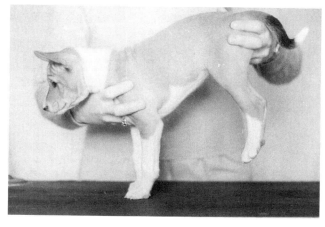

Figure III-2B

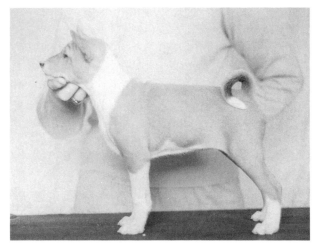

Figure III-3

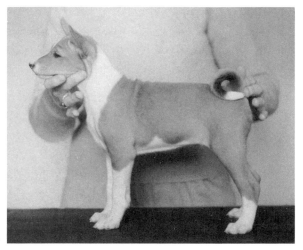

Figure III-4

Figure III-4—Move your left hand from under the legs to support the tail and hold it in position as shown, so that the puppy learns to support its own weight on the table.

Figure III-5—shows the puppy posed.

These are the basic procedures for setting up the the puppy. If you can accomplish all this in one session; excellent! Otherwise, work on the first position until the puppy assumes that pose without fussing, then go to the next position and so on. Each time the puppy assumes a correct pose, praise it lavishly. At all times when you are moving your hands to the various positions, be aware that the puppy might squirm and pull away, therefore you must be ready to recover it immediately by using the first position.

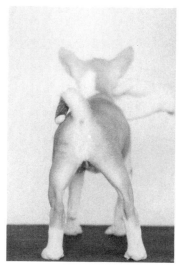

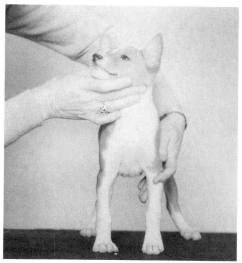

Figure III-5   **Figure III-6**

Figure III-6—To adjust the puppy's right front foot, control the dog by holding its head in your right hand. Release the hold on the tail with your left hand and allow it to grasp the right leg below the elbow and while pushing the puppy's head away from that foot, place the right leg down, then swing the puppy's head back into position to distribute its weight evenly again.

To adjust his left front foot (as shown), with the puppy's head still in your right hand, reach over the dog with your left hand, grasp the left front leg at the same point you did on the right. Twist the puppy's head toward you (putting the weight on the right leg) and correctly position the left leg, then return the head to its normal position.

Figure III-7—If you have a small dog with an excellent front, simply grasp the puppy under the neck, raise it off its front legs, then drop it back onto the table.

Figures III-8 & 9—To position each back leg, grasp the leg between the hock joint and foot and place it in the correct position. This procedure for positioning the back legs is used when you have the dog on lead or with your hand under the neck.

The procedure for posing a puppy on a lead begins by following the same steps as shown in Figs. III-6–9. Pick up the dog and place it on the table.

Holding the lead in your right hand with the head in an upright position, move your left hand between the dog's back legs. If the dog moves its left or right front leg, position them as described before. Corrections to the rear are done the same as instructed in Figs. III-8 & 9.

If the puppy has a tendency to lean back when being posed, grasp the puppy under the throat with the right hand and place your left hand between the hind legs. Draw the puppy slowly backwards off the table, and then place it back on the table so that its weight is distributed evenly on all four legs.

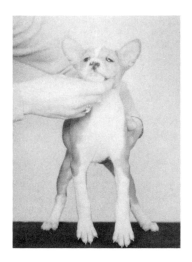
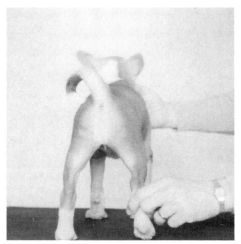
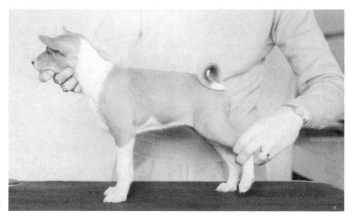

Figure III-9

If a large puppy has a tendency to lean back when posed on the table, take hold of the tail and apply a pulling back pressure which will make the dog lean into its front. Later on, when the dog is posed on the ground, this method also may be used to correct leaning back.

After your puppy learns how to stand properly, start posing it for longer periods of time. When the puppy can pose without fussing, the next step is to enlist the help of friends by having them go through the motions of lightly examining the dog—checking its bite and feeling the body—doing the things a judge will do in the ring. If you are training a male, in the ring the judge will check to see if both testicles are in place, so do remember to train your puppy to accept this procedure at an early age.

As the posing sessions progress, you can begin practicing the more subtle aspects of show posing, *i.e.*, setting up the puppy in a variety of situations and on different ground surfaces, especially grass.

Lead Training

Of all the steps necessary to prepare a puppy for the show ring, probably lead training is the most important because there have been many potentially fine show dogs ruined by improper lead training. So many exhibitors wait until the last minute to lead break a dog then expect it all to happen in one try. Then they become impatient and treat the dog roughly and the puppy's reaction to all this is fear. Do remember that extreme patience is necessary because introduction to a collar and a lead can be a frightening experience for a young puppy.

Most canine behavior experts agree that at 6 weeks, a dog can have a small soft collar put around its neck. The younger the puppy becomes accustomed to wearing a collar around its neck, the easier it will be to lead train it later on. Begin by placing the collar around the puppy's neck for short periods of time and only while someone is in attendance. The first few times the puppy wears the collar, it may roll on the ground or try several other things to get the collar off, so never allow a baby puppy to be unsupervised. Make the first lesson short, not more than 5 to 10 minutes, then remove the collar, play with the puppy and praise it for being such a good dog.

After a period of about a week (or when the puppy is relaxed about wearing the collar) snap a lightweight lead onto the collar and let the puppy drag the lead freely about the floor. Allow the puppy to walk wherever it wants to go. If it starts to follow you, fine; but the first time the lead is attached, don't pick it up and jerk and pull the puppy in any way. After a few times of allowing the puppy to drag the lead around the floor, pick up the lead in your hand and let the puppy take you for a walk. Speak gently and walk wherever the puppy wants to go. Once again, don't pull or tug on the lead in an attempt to make the puppy follow you until it is completely accustomed to wearing the collar and lead.

When this has been accomplished, the next lesson is to try to walk the puppy on lead. The first time you try this, don't be surprised if your puppy pulls back or rolls over on the floor. Don't panic, just learn to be patient and speak gently. Put the snap adjustment under the puppy's neck at first so it won't be tempted to look over its shoulder or try to bite the lead. Squat down and call the puppy's name and the word "come" in your most inviting voice, to get the dog to move forward to you. If it balks or sits, try coaxing it to come forward for its favorite tidbit. You may have to give a slight forward pull to the lead to start the puppy toward you but remember, a slight pull does not mean a neckbreaking jolt for you can injure the neck and the puppy will associate the resulting pain with an unpleasant experience. If this is done several times without thinking, it can develop into a deep seated fear of the lead.

When the puppy comes to you, pat and praise it; then walk ahead with the lead in your hand and repeat this action to make the puppy move forward again. It should only take a short while until the puppy follows you. Eventually, the puppy will learn that if it obeys and follows you, there will be no pulling or jerking of the lead and that it will receive plenty of praise.

Once again, we caution that because a puppy's attention span is short, try to make each session brief, 10 minutes at most, then remove the lead, praise and play with the puppy. The main idea at this stage of training is to make the first lessons a "train and play" time that the puppy looks forward

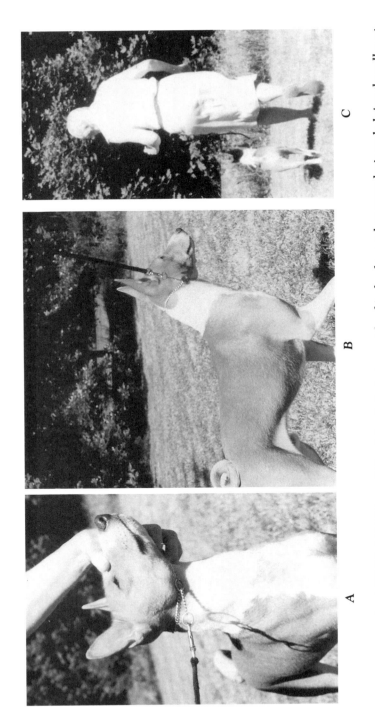

A   B   C

MOVING YOUR BASENJI. (A) Using a light choke chain just a couple of inches larger than your dog's neck, bring the collar up under the chin as shown here. (B) With the lead coming from the side, below the ear, any correction is easily and quickly felt by the dog. Get control of your dog before you try to move him fast. (C) The dog will learn to move by your side, collar snug under the chin, but with the lead loose. You will need practice to do this but it will be worthwhile. When your Basenji feels he is moving as freely as he wants to, he will move better.

to and not something it dreads. After a few lessons, you'll find your puppy can be lead trained rather quickly and what is more important, that it enjoys the experience.

At this point, we want to offer some advice about early training. Always try to train the puppy to move on a loose lead to help develop its natural carriage. In the show ring you will be asked by many judges to move your dog on a loose lead and you will be prepared if you accustom your puppy to do it at an early age. When a puppy is taught to gait only on a tight lead, it gets used to leaning into the lead and without that pressure, feels completely lost. There is nothing harder to break than a dog that is used to leaning into the lead for support. Dogs that are trained on a tight lead also lose their natural head carriage and they often learn many other bad habits including sidewinding. In the ring, it is not uncommon to see exhibitors string up their dogs so tightly that the front feet hardly touch the ground. There is a trend to show certain breeds on a tight lead to make a more positive topline.

However, if a knowledgeable judge wants to discover whether the dog's topline is natural or man-made, he will ask that the dog be moved on a loose lead and, if that fault is present, it will be exposed.

While the puppy is being lead trained, don't train it to be hand posed at the same time. At first, these should be two seperate procedures. Animals learn by repetition and, if each time you stop leading the dog and then get down and set it up, the dog will anticipate this action and will become discouraged from learning to stand naturally and pose itself without being set up by hand. So many exhibitors hand pose their puppies after each gaiting session and when this happens, a puppy soon gets the idea that every time it stops on lead, someone will bend down to hold its head and tail. In the ring, after you have individually gaited your dog, many judges will ask you to let the dog stand on its own. If your puppy hasn't learned to stand naturally at the end of its lead, it won't be able to do so in the ring.

As the gaiting sessions progress, teach the puppy to move on your left side (eventually the dog should learn to move on your right side as well as your left). Encourage the puppy to stand naturally at the end of the lead each time it stops. To help get the puppy to stand alert, try attracting its attention with a squeaky toy, a ball or by offering its favorite tidbit. Doing this will start to teach the puppy the fundamentals of baiting.

After a while you will be ready to begin more advanced training. Replace the training collar with a one-piece show lead or, on large breeds, switch from the training collar to a choke chain or a more substantial type of collar for better control. (As the dog grows older, remember that any collar or chain should be worn only during practice sessions and then removed to prevent the hair from wearing away around the neck.) Before starting advanced training, be sure that the lead is correctly positioned around the dog's neck. It should be high under the chin and behind the ears to keep the dog under control at all times. This position will also help to train the puppy to keep its head up because for the first few weeks, a puppy may need a gentle reminder under its chin to learn to keep its head up.

Next you should begin advanced training by teaching the dog to move down and back in a straight line. Once the dog does this well, then try moving it in a circle. As a prerequisite to executing the individual patterns, practice doing figure-eights because this will teach the dog how to turn smoothly. Then you can begin the other movement patterns that will be used in the show ring—the "L," the "T," and the "Triangle." Vary the movement patterns in each session and remember not to overtrain. Always end each session on a pleasant note and give the dog lots of praise.

As your puppy matures, it should learn to gait on grass, concrete floors and other surfaces including rubber mats (these are used at indoor shows). Once the lessons go well at home, take the puppy out and get it used to walking on a lead and being posed in new and different surroundings. Parking lots of supermarkets and department stores are excellent for this as there are usually lots of people and all kinds of distractions. For the first few outings, be patient and give the puppy plenty of time to adjust and respond to strange surroundings. Occasionally, because of a pup's insecurities, it may revert back to not being well trained for the first few outings.

The greatest pitfall for most young dogs seems to be going to indoor shows because the lighting is strange and the echoes inside a building can sometimes distract a young dog. The inside of a department store or shopping mall can help you to overcome this problem. Always try to anticipate experiences that might distract and frighten a puppy at a show and try to solve them while the puppy is young. If you live in a rural area and none of these suggestions apply to you, take the puppy to matches as often as you can for this is the best place to gain experience with the least amount of tension.

You must work with your dog to determine its best speed in gaiting. Each dog is an individual and looks best when moving at a certain speed and if you want to show your dog to its best advantage, you should determine that correct speed. Have a friend move your dog at varying speeds in front of a knowledgeable person to learn the right speed for your puppy. Then practice the movement patterns at that speed until the dog can do them smoothly. No dog can move at its best speed if the handler moves improperly, so you should take long strides when gaiting the dog. A common error of the novice is to move the dog too slowly. Short, stilted steps look clumsy and prevent the dog from moving smoothly. If you do not move fast enough yourself or with free and easy strides, you will prevent your dog from executing its most efficient movement. If you are showing a small breed take normal walking steps. For the medium or large breeds, move at a fast walk or run.

We should end the puppy lead training section with some advice about two common problems: sitting and sidling.

Sitting

When stopping, if you find that your puppy constantly sits, keep moving forward a few steps while attracting its attention at the same time with a piece of food or a toy, until the puppy understands that it must stand when it stops. If that does not work, bring the puppy forward a few steps, stop, then put your toe under its stomach to prevent it from sitting.

Another solution is to ask a friend to stand holding a long piece of rope or a show lead which encircles the dog's stomach. When you bring your puppy forward and it starts to sit, have your friend brace up its rear, but do not make this correction with a jerking motion. Breeds that sit when stopped are difficult to train to stand at the end of the leash with tail up (if that is desired in the breed). To remedy this, after you have trained the dog to stand when it has stopped, reach gently from a standing position and put up the tail, stroking underneath the tail until the puppy gets the idea of what you want it to do.

Sidewinding

A common characteristic during lead training is when a dog has a tendency to sidle. This can be caused by:

A. *The dog pulling away from you.* Solution: When the dog starts this habit on the lead or shows indications of doing so when moving individually, train the dog to move on your opposite side. In other words, if you are going away or coming back with the dog on your left side and it sidles, switch to going and coming with the dog on your right.

B. *A dog that has a tendency to look up at its handler while being gaited.* Solution: Never show a dog a toy or food while you are gaiting it as this can cause the dog to look up which may cause sidling. You can also try the alternate side method mentioned in (A) above.

C. *A dog is too short in back.* Solution: If you move at a faster speed, it will go sideways to be able to move at a faster speed. The best way to deal with this problem is to get someone to move the dog at different speeds so you are able to decide at what speed the dog levels off. Another solution to sidling is to put two show leads on a dog and have one person walk on either side of the puppy so that the puppy walks straight in the center. If after a few tries you feel this method is working, the best way to keep the problem from recurring is by constantly alternating the sides each time you take the dog up and back. Gaiting next to a fence or a wall so that the dog can only move straight ahead is another solution to sidling.

Temperament

Temperament plays a major role in puppy training. While most dogs need consistent training to learn what is required of them in the show ring, some dogs are "naturals" at showing. They are outgoing and love being the center of attention and always seem to show themselves off to the best advantage. While these extroverted dogs are exceptions, they always train quickly and easily.

If you experience a temperament problem ("sound" shyness or hand shyness for instance), try to determine what is causing the problem and especially whether you might be the cause of it, as poor temperament can be the result of environment as well as from breeding. In the event you have purchased an older puppy that exhibits temperament problems, consider obedience training for that is a good way for an animal to learn regimentation and to get out among people. Obedience training has been used successfully on dogs that were kennel raised without adequate human socialization at the proper time.

Another part of training your puppy for the show ring has nothing to do with the ring itself, but a means of making going to the show a lot easier on you and the dog. This part of the training has to do with getting the puppy "crate trained." At an early age the puppy should be introduced to the crate that will be his home away from home. One of the best approaches is to put the crate down on the floor near where the puppy has his water bowl. Leave the door open. Put a favorite tidbit inside and let the puppy size it up. Most puppies will be somewhat leery of this new object. However, the puppy—by its very nature—is a curious animal and so will begin to approach it, at first giving it a wide berth. Now this process may take hours as the puppy, often unsure of what this thing is will leave the room for awhile before screwing up its courage and coming back. Gradually, it will approach closer and closer until finally it will be within inches of the crate. Typically, this is when the puppy stops short and reaches out its neck and head while keeping the body ready for flight if this "thing" should prove to be unfriendly. If nothing jumps out of the crate the puppy will feel safe to try to go further and eventually get the tidbit. However, staying inside, oh no, not me!

With this first success you know you have him hooked. Leave the crate down and pay no attention to it or the puppy. A couple of times during the day, place a tidbit in the crate. You will find it gone sometime later. After a few days of this game and you are sure the puppy (and not the cat!) is eating the tidbits, place a favorite toy in the crate. Let this game go on for a couple of days as well. Your next step is to gently pick up the puppy and place it in the crate with a tidbit inside and gently close the door. Be sure the puppy can see you as you go about your daily chores. He will most likely fuss about being confined. Talk to him, tell him what a great fellow he is and—if necessary—give him another tidbit. He should be confined for only about 10 minutes the first time. When you let him out, praise him lavishly for being a good dog. Over the next weeks you can extend the time slowly until the puppy comes to accept a few hours confinement as natural.

Once you have gotten to this point you can begin to let him sleep in the crate. Be sure you get up early enough so he will be let out of the crate before he soils himself. It's a good idea to put in some rough toweling or carpeting. Later on you might want to use a wire bottom or papering.

Next, you want to take him for a car/van ride to accustom him to motion. One of the trips to a shopping center referred to above would be ideal. Don't make his first voyage out into the world too long, however. Many puppies get car sick rather easily so keep the trip short and talk reassuringly to the puppy the whole time you are on the road. If people pull up along side of you at stop lights and see you talking to yourself, don't be worried, just put your hand up to your ear and they will think you have a car phone.

Grooming and Conditioning

A Basenji, like a deciduous tree in the winter, has his structure and muscular condition exposed. Give your Basenji every advantage by being sure he is in top muscular condition. Some Basenjis seem to keep themselves in condition but others who may have just a small yard or who live in an apartment may need to be exercised. If you are a jogger it is fairly easy to take your Basenji along for his exercise. For those less athletic, a brisk mile or two beside your bike will bring your Basenji into good muscular condition within a couple of weeks or a month. Do not take a very out-of-condition dog on a brisk two-mile run but start him out leisurely and build up. Do not exercise a puppy this way but do be sure he has plenty of opportunities for play.

While a Basenji's short coat is one of his true advantages, it still requires some special attention in preparation for the show ring. Coat conditioning must begin long before the show debut with the best care given to keep the coat shining with good health. A proper diet, proper exercise and warmth are required. Since a Basenji sheds little, it can take months to develop a good coat on a dog who has grown a heavy winter coat or who has not been fed properly. If your Basenji's coat does not measure up to the dogs you see at the shows, consider a change of diet. Better food or perhaps additional oil can make a difference. The food requirement of each dog is a bit different and only you can find the optimum for your particular dog. A poor coat can hide the quality of wrinkle your dog carries as well as take away from the typical clean look of the Basenji. The dog in good coat is going to look better in the show ring.

Use a hard, rubber curry brush to remove the dead hair from your dog's coat when he is shedding. This will help massage the skin, and so, is valuable as a grooming aid at all times. The massage will also help keep dandruff under control. Any loose, flaky skin is especially noticeable on the black or tri-color coats. Last minute show preparation is pretty minimal. The day before the show, bathe your dog with a good dog shampoo to make sure he is clean and that the white really sparkles. Some dogs need a cream rinse, some do not. The tail hairs may need to be trimmed to give a tidy appearance. Some dogs can use a bit of chalk to brighten the white parts of their coats. Sometimes a nick in a black coat can be improved with a touch of black chalk. Always be sure that all loose chalk is brushed out of the coat and does not find its way onto the judge's hands as the dog will be excused from the ring if chalk is found. Some people still trim the whiskers from the Basenji's face but this is becoming less popular since many exhibitors and judges prefer the natural look. Other exhibitors can help you learn about trimming and chalking. You should practice these techniques long before the show.

How the Dog Show Game Works

The backbone of the the dog show is the individual, the all-breed and specialty dog clubs. By joining a dog club you begin to learn the ins and outs of raising and showing dogs. Boy, is there a lot of information waiting for you out there! Getting that information can sometimes be difficult. By reading this book you have shown you are interested enough to get going on your own.

Most dog clubs have educational meetings where you can learn interesting facts about the sport. The best entry point is a specialty club, that is, a club dealing with a single breed. For instance, The Basenji Club of America is the "parent club" for Basenjis. If you are not a member, find the club nearest to you and inquire about joining.

Specialty clubs are the best place to learn about your breed. Their major goal is to educate their membership and to hold American Kennel Club (AKC) licensed shows. Specialty clubs are under the overall "jurisdiction" of

their (parent) national club. However, in order to hold a dog show, they must be given approval by the AKC and hold the show under AKC rules. The club picks their own judges from a list of AKC-licensed judges.

It's apparent that the AKC is a pretty important organization, so let's talk about it before we go on to describing dog shows themselves.

The AKC is a private organization, not a government entity as is the case in many countries. The club is run by delegates who are elected by their local clubs. The local clubs in turn, are member clubs of the AKC. The delegates elect a Board of Directors from their own ranks. The Board is entrusted with formulating policy and direction for the club. The Board hires the President and he acts as its Chief Executive Officer. The AKC is over a 20 million dollar corporation and is located at 51 Madison Ave, New York, New York 10010. It is chartered in that state. The AKC only rarely puts on shows of its own. The major functions of AKC are:

- Registration of purebred dogs
- Publication of a stud register
- Keeping and publishing statistics through the AKC *Gazette*, its monthly publication
- Recognizing new dog clubs as show giving entities under AKC development rules
- Education of the public through publications, seminars, and audio/visual media
- Sponsorship of research into major medical/physical problems of dogs
- Sanctioning of dates and places for dog clubs to hold their shows
- Licensing of judges to officiate at AKC licensed events
- Providing oversight of the shows themselves through AKC field representatives
- U.S. representative to international bodies interested in promoting the sport of purebred dogs

Now, let's tackle the concept of dog shows themselves. Naturally, enough of you would like to participate. In order to do this you must have a purebred dog. By "purebred," it is meant that your dog must be eligible for registration by AKC. You will recall when you bought your puppy you were given registration papers. If you have not filled them out yet, do so now. Until your dog is registered with the AKC and gets an individual registration number, you can't show him. Once you have that magic piece of paper in your hands you can enter dog shows to your heart's delight. Of course, each entry fee will cost you a sum of money. The going rate today is about $16.00.

OK, now we get into it. Your local specialty club is going to hold a show and they are encouraging you to enter. So, nothing ventured, nothing gained. The show chairman makes sure you get an entry form and even waits around for you to fill it out. You need to put down your dog's registered name and number, his birthdate, his parents' names, who were the breeders (it's all on the registration form) and your name as owner. That's it—except for the check in the proper amount. Oh yes, you must select the class he will be in. Now what do we mean by class? Dog shows, like most sporting events, have various classifications—some by age and others by the amount of winning the dog has done. Let's take a look at the various classes offered and find out who is eligible for them.

The classes include:

- Puppy . . . . Over 6 months & under 9 months
- Puppy . . . . Over 9 months & under 12 months
- Novice . . . . Has not yet won a blue ribbon in adult classes, three first prizes in the Novice class, or one or more championship points prior to close of entry.
- Bred by Exhibitor . . . . Exhibited by the Breeder of Record (you must have bred and currently own the dog to show in this class)
- American Bred . . . . Must have been bred in America
- Open Class . . . . Open to all, including puppies
- Best of Breed . . . . AKC Champions only in this class

In certain specialty shows, there may be a class for 12–18 month old puppies.

Once entered, you need to make sure your dog is ready to be shown. If you have not learned to trim your dog, now is not the time to start practicing! Either take him back to the breeder or to a professional trimmer, one who knows about your breed. Observe them carefully; it's a good idea to learn to trim your own dog. Otherwise, it gets expensive. Consult the chapter, "As A Show Dog," to get a good idea what trimming is all about. That same chapter has very useful directions on training your dog for the show ring.

The dog show itself is a novel experience for the uninitiated. Sights and sounds like you've never seen or heard before. It's a good idea to latch onto a more experienced exhibitor to go with you the first time. Find your ring and be sure you carefully observe the time schedule, which you received from the show superintendent the week preceding the show. If you were lucky, there were even directions on how to get to the show site.

Since the dog show world still seems to cling to its male chauvinistic ways, dogs are shown first, followed by bitches. The procedure is to start off with the youngest age puppy classes and work their way through all the classes for males. (The classes are just like those listed above.) Once the judge has selected a winner for each of the classes, he brings back all the class winners to be compared against each other and the breed standard. Yes, there is a specific blueprint laid down by each breed's parent club and accepted by the American Kennel Club as to what each breed should look like. (Refer to the chapter on the standard for more in-depth information.) The judge's purpose in comparing all his male winners is to select the one closest to the standard to award AKC points toward his championship. The number of points for each breed is determined by the number competing on that day, in that geographic location. Look in front of a show catalog and you will find a schedule of points. It's different for each breed and each area of the country. It depends on the popularity of the breed and how many dogs were shown in this area last year. It's an intricate formula; all worked out by the statisticians of AKC.

To become a champion, your dog needs to earn 15 championship points, including two major wins. The major wins must be earned under two different judges and your dog cannot finish his championship without winning under a minimum of three different judges. A major win consists of 3, 4, or 5 points. The more dogs competing, the greater number of points awarded. Five is the maximum at any one show, no matter how many dogs are defeated.

After all the males have been shown, the judge repeats the same procedure when judging the bitches. After he has selected his point-winning bitch, the winners dog and the winners bitch come into the ring with the champions competing in the Best of Breed ("Specials") class to compete for Best of Breed (or in certain breeds, Best of Variety).

At an all-breed show where 130 AKC-approved breeds can be shown, the judge of each breed selects one animal as his Best of Breed winner, either the Winners Dog or Winners Bitch of the day as the Best of Winners, and a Best of Opposite Sex to Best of Breed. That means that if a male Champion won Best of Breed, then the judge would pick a bitch to be the best of her sex. It can happen the other way around, too. The judge, if he sees fit, does not have to pick a champion for these top awards. The Winners Dog and Winners Bitch can be selected to be Best of Breed and/or Best of Opposite Sex. Each of the breed winners go on to compete in the Hound group against the 20 other breed winners that make up its group. Before this gets too complicated, please refer to Figure III-10 which shows the classes and the winning progression at an all-breed dog show. In a way, it's like a basketball tournament. The seven groups make up the brackets and they move along until there are only seven finalists left. Then the judge makes the ultimate award of Best in Show. One last point, if the Best of Winners dog or bitch had earned fewer points by winning its portion of the competition than the animal it defeated, it will gain the greater number of points; *i.e*, the Winners Bitch won two points but the Winners Dog won five. By going Best of Winners, the bitch would pick up the three additional points awarded the dog and gain a major. The dog would still have his five points so the net effect would be that both took home five-point major wins.

All-breed shows are the most prevalent in this country. But, there is another type of show that is designed specifically for a single breed—it's called a Specialty Show. Any breed club that is recognized and licensed by the AKC to hold one may do so. AKC championship points (and/or obedience "legs" if obedience classes are being offered) are awarded at these shows. Specialty shows are a way of getting breeders and exhibitors together from perhaps all over the country in a "convention"-like atmosphere. Sweepstakes or futurity

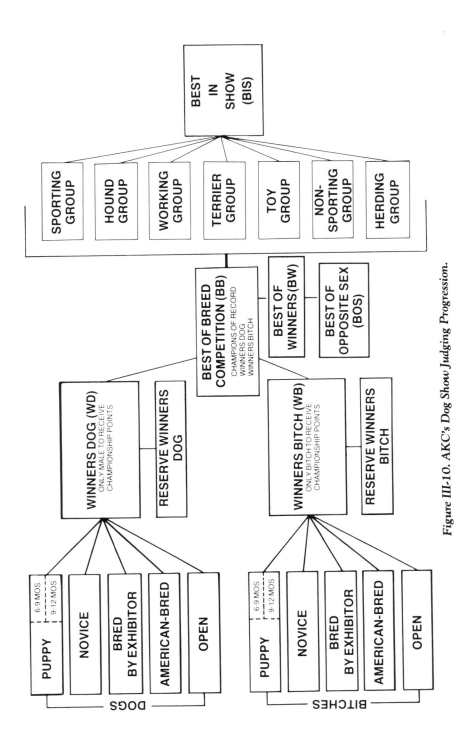

Figure III-10. AKC's Dog Show Judging Progression.

classes are often offered as well as meetings, seminars, banquets, picnics, dances or award dinners. A special form of camaraderie abounds at a specialty show that does not usually exist at all-breed events. Wins and placements at specialty shows are considered to be very important honors. As a result there are several of these shows held every year all over the nation.

A third type of show—and one that seems to be the kind of event for novice and expert alike—is the Sanctioned Match. Again, most of these are held under AKC sanction but no championship points are awarded. It's a practice ground. New owners can show their own dogs and make all the first-timer mistakes without penalty or embarrassment. Experienced breeders use it as a training ground for their newest show prospects. The judges are usually professional handlers or breeders who want to qualify to become regular judges. It's fun and a great learning experience. There are both all-breed and specialty sanctioned matches. Check with your local dog club for information on these events.

On several occasions, reference has been made to "the judge" who selects the winning dogs. These ladies and gentlemen are duly licensed by the American Kennel Club. They are usually persons who have been successful breeders or professional handlers of many years' standing. They have filled out arduous questionnaires about their involvement in dogs, taken tests on the breeds they wish to judge, and have been interviewed by an AKC Field Representative. Once they have passed these "hurdles," their names are published in the *American Kennel Gazette*, the monthly magazine of the AKC. Persons having knowledge of these candidates may write to the AKC either for, or against, them. The final step is a review and analysis by an AKC panel. Using prescribed guidelines, they grant a candidate one or more breeds. The candidate must go through similar subsequent applications in order to judge additional breeds.

Once granted his or her initial set of breeds, the fledgling judge must judge all of these breeds on five occasions to be eligible to apply for others. During this period, the judge is known as a "provisional judge." Their actions are carefully watched by an AKC Field Representative and a report is given on their ring procedure and general knowledge. Even after being granted status as a regular judge, all judges are periodically evaluated and a report submitted to the judge and to AKC.

At this point, I must warn you about a terribly infectious disease you could pick up by attending your first dog show. It's called the "BUG" and people who catch it can become dog show bugs for the rest of their lives. Their friends think they are off their rocker since they suddenly start talking about "bitches" and "points" and other stuff that makes no sense to normal people. Dog show bugs often give up golf and on weekends can be found out in the sun in the middle of a ring howling about what a great win they just pulled off. Have pity on them, but beware—it could happen to YOU!

Climbing the Ladder of Success

When people seek the services of a doctor or a lawyer, they usually look for one with a good professional reputation and avoid the "quacks" and "shysters." When shopping for major purchases, "brand names" and "quality" are sought in preference to the unknown and untried.

Then why, *oh why,* does the novice breeder select an often unproved, or less than adequate, breeder as their "mentor"? It is so often a case of the blind leading the blind!

This is not universal by any means. There are many novices who have had the good fortune of enjoying the association of respected, successful breeders. From them, the novice receives a valuable education about many aspects of breeding and showing dogs as well as the basic rules of sportsmanship. Oftentimes, this association comes about purely by chance. Very seldom is it sought.

Most experienced and successful breeders neither need, nor want, the "coat-tail crowd"—those that look to him for every assurance, opinion, and then reflect his exact thoughts back to him. Through experience, it is not difficult for this breeder to discern fairly easily those worthy of his time and efforts. Novices are NOT expected to know it all—and those who act as though they do are quickly given the cold shoulder. Novices ARE expected to ask questions and shouldn't feel their questions will be regarded as silly or insignificant.

Perhaps it is from the "fear" that the big-name breeder will not want to bother with him, that makes the novice seek out "second best." Or, more than likely, an association with a lesser breeder is sought because in the eyes of the novice ANY accomplishment looms large beside his own insignificant or fumbling beginnings. To the novice, the word "champion" is truly the magic word—this, before he develops the ability to discern that there are champions and *THERE ARE CHAMPIONS!*

There are many breeders, both successful and near successful, who are more than happy to lend a helping hand. They have usually reached their own pinnacle of success due to another's assistance along the way. However, whereas successful breeders desire to help those deemed worthy, many not-so-successful breeders encourage the association of one and all. In fact, the more the merrier! To gather a group of "disciples" around gives many less-than-successful breeders a prop for their sagging egos. It's not uncommon to find these breeders with their own personal retinue accompanying them everywhere, hanging onto their every word and taking all they have to say as the gospel truth. They are seen at dog shows clustered around the breeder's crates listening only to him. They pay no attention to the other dogs, rarely watch the judging (where they might actually *learn* something!), and have eyes only for the dogs belonging to their "friend."

The disciples end up with very little true knowledge of the breed which they originally sought. Actually, they have been "used" rather than helped. They are often kept within the fold by being made to feel obligated as a result of "free" stud services, "gifts" of dogs and "deals." If they would only look around them and see the light, they would realize that "free" stud services are rarely offered on GOOD dogs; dogs are not "given away" that possess a monetary value and for which there is a demand, and "deals" rarely work out to everyone's satisfaction.

Many of these people have long ago lost sight of their original goals and have become enmeshed in all sorts of dog activities that lead them nowhere. These are the ones who throw in the towel and become yet another "five-year statistic." (*Author's Note: The average person lasts only this long in the dog game.*) Very few go on to become successful breeders on their own, for that requires independent thought and they have not been conditioned to do this.

It should not be too difficult to establish criteria of some sort to distinguish between those breeders capable of assisting the novice and those who use the novice to further their own interests. First off, what constitutes success? What assurance can the novice obtain that his would-be "mentor" has something to offer? Is it because he has bred a champion? Realize, please, that many a champion is the result of luck in breeding or persistence in showing. Maybe he has bred several champions. Then ask, what kind of champions? Did they finish quickly in good competition or were they dragged through to their titles winning against even more inferior competition? Also, ask how others regard these champions. Do other well-known breeders desire their offspring or breed to them or does their "popularity" result from the novice and pet trade? Is this person known only in their own locale or known throughout the state and country as well?

Answers to these questions—honest answers, that is—should provide the beginning breeder with some insight as to where they should look for assistance. Then, there is the matter of integrity. Does this breeder constantly knock dogs belonging to others? Does he start, or perpetuate rumors based on heresay or inconclusive evidence? Does he, when selling his stock, "guarantee" that eight-week old puppies will finish their championships? Does he imply that his stud dogs will sire top quality—regardless of the bitches bred to them? Does he profess expert knowledge of bloodlines with which he has had no experience? If the answer to most of these questions is "yes," look elswhere for your guidance. If you chose this kind of person as a role model, your chances for success are slim and none.

To become completely dependent upon another for your success in dogs will—in the long run—not serve you well. To be a good breeder, you must be able to think independently and, when ready, begin to make your own decisions—to buy that puppy, to line breed correctly, to keep that *one great puppy.* Learn all you can from your competent mentor and then go out and apply that knowledge on your own. Of course, you will make mistakes, who doesn't? Remember, you can learn as much from failure as you can from success. Go over the dogs who are winning, find out why. Ask questions when you don't understand something. Have an inquiring mind. And, by all means, watch the judging and learn by observing where the judge puts his hands, what he comes back to when he goes over a dog a second time. Many judges "signal" the ringside what they are looking for.

Now you will find some top breeders who are leery of helping a novice. That is because they have no doubt had some bad experiences. They have run into the know-it-alls, the stubborn ones who will do it their way only, and the troublemakers. Unfortunately, there are always novices out there who—in order to make a quantum leap to stardom—set out to accomplish something that has never been done before. Maybe an experienced breeder with a good knowledge of genetics may hazard such a venture, but the rank novice is headed for disaster. And when he crashes on the rocks he blames all but himself.

Let us say you have been fortunate enough to get yourself a good mentor and have learned your lessons well. You set out on your own and Dame Fortune has smiled upon you. All is wonderful, you are a winner and you bask in the reflected glory of your winning dogs. Great, except something is not quite right! You have the uncomfortable feeling that all your winning is not going over too well with your fellow exhibitors. Where did you go wrong? After all, isn't the idea of this whole thing to be a winner? Let's look into that part of the game a bit more.

Much emphasis has been placed on the importance of being a good loser, but little or nothing is said about the difficulty of being a good winner. To be a good loser is not difficult; in fact, it happens frequently to most of us. But acting appropriately as a winner, is something else indeed.

At any show, whether it is a specialty or an all-breed show, there can only be a few winners. Should one exhibitor's entries account for more than one win, the leftover pickings become even smaller. This means only a small number of people go home perfectly happy from a dog show. The vast majority console themselves that there will be another day or, at least, the judge did a conscientious job and gave them a fair shake.

Let's face it, we would rather win than lose on any given day. In the dog game, we have learned that a top dog probably will win three out of five times and be close when he loses. The average competitor will probably finish in 15-20 shows, winning perhaps six times. So you see, losing is the norm. However, we go into each show with the expectation of winning and, as a result, we get disgruntled when we don't. Turn to the person standing next to you and remark about the poor job of judging that old Nicholas Applebee is doing today and chances are you will get full agreement. What's so strange about that? However, point out that old Nicholas is really on the ball today and is picking the top ones and you will most likely get a baleful stare, unless you happen to be standing next to one of the day's few winners.

You learn that it's hard to be a winner by any standard. Everyone's goal is to be a winner and get to the top. But, for many, that winning spirit can get us into trouble with our peers and reaching the summit can become a hollow victory. Your dog has won, you're thrilled, elated, on Cloud Nine and you want to shout about it from the rooftops and let the world know about your accomplishments. But you don't, because—let's face it—YOU are happy but most of the other exhibitors are not! So you adopt the reserve of the English and smile inwardly. To have your dog's wins greeted by indifference or snide remarks takes the wind out of your sails and much that should be joyous becomes just the opposite. After coming up against the "wet dish rag" form of enthusiasm, you keep your happiness to yourself to be taken out later and savored privately. While it will have to suffice, winning's not what it *should* be like. The losers of the day, on the other hand, are walking around muttering under their collective breath's that they "were robbed," or "the judge was stupid," or both. Perhaps some day there could be a cartoon that poses the question "Guess who the losers at the dog show are?" Not too long ago, a top-winning special went up for Best of Breed and one of the losers came over to the handler and said "Nice win. Too bad he didn't deserve it." Comments like this cannot help to make a winner's day!

As you can see, being a winner is not easy—no matter how desirable this position looks from afar. To come up with winning dogs, year after year, places many breeders in the position of being a prime target for all the unsuccessful, jealous and petty breeders still striving for success. Because of some quirk of human nature, it seems that people feel the need to elevate their own kennel's status—not necessarily by breeding better dogs—but by downplaying those belonging to others. Everyone, at one time or another, has been guilty of this to some degree. However, the driven ones give little heed to the feelings of others and strive to demean other's accomplishments at every turn. Perhaps this is their way of lessening the threat to their own aspirations.

This type of behavior is not soley confined to those engaged in dog activities. It is evidenced even more clearly in the business world by price-cutting, false advertising, and disparaging your competition. It's frowned upon by the Better Business Bureau. In dogdom, we have no BBB, only virtually "unenforceable" club codes of ethics.

By now, you must recognize that a healthy competitive spirit and a thick skin are prerequisites to success in the dog game. Obviously, when competitive spirit meets competitive spirit, some sparks are going to fly. Think of it as two terriers being sparred against each other in center ring. It's a good show but when it's over, it's over!

In order for any one breeder in an area to attain success, others must—by necessity—lose along the way. This cannot be helped, for it takes many losers to make a winner. Those on the threshold of success might do well to remember that the time will come when they must come face-to-face with some of these same losers—as they lose their grip on the top rung and slide downward. No matter how good we are as breeders, there comes a time when not every success is topped with yet another success and we lose our momentum and backslide a bit.

Very few, if any, have the good fortune of having their cake and eating it too. That is to say, few breeders can continually enjoy success without ruffling some feathers of their losing breeder acquaintances. Some people just can't take the slings and arrows that come their way as the winner. They have thin skins and suffer grievously. What to do? Some breeders just up and quit. To them, it's just not worth it. Maybe they feel they have achieved what they set out to do and don't want to settle for second best. Many learn to compromise. That is, they can share the winner's mantle with others without feeling they are a "failure." These are the ones who survive. Their accomplishments and abilities are recognized but they no longer hold a monopoly on success. As a result they have a degree of popularity with their fellow breeders and have gotten out of the crossfire allowing them to enjoy their hobby.

These "old timers" no longer have to prove themselves at every outing. The "comers," on the other hand, strive and claw their way at every step. These are the ones who "work" the judge and demean the competition. This aggressiveness is what makes them tick and can lead to "success." But at what cost? Many of you have run across such people in the dog show game. The desire for recognition is one thing, but you can carry the craving for success too far and alienate everyone around you.

Once you have climbed that mountain and become "top dog," you may well find out that it's very lonely on top of that peak. There just isn't much room at the top; the kind of personality that's driven you there doesn't allow for sharing the top perch. This fact is usually not recognized by those hell-bent on getting there. It can only be truly understood by those who have experienced this heady sort of success with all of its accompanying drawbacks.

It doesn't have to be like this. In fact, in many instances it's not. However, there are too many cases where this is the norm in the dog game. They'll all love you when you're a "point maker." In fact, your dogs may not be bad and—with a little help and some good luck—might do some real winning. On the other hand, just as soon as you do start that *real* winning . . . well, after reading this chapter, it should be all too familiar.

CHAPTER 14

The Basenji As An Obedience Dog

Ch. Pendragon's Sugarbabe of Kazor, C.D.X., F.Ch., doing the directed jumping exercise while in training for her attempt on a Utility Dog title.

In the 45 years since Phemister's Barrie, C.D. earned the first AKC obedience title for a Basenji (in 1942) through 1986, 334 Basenjis have claimed that same first title: Companion Dog. Just 47 of these obedient Basenjis have gone on to add the second title: Companion Dog Excellent. The real Basenji obedience elite gaining the Utility Dog title numbers 7 to date. Three of the seven Utility Basenjis were owned and handled by Rex Tanaka of Hawaii. Rex's star was Ch. Il-Se-Ott Golden Majorette, U.D.T., who gained her Tracking Dog title, the first given a Basenji, in 1972 and then became the third Utility Dog Basenji in 1974. There have been six Basenjis earning the working title in tracking and Spring's CC of Takuvik, T.D.X., F.Ch., is the only one who has gone on to gain the Tracking Dog Excellent title.

There is no question that Basenjis are not prime obedience trial prospects. This is a smart, independent and easily bored breed with a naughty, into everything character that does not lend itself to formal obedience work. The true obedience buff usually looks to the Golden Retriever, Doberman Pincher, Shetland Sheepdog, etc. types from the Working, Herding or Sporting Groups for obedience prospects. They want a dog that's easy to train and will win high scores in American Kennel Club trials. Just because Basenjis are not easy to train does not mean training will not be good for them. It will also help develop your understanding of your Basenji. Working in obedience really develops the bond between owner and dog and enriches the relationship immensely. As you come to know

Ch. Baranfield's Cyclone, U.D.—First Utility Dog Basenji.

Ch. Il-Se-Ott Golden Majorette, U.D.T.—Shows her tracking skills.

your dog better and your dog begins to understand what is expected of him, many of the rough, contentious points in your lives together may smooth out with a pleasant and rewarding pet emerging. The time you spend together will help fulfill the desire for human attention the normal Basenji has, making his life more satisfying. Like the child who is naughty just to gain notice, some of your dog's behavioral problems may be due to a need for more quality time with you. The formal trials are fun but the real goal in training is a better human/pet relationship.

Although there are very good books which present different systems of training, obedience classes are still useful to either experienced or inexperienced owners. Sometimes, no matter how hard you study training books, you do not get the desired results. Usually you have missed some very important point the author was trying to get across, and which an experienced instructor will be able to help you with. You may be amazed at how well your Basenji acts for the instructor compared to what he does for you. Your delivery of commands or your body language can easily confuse your dog. These are things that experience can teach and your instructor can help you with. There are classes for baby puppies called kindergarten puppy training (K.P.T.), and adult classes for "around the home" or trial training. Often obedience instructors are not familiar with Basenji temperament since they have primarily trained the "easy" breeds and have had few Basenjis come to their classes. This can be a problem, but usually the

The distractions of other dogs working in a class setting will help make your dog steady in his work.

pluses outweigh the minuses and you can still learn a great deal at class. Do not be discouraged when some other dogs seem to be advancing quicker than you and your Basenji. You are contending with a breed that learns quickly but becomes bored easily. Remember that YOU have the challenging breed and must learn to out-think your youngster. I have attended a number of obedience classes over the years and have found the quality and effort the handler is willing to put into the dog's training is far more important than the breed. Some owners cannot control their Labrador Retrievers, generally an easy-going and willing worker, while another more astute owner with a tough and busy little terrier graduates at the head of the class.

Obedience performance can be vastly improved by the way a Basenji is raised. However, even if your Basenji is already more than six months old, do not hesitate to give obedience a try. Obedience training may help solve problems you are having with your little wild creature and develop a rapport between the two of you that you did not think was possible. The following text will briefly discuss obedience at different points in your Basenji's life. Don't feel that because you have skipped an early stage that obedience will not be possible with your Basenji. It is just a bit more difficult.

Choosing A Puppy For Obedience

If you are interested in obtaining a Basenji pup for obedience work, do some homework before going to see any puppies. Study some good books on canine behavior and training. There has been a good deal of research on hereditary and environmentally-motivated canine behaviors, personalities and traits. Some of the work done by the guide-dog foundations is fascinating. When you contact Basenji breeders, be honest with them regarding

This female began her training at 3 years of age. *Photo courtesy of the American Kennel Club.*

your interest in obedience. Don't be surprised if most breeders are reluctant to let you have one of their pups. They know Basenjis are not great in obedience and want to make sure you are really getting the right breed and individual. They are concerned about the welfare of their puppies.

It is your job to really search your soul to determine if you will be happy to work hard to have a dog that places consistently in the mid to low 190's rather than a dog who wins class placings on a regular basis, highs in trial and obedience championship points. The Basenji obedience trainer must have determination, intelligence and, most of all, a sense of humor. If you can find a breeder who has some interest and experience in obedience you may get some good advice regarding your expectations of Basenji performance.

Every Basenji has a different personality and some of these traits show up in the very young puppy. Selection of the obedience potential pup should take place between 8 and 12 weeks. If you are dealing with an experienced breeder, take the breeder's comments and advice into account.

This breeder has watched many litters grow up and will have insights into behavior that you could miss. Your obedience prospect should be neither a pup that is retiring and shy nor the boss of the litter. If there is a shy pup in the litter, he may not be able to withstand the confusion of classes or obedience trials. He may well grow up to be a retiring dog who needs a very protected, quiet adult home. The bossy pup is continually bullying the other pups and he may be too aggressive to take your commands easily. You want neither a lethargic pup who has no energy nor a hyperactive pup. Again, the breeder may have noticed if any of pups in the litter have either of these tendencies. The hyperactive pup may not be able to concentrate on obedience exercises and they are usually a handful to live with as well. The obedience prospect is aware of humans and very interested in them. When you gently call them, they notice and are likely to come over for attention. If over the course of the visit you gently sit them several times, the obedience prospect may be sitting without too much resistance before the visit is over. If you roll a ball or a wad of paper, the obedience prospect will chase after it and perhaps even bring it back. Make some odd quiet and loud noises to see how he responds.

Take each pup alone and watch it in a new situation away from its littermates if possible. The pup should be cautious but not fearful. He should look over the new situation with interest. A responsible breeder will not mind taking the extra time for you to decide which pup, if any, in a litter is what you are looking for. Don't be rushed.

The obedience dog that will be going into advanced training should be structurally sound to withstand the rigors of the jumping exercises. A strong topline and sound movement can make a difference over the years of obedience training. If you are not experienced in selecting a pup for soundness, the breeder may be able to help. Each line of dogs develops differently and only those very familiar with the line will be able to make an educated guess as to how a particular pup will develop physically.

A pedigree full of past obedience dogs would be a great help in choosing a potential obedience competitor if one were especially interested in formal obedience. Such pedigrees simply do not happen in Basenjis because there are so few Basenjis with obedience titles. If you deal with a breeder who has worked in obedience, you will probably make out well enough.

These are suggestions and guidelines. Perfect dogs rarely exist. Don't forget that obedience is not a true Basenji trait. Reread the section on Basenji history, noting the thousands of years of natural selection which have gone into developing a breed that thinks for itself on the hunt. Breeds which star in obedience have hundreds of years of selection behind them for a dog that will do what its master tells it to. If you are not going to be happy with moderate obedience scores and an intelligent clown for a dog, perhaps you really should consider another breed.

Directed Jumping   *Scent Discrimination*

Stand for Examination

These are some of the Utility level exercises at an obedience trial. "Sugarbabe" needs to be of sound mind and body to perform well.

Early Training

Consider the way a puppy learns. When the pups are first let out to play in the kitchen they run all over without much regard to kitchen chairs. Soon you hear a crack—the first pup has discovered just how high off the ground the chair braces are. The pup picks himself up, shakes and dashes off. It certainly doesn't take long for him to be conditioned to the height of the braces and he ceases to have trouble with them. When a pup tastes a new object, if it is good he continues to chew and if it tastes bad, he quickly learns the shape, smell, color or combination that produces that taste, and leaves it alone. Does he resent the chair or the bad tasting chewed object? No, he is just experimenting, and he accepts the results as the way things are. A puppy is always trying out new solutions to the problems of his life, and he accepts what works after a few tries. This is the time to introduce the basic obedience exercises and show him what fun they are to perform and to condition in him the correct responses. He will accept obedience as another part of his life with the introduction of early obedience training.

The point of training the baby puppy is to develop its natural inclinations and direct its learning experiences. Since a Basenji is not an obedience natural, early training is vital. The pup should be well socialized and accustomed to human handling while still with littermates. If the pup is removed from his littermates too soon, he may not develop normal canine associations and be insecure. Training techniques for babies have changed over the years, and videos can be especially helpful in teaching the proper use of toys or food as rewards. Plan ahead and investigate information sources before the puppy arrives.

Basenji puppies seem to become mentally ready for training much earlier than some other breeds, especially larger dogs. Training should begin almost as soon as a pup arrives. Allow time for rest and an investigation of the new environment. Then introduce the puppy to the regular wearing of a buckle collar. When he is used to his collar, the lessons can begin. Introduce and condition the pup to each exercise in a quiet place away from distractions. You and your lessons should be the most interesting things available to the pup. Always be gentle, consistent and positive.

The following exercises and training procedures have been adapted from an article by Joyce O'Kelly which appeared ten years ago in *Off-Lead* magazine.

Keep all training sessions short and sweet. Five minutes several times a day is much better than a long session because puppies have a short attention span. The sessions will become a bit longer when various exercises are combined later. Avoid the word "no" in the training sessions. Repeatedly show the puppy what you want and praise it lavishly for any positive work it does.

To teach the sit, place your right fingers under his collar and place your left hand on his shoulders. As you say "sit," slide your left hand down his back, over his rump and apply gentle pressure just above his hocks. He will sit on your hand. Let him sit very briefly while quietly praising him. When he accepts the sit, try removing your left hand while loosely holding the collar. Try to keep him sitting for a count of ten while you quietly praise him. Excited praise will encourage him to stand up and bounce around. The second step in this first exercise is the "stand" command. With the pup in a sitting position, slide your right hand, with fingers still under the collar, under the pup's chin. Keep your palm down. Put several fingers of your left hand, palm down, under the pup and just behind the front legs.

TEACHING THE SIT

TEACHING THE STAND

As you say "stand" and pull gently forward with the collar, slide the left hand, with very slight upward pressure, from behind the front legs along the tummy to just touch the rear legs. This will cause the pup to stand, and a very slight stroking of the tummy will keep him standing. Again, don't forget the quiet praise for the count of ten.

Continue the sit and stand training for several days. The pup will usually start responding to the sit command sooner than the stand command. But, as you work with the puppy, you will notice he is beginning to respond to the word. Reduce the hand pressure and motions as his response develops.

Introduce the "down" command with the puppy in a sitting position. Place one hand along the pup's back applying a little pressure downward while the other hand slides his front feet forward as you say "down."

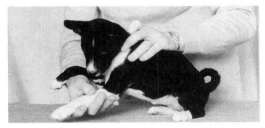

TEACHING THE DOWN

When the pup is responding to the spoken words and you are able to remove your hands without having him immediately change positions (this may take several weeks), begin introducing the "stay" command. With the pup in a sit position, bring the right hand, palm facing pup, to within a few inches of his nose and say "stay." Have him stay a very short time—less time than you expect he could. This is so that you can release him from the stay before he makes the mistake of breaking the command. If he does break the stay, repeat the exercise with a shorter time in the stay command. When the pup understands the command and is staying briefly as commanded until released, introduce the stay for the "down" and then the "stand." Don't be in a rush to advance the length of time in the stay or rush to move away from the pup while he is staying. The pup's understanding of the command and correct response to the "stay" in his future obedience work is too important. This foundation work cannot be rushed.

You may begin retrieving in the same distraction-free environment at the same time as you work on the sit/stand exercise. Begin with a ball reserved for these occasions. Roll the ball along and praise him for even going after it. If he picks it up, more praise. Don't worry about the pick up or bringing it back at the beginning. If he doesn't bring it back, just go pick

Don't change from retrieving the ball to working with a dumbbell too soon. The puppy shouldn't learn to chew the dumbbell.

it up and roll it again. Most puppies will begin chasing the ball and picking it up. Other toys can be introduced. When he is happily chasing these items and enjoying this game, try to coax him back to you by calling or patting the floor. A glance or step in your direction should earn praise. He may begin bringing the items back to you to throw again. If he doesn't but is busy playing with the item in question, sit quietly and wait for him to get bored of playing by himself. If he is close, you may pull him gently over by the collar and gently take the retrieved article away with maximum praise. Immediately toss the item again so the game can continue. Don't ever chase the puppy to get the item back as we are not interested in "keep away." This exercise is a game unto itself and boisterous praise and good cheer is in order. Always quit while the pup still wants to play more. Don't allow him to become bored. You'll find the game of fetch with a toy or ball useful for many years of your Basenji's life when he wants to play while you'd rather be sitting in your favorite chair.

Leash work can begin when the outside weather is acceptable. Attach a six-foot long lightweight leash to the collar and carry the pup outside to a quiet area. Put the pup down on the ground and just stand there. When the pup is ready he will investigate the surroundings. Simply follow him. When he enjoys his outings and moves freely about on the leash you can begin to use the leash to control him.

Remember, this is a baby puppy. Any force used during this leash work is *very* gentle. Quick and tiny tugs are all that are required.

On the day leash control is to begin, attach the leash and carry the puppy outside as usual and then stand still. This time do not follow the puppy as he moves about. When the pup reaches the end of the leash and it grows taut, give a gentle, quick tug then release and praise the pup as the pressure is released. Be silent as you tug on the leash and he will not associate the tight leash with you—only the praise. If you consistently repeat the tug, release and praise each time the leash becomes tight you have become like the chair we mentioned at the first of this section—a fact of life. The pup assumes he is causing the tug and associates it with the tight leash, and since it isn't particularly pleasant he quits pulling. Move about a bit when the pup is no longer pulling on the leash. If the leash is pulled tight while you are moving, use the same gentle tug, release and praise. Your pup should be staying within six feet of you within a few sessions. When he is aware of the leash length, shorten the leash to four feet, then three feet, then two feet. This should put him in a position very close to the formal heel position. You may introduce the sit at heel when the pup is walking beside you in a position approximately like the formal heel position. He won't be used to sitting outside so he will probably need to be placed in the sit position at first.

Remember the tiny tugs of correction are silent but after the immediate release the praise is lavish. Remember this is a young pup with a short attention span so keep the sessions short and fun. Do not rush to the next step in training. Take your time.

After he is working well in his distraction-free work area, take him to more and more distracting work areas and begin combining all the exercises: sit, stand, down, heel, and stay. The owner who is enthusiastic about gaining control over his Basenji pup should study books on dog training and dog psychology. The best dog trainers really understand their dogs. If you continue your regular, short training sessions and are interested in going further, the pup should be ready for training classes as soon as you can find a suitable class starting up.

Obedience Training Adults

The increased study of behavior in wild and domestic animals has had a great influence on dog training. These advances in training techniques based on the natural behavior of animals seem to be better suited to the Basenji's temperament. As a result, there have been significant increases in the number of obedience trials won by Basenjis in recent years.

After a break of many years, three Utility Dog titles were earned, increasing the total number of Utility Dog Basenjis to 10. Both trainer-handlers of these dogs said they had begun in obedience because they had an adult Basenji who was a problem dog. They stuck with it to learn about various training methods, and their efforts made their stubborn dogs much better pets. Each found that their second dog was a joy by comparison because they started out right and used modern training techniques.

The first new Utility Dog was the black-and-white bitch Jonang's Basic Blac, UD, CGC, who completed her title with owner-trainer Cindy Griswold on December 5, 1993. Margot Fusci has won Utility Dog titles on two Basenjis, Quietus Bonga, UD, F.Ch., and Sukari's Akuaba the Hustler, UD, CGC, F.Ch. Bonga was in training for many years but did not reach qualifying levels until Margot received help from an experienced trainer who helped correct improper responses or behavior that had been taught to the dog.

A group of Basenji owners have gotten together to work with their dogs in obedience. These four all started their formal training as adults.

Hustle won her utility title in nine trials with nine qualifying scores when she was just two years old. Hustle was chosen for her compliant attitude as a pup and was raised with careful training from the day she arrived in Margot's home. (By the way, the CGC after the dog's name is the AKC Canine Good Citizen title.)

Back to your naughty, hard-to-live-with adult. If Margot can gain a utility title on the once-incorrigible Bonga, surely you can try to teach your Basenji some manners. Current techniques are based on the normal interaction between dogs and of a dog with the overall environment. These natural techniques do not require rough handling and are generally labeled as positive motivation. They do require patience, correct techniques, rewards and some corrections.

When we started trying obedience more than 20 years ago, one did not train with food rewards or lures. One either nagged the dog into obeying, which didn't work well with Basenjis, or one carefully presented each exercise to the dog in a set number of repetitions. The dog received praise and a pat for a reward or corrections when he did not respond correctly to a command.

The second method is still part of modern training, with changes in the presentation of exercises. Each exercise is still carefully broken into parts the dog can understand. Food, or even a toy with some dogs, is often used as a lure. The timing of rewards is very important. The dog needs a carefully timed reward to understand what behavior is being rewarded. A small amount of a preferred food along with praise is used when the correct response is given with some dogs. The teaching is tailored to each dog, with the number of repetitions depending on how rapidly or slowly the dog gives the desired response. There is more emphasis now on making the dog happy to respond.

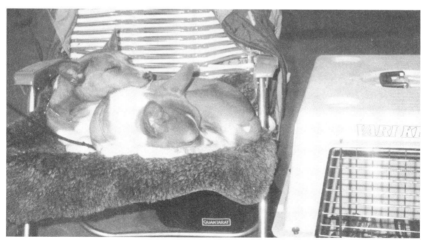

Sukari's Akuaba the Hustler, UD, CGC, F.Ch., and Quietus Bonga, UD, F.Ch., relax while waiting to perform at an obedience trial.

The goal is to make the two of you into a team instead of developing a contest of wills between dog and trainer.

There are many books and videos available about training dogs. Some trainers feel videos are far more useful than books. There are classes given by local kennel clubs and professional trainers. Visit the training classes before you enroll if possible. See how the dogs are taught. See how the trainer relates to both dog and owner. Discuss your breed to make sure the trainer does not have a totally negative attitude toward Basenjis. This is not uncommon among trainers who prefer the "easy" breeds.

There is a real advantage in attending classes with your dog. Yes, a trainer can take your dog and teach it all the exercises, but you need to learn how to get responses from the dog as well. Most trainers admit it is easier to train the dog than to train the owner. If you attend the classes together, you'll both learn what to do. And you'll be spending some quality fun time with your Basenji. Both you and your dog can avoid picking up additional bad habits. You will learn how to train your Basenji, which can be useful in teaching additional manners for your daily life. Dog training classes are wonderful places for you and your dog to get used to meeting other dogs and people under controlled circumstances.

In recent years, dealing with problem dogs has become a more common veterinary specialty. These doggy psychiatrists will help you modify your dog's bad behavior by changing the physical situation, by altering your responses to your dog's behavior and/or by using conditioning exercises. This is a relatively new endeavor which you should consider if you are experiencing serious behavioral problems. These people offer much more than obedience classes. They will request a lot of information about you and your dog; they will come to your home and observe the actual situation, and they will give you sound advice about how to change your dog. Their suggestions may be simple to follow or may require a great deal of dedication on your part.

A stay with difficult distractions can prepare your dog to accompany you anywhere.

SECTION IV
Influences on the Breed

- *Early Influential American Breeders*
- *Top Producing Bitches*
- *Top Producing Dogs*
- *Top Winning Show Dogs*

Miss Veronica Tudor-Williams awards the Breed to Mrs. McGrory's Ch. Risregor Regal Dalabu in Australia in 1975.

CHAPTER 15

Early Influential American Breeders

Looking back to the earliest breeders we find that Dr. Richmond's Windrush Kennel, in Canada, was an important exporter of Basenjis to the United States in the years before Basenjis were even recognized by the American Kennel Club. Al and Mary Phemister, of Massachusetts, were very actively promoting the breed from the beginning. Their dogs came from a variety of sources including Dr. Richmond, Veronica Tudor-Wiliams (England), as well as the rediscovered Phemister's Bois and the stowaway, Congo. Some of the

The last photo taken of Al and Mary Phemister together.

other names one runs across frequently in reading old letters and Basenji Club of America reports include George Gilkey's Rhosenji Kennels of Wisconsin, whose Ch. Rhosenji's Beau was Best of Breed at the first Basenji Club of America Specialty in 1950; Mary McWain's Haku Kennels of New York state, who worked hard to bring tri-color Basenjis to America; Mrs. Taffee, of California, who was instrumental in saving the Kindu and Kasenyi imports; Dr. Eloise Gerry of Wisconsin, and Forest Hall (Hallwyre Kennels of Texas), who gave us Ch. Kingolo. These were the active people who helped get the Basenji breed off the ground.

The first champion and obedience-titled Basenjis listed were the Phemisters' breeding. Entries were generally very small at the early shows in the 1940's except at a few Eastern shows. The small number of Basenjis competing in certain areas had some curious effects. For example, it was noted in a letter that Mr. H.N. Francis of Portland, Oregon, had the only Basenji entries at 46 shows in his area and he finished eleven Basenjis from his How-Gert Kennels in the 1940's, while competing just once with someone else's dogs. Miss Tudor-Williams came from England to judge at Batavia, New York, in 1947 and drew an entry of 20, the largest entry anywhere to that date. The first National Specialty at Batavia, New York, June 11, 1950, had an entry of 23 which, by the way, was the third highest breed entry at the show that day.

This early group of breeders seem to have been strong-willed and quite opinionated about our breed. Early private correspondence was quite lively regarding quality and history with many discussions on color and temperament. These breeders were faced with the difficult task of establishing a breed with consistent quality based on a very limited gene pool. Miss Veronica Tudor-Williams played a major role in early American Basenjis, with her many "of the Congo" exports from Britain supplying most of the early breeders with much needed diversity. She worked diligently for many years locating top-quality Basenjis in Africa which she then had sent to England. These dogs helped the breed all over the world. Miss Tudor-Williams wrote in 1973:

> I often think how courageous the few early breeders were, and I am proud to have been one of them. We coped with all sorts of difficulties which the present-day breeders know nothing about, and I often think if I had not been very young, and very enthusiastic, I could not have gone on.
>
> To give brief instances of some of the problems: In the 1939–1943 period, at least 20% of all puppies born were undershot. At first about 50% of all pups born had bad inguinal or scrotal hernias, but thank goodness, this was under control quicker than bad mouths, though bad umbilical hernias persisted for a long time. And by bad, I mean bad, with hernias sometimes the size of walnuts. Then we had the cream problem—cream being a pretty colour, but quite ruined by pink noses, pink eye-rims, and yellow eyes. I would say at least 20% of the early puppies were cream, and sometimes there were more creams in a litter than reds. On top of this, we had a few cleft palates in the early days, but these did not persist. And we had "sprawlers" which are puppies which cannot get up on their feet, not many of them, but enough to be a problem, and I am glad to say these have not been seen for many years.

As can be well understood, all these major problems did not allow very much scope for selecting show points, nor being hypercritical over temperament . . . We had to work out which were sweet tempered dogs with native apprehension, and how the six-month solitary confinement of quarantine required before entry was allowed to Great Britain had affected them; and which were naturally not so good tempered, and this, with the best intentions in the world, could only be found out by trial and error.

It isn't easy to find concise statements from these early breeders listing their goals for the breed. In 1958, Al Phemister wrote in a column:

. . . when a well-trained Basenji, of correct type, steps into the show—full of confidence—he draws the eyes of the spectators . . . On the subject of "Show Ring Judging," I would like to see both judges and exhibitors follow the context of the standard more closely. The Basenji standard is clear and concise; it leaves absolutely no room for doubt. However, imagine the bewilderment of the judge when he sees Basenjis brought before him of various sizes and types, some who have little semblance to the Basenji of the standard . . . There is no advantage to changing the Basenji Standard . . ."

The 1950's found the Phemisters and George Gilkey still active. Mary McWain was working toward desirable tri-colors with the imported Black Idol, English Ch. Black Ace and Black Mist of the Congo some of the earliest tri-colors with excellent coats. Ace and Mist were the Winners Dog and Winners Bitch at the first National Specialty in 1950. Sheila Anderson's Glenairley dogs from western Canada began making an impact on the American scene introducing progeny of Widgeon of the Congo, daughter of the African import, Wau of the Congo. Sheila Anderson was a dog show judge in 1965 when she answered some interview questions:

(1) In my opinion type must take precedence over soundness. It is the unsure judge who takes refuge in making the decision rest on soundness. Without type, it surely does not matter if the dog moves soundly or not . . . it could be a sound mongrel! (2) I prefer the gait around the ring to be fast so that one can assess the long, far-reaching action which is characteristic of the breed. This gait is not seen on a slow-moving dog. (3) Coat colour has a very great influence on my decisions. Unless a red Basenji has a real red shade in its coat (no muddy, wishy-washy, brownish shades), it fails badly in respect to our standard of perfection. The black of a tri-colour must be a real shiny, dense black.

Mrs. Anderson was still judging up to a few years ago but is rarely heard from now.

In the 1950's, Norm and Mae Wallace of Washington state began their Tinas Coma Basenjis with Ch. Glenairley Black Munia, who they got from Sheila Anderson. Their import, Ch. Flageolet of the Congo, produced 24 champions which still puts him in the top dozen producing stud dogs in a tally today. Tinas Coma Kennels supplied many new breeders with their foundation stock through the 1960's and into the 70's. Then they began to take AKC judging assignments and reduced their breeding activities. One of Norm Wallace's last important judging assignments was on the judging panel for the

Mrs. Sheila Anderson awards Best of Winners to Kenset Age of Aquarius in Seattle, Washington, in 1980.

1984 Basenji Club of America National Specialty. Mae Wallace is still judging all the Hound breeds and some of the Sporting breeds.

Margaret Robertson's Merlea Basenjis of British Columbia, Canada, also started out with Glenairley stock. Many breeders from the U.S. and Canada went to Mrs. Robertson for foundation stock based on the famous Am./Can. Ch. Dainty Dancer of Glenairley. The Merlea "Dancers" could be found everywhere in the 1960's. Although Mrs. Robertson did not breed as much in the 1970's, her stud dogs still were often used, particularly by Canadian fanciers.

Bettina Belmont Ward started the strong Bettina lines from "of the Congo" stock blended with Ch. Kingolo and maintained a showing and breeding kennel into the 1960's. Her import, Ch. Brahme of Syngefield produced 19 champion offspring. Although Bettina Ward has not been active in Basenjis for many years, she did honor the breed by judging the Sweepstakes at the 1987 National Specialty. She continually commented, with

Mrs. Mae Wallace examines the Veteran Dog winner, Ch. Khani's Lucky Temptation, C.D., F. Ch., handled by Debra Blake, at the 1986 Evergreen Basenji Club Specialty.

Bettina Belmont Ward awards 1987's Best in Sweepstakes to Edgie's Cordero of Maggie, handled by Jim Edgerton.

obvious pleasure, on the numbers of Basenjis being shown and the wonderful temperaments of the exhibits.

Damara Bolte got her start in Basenjis as kennel manager for the Bettina Kennels in the 1950's. Her foundation bitch, Ch. Bettina's Fedha can be found behind her many top-winning and top-producing Reveille dogs through the years. Ch. Reveille Recruit is ninth all-time producing sire and is closely behind seven of the eight dogs ahead of him in our Stud Dog Honor Roll as of 1987 while his son Ch. Reveille Re-Up stands at number two producer as well as having held the Basenji record for all-breed Best in Show wins (14) from 1970 into 1988. Her top brood bitch (and dam of Re-Up), Ch. Reveille Ruffles of Rose-Bay, is number two all-time top-producing brood bitch. But more on these winners and producers in the following chapters. In 1979, Miss Bolte wrote this brief description of a Basenji:

> The Basenji is an elegant alert little dog that stands about 17 inches at the top of the shoulder, has short hair, a foxy face, wrinkled forehead, nice little eyes, stick-up ears and a tail that curls like a doughnut. The legs are long and straight, the body short coupled and level with deep ribs tucking up in the loin. The neck is arched and fits smoothly into clean shoulders. The front and rear should match with a fair amount of angulation to permit the flowing stylish movement that really characterizes the breed.

In talking with Miss Bolte, it doesn't take long to notice her emphasis on good front structure and movement in Basenjis. Damara Bolte is still very actively showing and breeding in Virginia.

Miss Damara Bolte is relaxing with the camp manager and a Zande chief while on expedition in Africa in search of Basenjis in 1988.

Bob Mankey started out in the 1950's by obtaining the young male, Ch. Phemister's Kedar, from the Phemisters' in Massachusetts and taking him out to California to his Cambria Kennels. This handsome and showy youngster did a great deal to introduce Western exhibitors and judges to Basenjis as Bob Mankey exhibited him at many shows. The two of them made a striking picture in the Group ring. The Cambria Basenjis originated with Kedar, Ch. Katema of Carmel, who had a pedigree almost identical to Kedar, Ch. My Love of the Congo and Ch. Bettina's Oryx, a tri-color. The Cambria Kennels produced well over a hundred Basenji champions in their active years, (1951–1986), with Ch. Cambria's Ti-Mungai being clearly the best known. Sheila Anderson once told me that it was through Bob Mankey's efforts, and Ti-Mungai in particular, that length of leg and correct overall proportions of Basenjis improved in the l96O's. Ti-Mungai produced 52 American champions and is still in fifth place among the all-time top producing Basenji stud dogs. Additionally, Bob Mankey exhibited this fine tri-color at many shows, to the advantage of the breed.

Ralph and Joe Lepper had the dominant kennel in the Midwest in the 1950's and early 1960's. Ch. Lepper's Nik Nak was the breed's third Best in Show winner when she picked up two in 1962. Ch. Lepper's Red Pepper,

Mr. Robert Mankey awards Reserve in the 1984 Evergreen Futurity to Jato J'Mira, handled by breeder-owner Sandra Bridges.

C.D., was their movie star. Pepper was one of the dogs used in the movie "Goodbye, My Lady." Her big scene was the one in which Lady retrieves an egg. Watch for her. Lepper Basenjis were the foundation for the Lutes Basenjis, Alice Bair's Sashalia Basenjis and the Woz Basenjis, among others.

There was an influx of new breeders in the late 1950's and the 1960's as well as the introduction of many new dogs from England with the "Fula" breeding. Fula of the Congo was brought back from Africa by Veronica Tudor-Williams in 1959. In looking through the book *Basenji Champions, 1937–1977,* (British) the change in type to a lighter-built Basenji is quite clear with the introduction of the Fula breeding, particularly through Eng. Ch. Fulafuture of the Congo. Some of Fula's early exported descendants—Ch. Fula Hazard of the Congo, Ch. Fula Hill of the Congo, Ch. Fulafaun of the Congo, Ch. Fulaflashi of the Congo, Ch. Fulafriend of the Congo, Fula Reveille of the Congo and Ch. Fulafrown of the Congo—had a very great impact in America in the 1960's and 1970's. The Fula imports went all over the country to many prominent kennels. Ch. Fula Hill of the Congo, for example, went to live with Minnie and Francis Hill in Florida and was a strong influence on their Hills Half Acre Basenjis. However, the Hill's are probably better known for their dedicated work on *The Basenji* magazine which they pioneered in 1964.

Shirley Chambers started her Khajah Kennels in Pennsylvania in 1955 with Eastern dogs, as well as some from the Wallace's Tinas Coma Kennels. She imported Fulaflashi of the Congo in 1963. Flashi won her championship easily and went on to produce 17 American champions for the Khajah prefix. When bred to Ch. Reveille Recruit, she produced the top Khajah sire, Ch. Khajah's Gay Flambeau of Ed-Jo. Flambeau produced 59 champion children, with his breeding to Ch. Tinas Coma Ouimac A-Okay probably the most important to further development of the Khajah Basenjis.

Shirley was successful in having the descendants of the pure black and white Liberian dogs registered with the American Kennel Club by working with the English breeders Commander and Mrs. Stringer of the Horsley prefix. The black and white Ch. Sir Datar of Horsley was registered in the United States in 1969. He went on to produce 13 American champions. The Khajah Kennels were important in supplying stock to many new and existing breeders in the 1960's and 1970's. Her top-producing sires, Flambeau and his double grandson, Ch. Khajah's Gay Excalibur (sire of 54 champions), were very influential. The following quote from Mrs. Chambers may help us grasp her goals in breeding Basenjis:

> The Basenji is a small, proud dog carrying its head high on a long, gracefully arched neck which flows very smoothly into its short level topline. The well-curled tail sits tightly over to one side making a smooth seat flowing into the shelf made from the pelvis. The chest is deep and there is a good tuck-up in the loin adding to the leggy, square appearance of the dog. The long straight and fine legs are set well under the body in front indicating a laid-back shoulder blade with a long well-angled upper arm. The rear legs show an

equivalent bend of stifle with a long second thigh to maintain balance in the whole. The dog moves as you would expect based on its construction—easily, proudly and with long strides. As the dog moves faster, it single tracks in both front and rear. The feet should be tight, compact and dainty. Wrinkles should be fine, while not distorting the shape of the head. Eyes are dark and almond shaped and the ears are set well on top of the head. The head is also smoothly put together with well-defined planes.

Shirley is probably the only breeder who can approach Bob Mankey's record for production of champions and she may well surpass him as she is still breeding and showing on a smaller scale from her new home in Georgia.

Mrs. Shirley Chambers wins Best of Winners with the puppy Khajah's Gay Jessica at the Eastern Regional Specialty in 1978.

Marianne Grybinski started her Luddymarie Basenjis with Tinas Coma, Phemister and Bettina crosses in 1960. She became a judge and some quotes from an article published in 1965 in *The Basenji* magazine may bring some of her priorities forward:

> I would like to state emphatically that I do not like big dogs, however, my interpretation of "big" might very well be different from yours. To me, a big dog would be a massive, huge, bulky type . . . But if you are referring to a "high on the leg," lightly-built dog, then I would say you were correct as I do like plenty of leg on my Basenji, my ideal being a 17-inch dog and a 16-inch bitch. On evaluating the Basenji, I put great stress on general appearance, in fact, as I parade the dogs around the ring, I have tentatively selected my first four placements . . . I like to see a swift far-reaching gait, with head held high on a well-crested neck. I like to see an assured dog whose whole demeanor is one of alertness . . . On closer examination, I evaluate all the good points while making a mental note of any serious fault . . .

Mrs. Marianne Grybinski awards Best in Show to Robert House's Ch. Kstar's Adonis of Anubis in 1981.

We probably find the Luddymarie dogs most strongly represented today in the line that Ross and Betsy Newmann developed with their Betsy Ross

Basenjis in Maryland. They started with Ch. Feruzi of the Zande, a very nice specimen, and combined with Bernice Anderson's primarily Reveille-based Ber-Vic Basenjis and the Luddymarie stock to develop a very showy and winning line of Basenjis who can still be found in pedigrees today. A 1979 quote from Ross Newmann summarizes his ideal Basenji:

> As a short summary, I would describe the Basenji as high on the leg, alert and intelligent looking, fine boned, and a long, arched neck giving the appearance of elegance.

Ross Newmann has now retired from the dog show scene and lives with just a few Basenjis in Hawaii.

Ross Newmann with his first champion, Ch. Feruzi of the Zande, winning a Breed from judge W.F. Gilroy.

Californians Jim and Carol Webb started their Kazor Basenjis in 1962 with Cambria stock. They finished their first champion in 1966 and soon started to put their own stamp on their dogs with crosses to other lines. They have had a number of Top Ten placing Basenjis beginning with Ch. Kazor's Watsie Kengo. Ch. Kazor's Dandy Deerstalker, Ch. Kazor's Intrepid Icebreaker and Ch. Kazor's Lime Lite continued the tradition. The influence of the Kazor Basenjis has been growing in recent years.

Cecelia Wozniak's Woz Basenjis started up in the Midwest in 1965 and continues to this day. She started with Midwestern lines which were already

Judge Nicholas Kay awards Carol Webb's Ch. Kazor's Lime Lite a Group II.

well developed from early stock. She obtained a dog from the Lepper's and bitches from the Lutes' kennel (who had produced the early Best in Show winner, Ch. Lutes Mona Lisa). Another bitch came from the hunting lines of Al and Kitty Braun's Henty P'Kenya Basenjis. Her first well-known Basenji was the typey Ch. Black-Eyed Susan of Woz. Cecilia bred to Cambria, Khajah and Reveille studs among a few others. Working from Black-Eyed Susan, she developed some very pretty Basenjis including the top-winning and top-producing black, Ch. Black Power of Woz (a Sir Datar grandson), and the top-producing Ch. Flower Power of Woz. Each was the sire of 15 champions. The Woz Kennel was less active early in the 1980's but again become prominent with the introduction of a variety of combinations of blood lines.

As we reach the 1970's it becomes more difficult to discover which new

Mrs. Cecelia Wozniak awards Sally Wuornos' Sonbar's Celestial Tania at the Cincinnati Club Specialty in 1988.

kennels will have the most impact, as only time will allow us to see which kennels produce the stock that will make a lasting impression on the breed. The popularity of air shipment of dogs and the ease of long-distance travel has changed the face of breeding, allowing a few individual sires to have a great deal of influence. The Reveille, Cambria, Woz, Khajah and ''of the Congo'' kennels continue to exert tremendous influence on the breed with their stock; the starting point for many new breeders in the 1970's and 1980's.

Ch. Makila Motane Moke

CHAPTER 16

Top Producing Bitches

A good brood bitch is invaluable to any breeder. A bitch of sufficient quality and strength of pedigree should be able to produce when bred to a dog of any line. The acquisition of such a bitch can save a breeder the many years of effort necessary to establish a winning and producing line of Basenjis. These top bitches are usually bred down from generations of well known producing sires and dams and then go on to become dams of many of the top producers and top winners in the Basenji breed.

These records were compiled during 1988 and will change over time.

Ch. Makila Motane Moke

(Orion's Fula Andante ex Ch. Sashalia Fair Sharon)

"Flame" is the top-producing Basenji bitch of all time. She was bred by Joseph and Bernice Walker and owned by Michael Work, of Sirius Basenjis. Mike's parents bought Flame as a young puppy for Mike's 14th birthday; she was shown and finished by Mike, who has since become a professional handler. She was bred to Ch. Reveille Re-Up (a top producer himself) for her first litter. The pups were so outstanding that the breeding was repeated six more times. There were a total of 35 puppies born to these two with 23 champions, 6 Group winners and 2 Best in Show winners plus a few more with points. Flame was named a top-producing bitch by *Kennel Review Magazine* in 1975, 1977 and 1978 and was tied with the Saluki, Ch. Jen Araby Taruna of Srinagar, for top-producing Hound bitch.

Ch. Reveille Ruffles of Rose-Bay

(Fula Reveille of the Congo ex Ch. Rose-Bay's Gay Buta)

The number two bitch was bred by Mr. and Mrs. David Hill and owned by Damara Bolte of Reveille Kennels. "Ruffles" was the only bitch puppy in a litter of seven born in May, 1964, and was chosen by Damara as a stud fee puppy. Ruffles and Flourishes is the bugle arrangement hailing, honoring and presenting flag rank; a fitting tribute to a special bitch. However, Damara had to settle for the shorter name of Ruffles. Ruffles' own show wins included Best of Breed at the Basenji Specialty at Westchester, New York, in 1966. Ruffles has 21 champions to her credit after whelping 32 puppies in five litters. Two litters were by her grandsire, Ch. Reveille Recruit. This breeding produced her best known offspring, Ch. Reveille Re-Up. Two other litters were by Ch. Pooka's Cadet with one litter by Ch. Khajah's Flambeau of Ed-Jo. Both these sires were themselves sired by Recruit. Ruffles passed away in May, 1974, at the age of 13.

Khajah's Gay Amethyst
(Ch. Khajah's Gay Trojan ex Ch. Khajah's Gay Samantha)

"Amy" is in third place with 18 champion offspring. She was bred by K. Anne Evans and owned by Bill and Doris Kukuk, Kukuk Kennels. Born November 17, 1971, she died of cancer January 9, 1980. Amy was purchased from Shirley Chambers as a 15-week old puppy. She whelped six litters with a total of 30 puppies although her last litter consisted of only one puppy. Amy was bred three times to Ch. Khajah's Gay Excalibur, her half-brother, producing 11 American and 2 Canadian champions. Doris Kukuk relates that the first litter was probably the most exciting with five finishing for a great beginning. She produced 4 champions with Ch. Kukuk's Colonel Bogie and 3 champions with Ch. Kukuk's Barnstormer. Doris feels that her most outstanding trait was her loving disposition which she passed on to all her pups. Amy was a *Kennel Review* Top Producer for 1974, 1977 and 1978.

Ch. Fulaflashi of the Congo
(Fulafire of the Congo ex Fulafancy of the Congo)

"Flashi" was bred by Veronica Tudor-Williams and was imported by Shirley Chambers of Khajah Kennels, as a ten-month old puppy in 1963. Flashi whelped six litters for a total of 33 puppies with 17 gaining their championships. She was bred to Fula Reveille of the Congo, Ch. Dark Ringo of Cock's Crow, Black M'Binza of the Congo, Ch. Bazimba's Pride 'N Joy (her grandson), Ch. Reveille Recruit and Ch. Khajah's Gay Flambeau of Ed-Jo (her son). Flashi has made a lasting impression on all who knew her with her outstanding disposition. She has passed this characteristic on to her offspring. Probably her best known sons are Ch. Khajah's Gay Fula Cadet, who was one of the first Basenjis to be in the Top-Ten Hounds, and Ch. Khajah's Gay Flambeau of Ed-Jo, a top-producing sire.

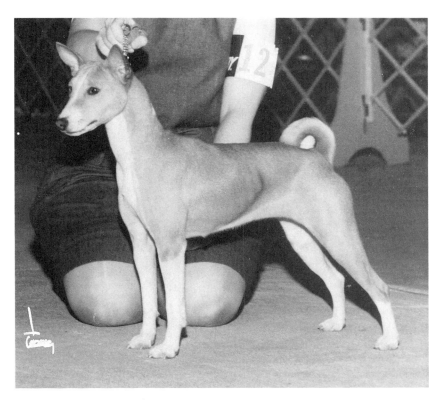

Ch. L's Fawn of Papalote

(Ch. Shadowbye's General Business ex Ch. Shadowbye's Vamp of Tamarango)

"Toppy" was bred by Loretta Kelley and was born on November 14, 1975. The Spring of 1988 finds her alive and well at 12 years old. She was the pride and joy of Bob Carlisle, Papalote Basenjis. Bought as a pet, Toppy exceeded everyone's expectations as she produced 16 champions from 22 puppies. Fourteen of her champions were sired by her grandfather, Ch. Shadowbye's Mitty with the other 2 by Ch. Fireworks of Papalote. Her best known offspring was Ch. Kiowa Warrior of Papalote, who won the Wessman Award for defeating the most Basenjis in 1980 and 1981. Other Group winning and placing children were Ch. Commanche Brave of Papalote and Ch. Karankawa Scout of Papalote. Toppy was a wonderful mother and was never happier than when nursing a litter of puppies. Being a tad bit lazy, lying in bed, nursing puppies and having all the food she could eat seemed to appeal to her.

Am./Can. Ch. Glenairley Black Munia
(Ch. Glenairley Black Trellis ex Widgeon of the Congo)

"Mama Munia" was bred by Sheila Anderson and was one of the first two Basenjis acquired by Norm and Mae Wallace of Tinas Coma Kennels. Munia produced 10 champions sired by Am./Can. Ch. Flageolet of the Congo, 2 champions sired by Ch. Cambria's Ti-Mungai, and 3 champions sired by Am./Can. Ch. Merlea Sundancer for a total of 15 champion offspring. Among Munia's many qualifications, Norm and Mae place her beautiful and loving temperament first. She is a granddaughter of Wau of the Congo (African import) and the first-line progeny of Wau's to be registered in the United States. Munia's descendants can still be found among the top-winning and producing Basenjis.

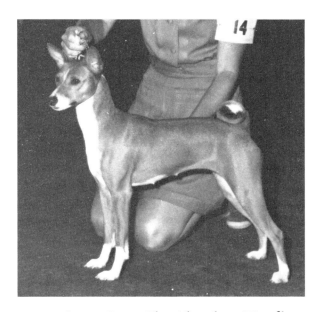

Am./Can. Ch. Akuaba's Firefly

(Ch. Luzambo's Frostfire ex Ch. Khajah's Gay Madeira)

"Firefly" was bred and is owned by Jon and Susan Coe. She was one of the foundation bitches for their Akuaba Basenjis. Firefly is a living example of the value of breeding down from top-producing Basenjis. Her pedigree contains and doubles back on many of the top-producing sires and dams from this listing and, in fact, carries back in a direct line along the dam's side of the pedigree through seven generations of Honor Roll (4 or more champion offspring) dams back to the English import Widgeon of the Congo. This sweet-tempered lady's ability to produce decent shoulders, good length of neck and nice movement has been passed on to some of her offspring who are also now producing champions. Firefly has 13 champions to her credit with a few more still being shown. She was born on December 26, 1976, and is alive today approaching 12 years old.

Ch. Kazor's Xenia
(Ch. Asari's Ntare ex Ch. Kazor's Panzi)

"Xenia" was bred and owned by Carol Webb of Kazor Basenjis in California. Xenia was bred primarily from early Cambria stock. Her sire, Ntare,
produced 9 champions while her dam, Panzi, produced 5 champion offspring.
Xenia is a very nice typical red and white bitch who produced 13 champions
from a variety of sires. Her first litter sired by Ch. Kazor's Watsie Kengo
doubled on Ch. Kazor's Panzi producing 2 champions. She also produced
champions when bred to Ch. Aleika-Absinthe Rajah's JR, Ch. Vikentor's
Lucky Mountaineer, Ch. Asari's Envoy and Ch. Arabrac's Run for the Roses
(son of Mountaineer). Among her children were a number of Top-Ten placing
show dogs including Ch. Kazor's Dandy Deerstalker, Ch. Kazor's Jazzy Jezebel
and Ch. Kazor's Intrepid Icebreaker. Icebreaker just recently claimed 2 Best in
Show wins.

Ch. Khajah's Gay Balalaika

(Ch. Sir Datar of Horsley ex Ch. Khajah's Golden Angel of Javad)

"Laika" was born January 2, 1970. Shirley Chambers, Khajah Kennels, was breeder and owner of this elegant bitch with her exceptionally lovely coat. This photo is unfortunately the only existing one. It was taken while Laika was quite in season. She simply would not hold her tail still! In an effort to combine the new black, Datar (an English import), with her existing stock, Shirley bred Laika to Ch. Khajah's Gay Flambeau of Ed-Jo twice with 7 champions resulting. Her next litter was sired by Flambeau's double-grandson, Ch. Khajah's Gay Excalibur with 4 champions produced. Since both these litters were so successful, Shirley had Laika bred to Excalibur's sire, Flambeau's son, Ch. Questt O'A-Talisman for her final litter. Laika produced a total of 13 champion offspring from these three sires.

Ch. My Love of the Congo
(Piccolo of the Congo ex Gold Pippin of the Congo)

"My Love" was bred by E.A. Collins in England and imported to America by Bettina Belmont Ward. Bob Mankey and Jack Shafer obtained her after she had had one litter. She was born on January 12, 1955. Her pedigree combines early "of the Congo" stock with the American import to Great Britain, Ch. Kingolo. My Love produced 13 champions from four different sires with 8 of her champion offspring sired by Ch. Bettina's Oryx. One of these was the well-known tri-color winner and top producer, Ch. Cambria's Ti-Mungai. A study of the early Cambria pedigrees shows many champions with My Love repeated several times in the background.

Ch. Riviana Jollity of the Congo
(Riviana Red Flame ex Gambol of the Congo)

"Jollity" was bred by Miss P.M. Cook in England and imported by Bettina Belmont Ward. She is the granddaughter of the African import Wau of the Congo and is bred from primarily "of the Congo" stock. Born in 1955, Jollity became an American champion before she was one year old. She produced 13 champions from breedings to these sires: Ch. Gold Pip of the Congo, Ch. Brahme of Syngefield, Ch. Bettina's Ebony, Ch. Glenairley Golden Fresco and Ch. Bettina's Oribi. Her daughter, Ch. Bettina's Fedha, became the foundation for Damara Bolte's Reveille Basenjis.

17

Top Producing Dogs

The Basenji male, unlike the brood bitch, usually has many more opportunities to produce puppies. The percentage of offspring who complete championships is generally smaller although the totals on the top sires are incredibly high. These top sires are almost entirely made up of a tight family. An extended pedigree of these dogs would find the same males repeated over and over with the younger among them all linebred upon the older males. A few of these dogs still have puppies in the show ring so these statistics will change in the next few years.

Ch. Shadowbye's Mitty

(Ch. Reveille Re-Up ex Ch. Lihu's Si-Kitu of Flambeau)

"Mitty" is the sire of 100 champion offspring clearly qualifying him as the top-producing Basenji sire of all time. Since Mitty's birth on December 7, 1971, he was always owned or co-owned by his breeder Lannis Kircus. Mitty was chosen, from a litter of six males, at three months of age by Diane Laue who first became his handler and later his co-owner. He died of cancer July 25, 1982. Mitty is a good example of a linebreeding on top-producing sires with his dam sired by Ch. Khajah's Gay Flambeau of Ed-Jo, the number three sire and Mitty's own sire, Re-Up, being the number two sire with both Re-Up's and Flambeau's sire being Ch. Reveille Recruit, the number nine sire. Two of the top four brood bitches can also be found immediately behind Mitty. Mitty was also a top winner in the conformation ring. His offspring are known for their free movement.

Ch. Reveille Re-Up
(Ch. Reveille Recruit ex Ch. Reveille Ruffles of Rose-Bay)

"Uppity" was bred by Damara Bolte and purchased by Col. Hoffman for his wife, Ellen. Uppity was the only boy in Ruffles' first litter of seven puppies. Born in November, 1966, Uppity died in April, 1979. He had always lived with Damara and when Mrs. Hoffman died, his ownership was given to Damara. His show ring record was unmatched from his career in the early 1970's until 1988. Uppity was the sire of 85 champion children including 2 on this list of top-producing sires: Ch. Shadowbye's Mitty and Ch. Reveille Do Be Sirius. The features Uppity produced most in his offspring were overall balance and substance, but above all, true movement with a level topline and nice head carriage.

Ch. Khajah's Gay Flambeau of Ed-Jo

(Ch. Reveille Recruit ex Ch. Fulaflashi of the Congo)

The number three dog, "Beau" was bred by Shirley Chambers and owned by Robert and Betty Yanowitz. Most of his years, from his birth in November of 1967, were spent with his breeder-handler. He died, in 1978, from a heart attack. He was from the first litter out of Fulaflashi, the number four brood bitch, and he and his litter sister, Ch. Khajah's Gay Firenza, both finished their championships the same day at nine and one-half months of age. Due to his handler's reluctance to campaign a special, Beau was specialed only a few times. Beau contributed many assets to the breed, including outstanding rear angulation with long second thighs, a very tractable, calm disposition, elegance, and a truly gazelle-like appearance. Ch. Khajah's Gay Excalibur, number four on this list, is a double-grandson of Flambeau. Beau was honored as a top producer for six straight years by *Kennel Review* and three times was awarded a Producer of Distinction award.

Ch. Khajah's Gay Excalibur
(Ch. Questt O'A-Talisman ex Ch. Khajah's Gay Samantha)

"Sam" was bred, owned and handled by Shirley Chambers. Despite her reluctance to campaign a special, Shirley felt that Sam deserved the exposure and campaigned him actively for one year with the result that he was number one Basenji as well as number seven all Hounds in 1975. This exposure brought him to the attention of many breeders and he was able to produce 54 champion offspring from a variety of bitches. He was number one Basenji sire and number one Hound sire as well as number three sire All-Breeds for 1977. Sam was honored for four straight years as a top producer by *Kennel Review* and was given a Producer of Distinction Award in 1979. Excalibur's offspring were noted for their good movement and excellent type.

Ch. Cambria's Ti-Mungai
(Ch. Bettina's Oryx ex Ch. My Love of the Congo)

"Ti-Mungai" was bred directly from the foundation stock obtained by Bob Mankey and Jack Shafer's Cambria Kennels and was owned by Bob and Jack. He was born on December 12, 1959. Ti-Mungai and Bob were often seen around the West Coast show rings, thus bringing the tri-color Basenji before the public. He was Top-Winning Basenji (Phillips System), in 1962, and won two National specialties and three Group Firsts. His record of 52 champion offspring is outstanding for an era when air shipment of dogs was not common. His offspring are known for their elegance and outstanding tri coats.

Ch. Djakomba's Spotlight
(Ch. Sirius Half-Back ex Ch. Caucasian Ruffles)

"Spot" was bred by Doris Daniels, Djakomba Basenjis, and Michael Work, Sirius Basenjis, and is owned by Doris Daniels. He was born on December 12, 1977, and after an easy trip to his championship, he was retired from the show ring due to his owner's inexperience in showing. Spot's sire is one of the illustrious pups from the Re-Up ex Ch. Makila Motane Moke breedings. Spot's pedigree has Re-Up as the double-grandfather. He has produced champions from a variety of bitches but some of the nicest have come from bitches from the Khajah lines. Perhaps it is the doubling up on Ch. Reveille Recruit from the two lines which makes those litters so successful. Spot, at 10½ years old is currently the sire of 35 champions with others being shown. He has been strong in throwing his high head carriage, movement, high-set tails and superb temperament.

Ch. Vikentor's Lucky Mountaineer

(Ch. Sirius Gold Rush at Vikentor ex Ch. Changa's Mamba Luckalot)

"Spunky" was born November 11, 1975, and was alive and well at 12½ years old, in 1988. He was bred and is owned by Judy Cunningham, Vikentor Kennels in California. His pedigree combines Reveille, Betsy Ross and "of the Congo" lines. Spunky first attracted attention as a stud dog among the many admirers of his dam, Lucky, who had been successfully campaigned as a special for several years. They were looking for her showmanship, her rich color and her well-wrinkled expression. As luck would have it, Spunky was able to produce those features and he continued to attract bitches from a variety of lines. He has produced a total of 38 champion offspring to this date including 10 Group winners and 26 Breed winners. Some of his well-known offspring include Ch. Arabrac's Mountain Mamba, a Best in Show winner, and these are among his 12 Group winning offspring: Ch. Sunhue Tony Vikentor, Ch. Darp's Mlima Ukungu Vikentor, Ch. Jerlin's Mystic Mountain, Ch. Jerlin's Reckless Richochet, C.D., and Ch. Jerlin's Best Juan Yet.

Ch. Reveille Do Be Sirius

(Ch. Reveille Re-Up ex Ch. Makila Motane Moke)

"DoBe" was from the final breeding between these two. Michael Work is the breeder and DoBe's owner was Mrs. J.H. Symington. DoBe, born December 31, 1975, resided with his handler and agent, Damara Bolte, until his death in April, 1986. Finally getting his turn after his sire, the ever popular Ch. Reveille Re-Up, passed away, DoBe produced 36 champion offspring. His best known daughter is the Best in Show winning Ch. Thackeray Toast Reveille and his best known sons are Top Ten winners, Ch. Reliant Intoxication and Ch. Reveille Skip to Sundance.

Ch. Arabrac's Mountain Mamba
(Ch. Vikentor's Lucky Mountaineer ex Ch. Fleeting Fancy of the Nile)

"Mamba" was bred and is owned by Barbara and Carlos Jiminez, Arabrac Basenjis. He was born November 26, 1978, and posted an outstanding career both in the show ring and as a sire. His show career ended in 1987, when he was the winner of the large Veteran Dog class at the Basenji Club of America National Specialty. While Mamba's pedigree is not a strong line-breeding, he has produced many of the same features his sire did. His pups are well known for their showmanship, their beautiful coats and expressive heads. Among Mamba's 32 champions, the best known offspring are two Best in Show winners, Ch. Arabrac's Evening in Paris and Ch. Reliant Inferno. One sees many pedigrees now with Mamba being used to linebreed on Mountaineer and Luckalot. These three dogs combined are having a tremendous influence on the breed today.

Ch. Reveille Recruit

(Ch. Reveille Rifleman ex Simba III)

"Rookie" was bred by E. Mervin and owned by Damara Bolte. Born January 11, 1960, he died one day short of his eleventh birthday, in 1971. From the 20 litters he sired, 29 of his offspring finished their championships. But what greater proof of his ability as a sire than to be surpassed on this list of top producers by his own children, grandchildren and great grandchildren. The only dog in this listing of eleven top male producers who does not trace back to Recruit is Ch. Cambria's Ti-Mungai, Rookie's contemporary.

Ch. Shadowbye's General Business
(Ch. Flower Power of Woz ex Ch. Lihu's Si-Kitu of Flambeau)

"General" was bred by Gene Litchfield and Lannis Kircus, Shadowbye Basenjis, and is owned by Loretta Kelley, L's Basenjis. General was born November 21, 1972, and is still thriving at almost 16 years old. General and number one producer, Mitty, are both sons of Ch. Lihu's Si-Kitu of Flambeau. When General was bred twice to the Mitty daughter Ch. Shadowbye's Vamp of Tamarango, 11 champion offspring from a total of 13 pups were produced for the L's Basenjis. One of these, Ch. L's Fawn of Papalote, is one of our top-producing brood bitches. Two of General's well-known offspring are Am./Can. Ch. Shantara's Gentaa Snowdancer, Can. C.D. and Am./Can. Ch. Shantara Gentaa Snowflurry, who is the sire of Ch. Music City Serengeti Jazzman, the breed's new all-time Top Winning dog. General was honored three times as top producer by *Kennel Review* and given a Producer of Distinction Award in 1985. While siring relatively few litters, General has produced a total of 29 champion offspring.

CHAPTER 18

Top Winning Show Dogs

Photos of the Best of Breed "class of champions" at the 1985 Basenji Club of America's National Specialty. The show was held in Leesburg, Virginia, and was judged by Thelma Brown.

United States

The very first Basenjis to win at an American Kennel Club show were Thurza of Windrush and the African export Kindu. They were entered in the Miscellaneous Class at the 1945 Westminster show under judge Alva Rosenberg. Kindu won Best Dog in an entry of three while Thurza was Best Bitch from an entry of two females. Basenjis reached the required 100 registrations and moved into the Hound Group and regular competition in the spring of 1945. The first point-winning Basenjis were shown at the Vancouver, Washington show on July 15, 1945 by H.N. Francis (How Gert Kennel) of Portland, Oregon. Best of Breed went to Andy of Glen Ho and Best of Opposite Sex went to Rwanda. Andy of Glen Ho quickly became the first Basenji to win the Hound Group when he took it at Vancouver.

While many Basenjis placed in the groups in the early years, none were really campaigned until Bob Mankey, Florence Wolman and Jack Shaffer purchased the young Ch. Phemister's Kedar from Al and Mary Phemister. Kedar appeared at all the California shows from 1953 to 1956. He earned a total 75 Bests of Breed with 19 Group placements including 3 Firsts. While Basenjis in later years had more outstanding records, Kedar was the pioneer in introducing judges to Basenjis. It was Bob Mankey who changed the way Basenjis are shown. Previous Basenji exhibitors had shown the Basenji like a terrier; strung up on a tight lead and walked around the ring. Bob took his dogs around the ring with a fast gait on a loose lead which emphasized their reaching, flowing movement.

Ch. Pemister's Kedar was the first Basenji to be campaigned as a "special."

The first Best in Show won by any Basenji in the world was won by Crackerjack of the Congo at the Basingstoke Show, 1943, in England under judge Leo Wilson. This, however, was not a championship show as there were no championship shows in England during the war years. In fact, the first Championship Certificates won by Basenjis in England came in 1946. Breeder-judge Forest N. Hall awarded the first Best in Show at a championship show and the first American Kennel Club Best in Show to Philo's Blaze of Koko Crater in Hawaii on October 13, 1956, at the Maui Kennel Club's 13th all-breed show over an entry of 80 dogs. Blaze was bred by Helene Vaughan and handled by Lyle Vaughan of Koko Crater Basenjis. The second American Best in Show went to the lovely bitch Ch. Dainty Dancer of Glenairley with a decisive win in Washington state over an entry of 557 dogs, in August, 1958. She had already won two Bests in Show in Canada on the way to her Canadian championship. Dainty easily became the top Basenji in the Hound Group for 1958, with 7 Group placements including 5 Firsts! She was not campaigned regularly in the United States. The main focus of her Canadian owners was showing in Canada, where she picked up additional Best in Show wins.

Ch. Miacor's Zuchil won 105 Bests of Breed with 49 Group placements including 8 Firsts in the Midwest and was Best of Breed at the 1959 Midwest

Philo's Blaze of Koko Crater winning the first American Kennel Club Best in Show. Handler, Lyle Vaughn with judge Forest N. Hall. Presenting the trophy, Roger Knox.

Ch. Miacor's Zuchil was campaigned in the midwest.

Ch. Bettina's Oribi was campaigned in the east.

Specialty. Ch. Bettina's Oribi was campaigning in the east at the same time taking a similar number of breed wins, and was the top-scoring Basenji in the Hound Group in both 1959 and 1960. Oribi was Best of Breed at 5 different

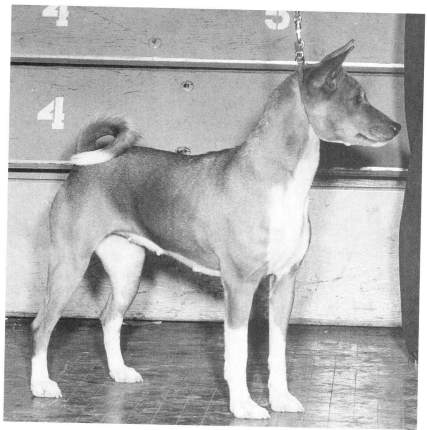

Ch. Lepper's Nik Nak won two Bests in Show. She was the third Basenji to win a Best in Show in the United States.

specialties, including all three regional specialties in one year. His final specialty breed win was from the Veteran Class at the Eastern Specialty in 1963. Ch. Lepper's Nik Nak, a bitch, followed Zuchil in the midwest with 75 Bests of Breed, 26 Group placements with 7 Group Firsts and finished with 3 Bests in Show.

Ch. Cambria's Ti-Mungai was being campaigned in California by Bob Mankey at the same time and was the top-winning tri-color until the 1980's. Ti-Mungai was the top-winning Basenji in the Hound Group in 1962 and won the Western Specialty in 1960, 1961 and 1962!

Ch. Reveille Recruit was the first of many Reveille champions campaigned by Damara Bolte to top honors. "Rookie" won 109 Bests of Breed with 61 Group placings including 6 Group Firsts. His major triumphs were such wins as the 1961 and 1962 Eastern Specialties, Group First at the Philadelphia Kennel Club in 1961 and Group Second at Westminster in 1962.

Ch. Cambria's Ti-Mungai introduced tri-color Basenjis to many while being campaigned in the west in the early 1960's.

Ch. Khajah's Gay Fula Cadet started out in the classes like a rocket. He was handled by his owner to two 5-point majors, one over 5 champions, and two 3-point majors in four consecutive shows when he was only 7 months old. Put into the hands of professional handler Ed Bracy, Cadet was the top Basenji in the Hound Group for 1965 after placing 65% of the time following his 28 Breed wins. Cadet's top year was 1966 when he was top Basenji with 68 Breed wins and 51 Group placements including 5 Firsts. He won the Breed at all ten shows on the Texas circuit and placed in 8 Groups with six of the top-ten Hounds for the year on that circuit. This was the first year a Basenji had sufficient Group points to place among the top-ten Hounds in the country. He was #10 Hound. Cadet defeated 4,131 hounds in 1966. His lifetime record includes competing at 152 shows with 135 Breed wins. He won the breed at 4 BCOA regional specialties and placed in the Group 83 times.

Ch. Khajah's Gay Fula Cadet with judge Vincent Perry and handler Ed Bracy.

All the dogs that came before seemed to set the stage for Ch. Reveille Re-Up. "Uppity" finished his title as a puppy. Judge Maxwell Riddle awarded him Best in Show the first time he was shown as a special just 9 days short of his first birthday. His lifetime total of 140 Bests of Breed may not seem exceptional in some breeds, but those wins lead to 60 Group Firsts and 14 Bests in Show. His ratio of group placements to breed wins was phenomenal. His record as top-winning Basenji stood until 1988! He was the winner of the first Wessman trophy for defeating the largest number of Basenjis at AKC shows in a single year. Uppity was retired after becoming the only Basenji to win the Hound Group at Westminster. The year was 1972 and Uppity was five years old.

Seven Basenjis in the 1950's and 1960's won the coveted Best in Show

Ch. Reveille Re-Up winning one of his 14 Bests with handler Damara Bolte. This is the Twin Brooks Kennel Club on July 13, 1969, with judge Anne Rogers Clark presiding.

Ch. Betsy Ross' Joyful Saint with owner-handler Ross Neumann being awarded with a Best in Show by judge Ted Wurmser at the National Capital Kennel Club.

award while 13 took top honors during the 1970's. Ch. Betsy Ross' Joyful Saint was the third "Betsy Ross" Best in Show winner. He and owner-handler Ross Newmann won a total of 6 Bests during 1973 and 1974. The top-winning black and white Basenji to date also emerged in 1973, Ch. Black Power of Woz. He earned 35 Breed wins with 19 Group placements, including 4 Group Firsts, when campaigned for six months in 1973. He was a grandson of the first black and white American champion Basenji, Ch. Sir Datar of Horsley. Ch. Changa's Mamba Luckalot was the top-winning bitch during 1974, 1975 and 1976. Lucky was campaigned on the west coast. Lucky's son, Ch. Vikentor's Lucky Mountaineer, was also in the top-ten Basenjis and has become one of the top-producing sires in the breed.

Ch. Black Power of Woz, shown by handler Carol Schubert, is the all-time top winning black and white.

Ch. Changa's Mamba Luckalot is shown with handler Ric Byrd.

Ch. Khajah's Gay Excalibur was the sensation in 1974 and 1975. "Sam" finished his title at 10½ months old with several breeds and group placements from the classes. Specialed by owner-handler Shirley Chambers for two years, Sam won a total of 119 Bests of Breed with 69 Group placements including 20 Firsts; leading to 3 Bests in Show. He was #1 Basenji in the Hound Group in 1975 and #7 among all the Hounds competing in the country.

Ch. Shadowbye's Mitty started his specials career in May of 1973 and was handled by Diane Laue through 1979 when he was seven years old. This was a

Ch. Khajah's Gay Excalibur, with owner-handler Shirley Chambers, was campaigned in 1974 and 1975.

Ch. Shadowbye's Mitty winning the Breed under judge Derek Rayne in 1977 with Diane Laue handling.

dog who loved what he was doing and simply would not quit. "Mitty" was the Wessman winner for having defeated the greatest number of Basenjis for four years. He was also the top Basenji in Hound Group placings in 1976. His lifetime record includes several all-breed Bests in Show and specialty breed wins.

The 1980's were led off by a specials bitch. Ch. Thackery Toast Reveille was #1 Basenji in group competition in 1981. Her career ended after 1983 with 2 Bests in Show.

Ch. Thackery Toast Reveille was Number 1 in 1980.

Ch. Arabrac's Mountain Mamba surpassed Ti-Mungai's record to become the top-winning tri-color Basenji while being breeder-owner handled by Carlos Jimenez in 1981, 1982 and 1983. Mamba was the winner of 3 Bests in Show and 5 Specialties. He was shown sparingly in 1984, but won the Basenji Club of America Specialty that year for his final show. Mamba appeared again at the 1987 National Specialty to win the Veteran Class. He still looked in great condition. Mamba's record might have been challenged by his own tri-color daughter, Ch. Arabrac's Evening in Paris. "Eve" started off a specials career with 6 Group wins and an early Best in Show but she was tragically lost when she slipped out of her collar and was killed by a car.

***Ch. Arabrac's Evening in Paris** with owner-handler Carlos Jimenez receiving Best of Breed from judge Del Glodowski.*

Ch. Aleika-Absinthe Rajah's JR was the top Basenji in 1982 and 1983. "JR's" two-year record includes 152 Breed wins with 101 Group placements including 36 Firsts leading to 7 Best in Show wins. He won the Basenji Club of America National Specialty in 1982 and 1983 plus 3 other regional club

Ch. Aleika-Absinthe Rajah's JR is shown with handler Michael Work and breeder-judge Melody Russell.

specialties. JR won the Wessman award for most Basenjis defeated each year as well. This is a particularly sweet record for his owner, the son of the original Mr. Wessman in whose memory the plaque is awarded. JR and handler Michael Work would probably have gone on to set records if JR had not died in a tragic car accident in December, 1983, a month past his third birthday. His record of 22 champion offspring is also indicative of his quality when you consider he was only available at stud for three breeding seasons.

Ch. Rameses Golden Phoenix, F. Ch., was a west coast contender between 1983 and 1986. "Nikii" was the first dog his owner, Ken Leighton, ever handled. Ken handled Nikii for his entire career. Nikii was #1 Basenji in the Hound Group, in 1984, having taken a Best in Show win. He was also the Wessman winner for that year. Nikii also has the distinction of being the only Best in Show Basenji to carry a second title, namely, field champion.

Ch. Music City Serengeti Jazzman won his first Group First from the puppy class at his second show when he was just 9 months old. This was a clear indication of the future. "Jazz" first appeared among the top-ten Basenjis in 1984, before he was a year old. Back-to-back Best in Show wins, in 1985, with numerous other Group placements made him #1 Basenji in the Hound Group for the year. He has never looked back, and each year's record surpasses the last. He was #1 Basenji in all categories, in 1986, with 2 more Bests in Show. The year 1987 was outstanding for Jazz and his handler Wendy Wolforth. He took 9 more Bests in Show, was #1 Basenji in all categories and #2 position among all the hounds. Jazz tied the record for Best in Show wins at the Greater

Ch. Rameses Golden Phoenix, F.Ch.—the only Best in Show winner who is also a Field Champion.

Ch. Music City Serengeti Jazzman winning Best in Show in Connecticut in 1987 is the breed's top winner in the United States.

Miami Dog Club show on April 24, 1988, and surpassed it at the Treasure Coast Kennel Club of Florida show at Fort Pierce, Florida, on April 30, 1988. Jazz ended his campaign with his 20th Best in Show, the new breed record, at his last show in 1988!

American Kennel Club All-Breed Best in Show Winners

1950's

Philo's Blaze of Koko Crater — October 13, 1956
(Akamai of Koko Crater ex Hottentot of Koko Crater)
From the American Bred class at the Maui Kennel Club.
Judge: Forest N. Hall—Entry of 80 dogs.

Am./Can. Ch. Dainty Dancer of Glenairley — August 1958
(Drumadoon Ducat ex Glenairley Melodious)
Entry of 557 dogs.

1960's

Ch. Lepper's Nik Nak — 1962
(Ch. Andersley Amazala ex Lepper's Small Wonder)
Twice—June & September in Michigan

Ch. Lutes Mona Lisa — August 31, 1963
(Ch. Lepper's Mr. Spats ex Lute's Sweet La-Lonnie)
Matoon Kennel Club — Judge: Dr. Frank Booth.

Ch. Betsy Ross Kingola of Ber-Vic — 1967 & 1969
(Ch. Feruzi of the Zande ex Ch. Ber-Vic's Memory of Nyoka)
Twice—October 28, 1967 and August 29, 1969

Ch. Reveille Re-Up — 1967–1970
(Ch. Reveille Recruit ex Ch. Reveille Ruffles of Rose-Bay)
1st Wessman Trophy winner.
Held a long-time record of 14 Bests in Show

1970's

Ch. Betsy Ross Melissa — 1971–1972
(Ch. Feruzi of the Zande ex Ch. Luddymarie's Miss America)

Ch. Reveille Be Sirius — 1972–1973
(Ch. Reveille Re-Up ex Ch. Makila Motane Moke)

Ch. Betsy Ross' Joyful Saint — 1973–1974
(Ch. Coptokin The Veldt Sir Lantic ex Ch. Betsy Ross Nikki of Ber-Vic)

Ch. Khajah's Gay Excalibur — 1975
(Ch. Questt O'A-Talisman ex Ch. Khajah's Gay Samantha)

Ch. Reveille Recycle Pikwik — 1976
(Ch. Reveille Be Sirius ex Ch. Reveille Rumors Are Flying)

Ch. Shadowbye's Mitty — 1976–1977
(Ch. Reveille Re-Up ex Ch. Lihu's Si-Kitu of Flambeau)

Ch. Tri-Tan's Uzuri Supow Lihu — 1976–1977
(Ch. Flower Power of Woz ex Lihu's Susu Yumdrum)

Ch. Camp's Dazzling Nazimba — 1976
(Ch. Khajah's Gay Saracen ex Camp's Tex Kan Baby)

Ch. Reveille Do Be Sirius — 1979
(Ch. Reveille Re-Up ex Ch. Makila Motane Moke)

Am./Can. Ch. Burgundy Wine Sir Gay of Linlo — 1979
(Kadee's Kenya Benji Sen ex Shajo's Sweet Burgundy Wine)

Ch. Darp's Kamili M'Wana — 1979
(Ch. Darp's Re-Up of Sowega ex Ch. Darp's Isis of M'Bwa Wazuri)

Ch. Libra's Apollo of Delahi — 1979
(Ch. Delahi's Fortune Hunter ex Ananka's Lady Nepha)

1980's

Ch. Hai Aari Golden Dybbuk — 1980
(Ch. Hai Aari Golden Dancer ex Petter's Lady Conniver)

Ch. Pero's Krugerrand — 1980
(Ch. Enzi Kidogo of Sun Diata ex Ch. Pero Precious Charm)

Ch. Akuaba's Mistral — 1981
(Khajah's Gay Martin ex Am./Can. Ch. Akuaba's Sungora, C.D.)

Ch. Arabrac's Mountain Mamba — 1981–1982
(Ch. Vikentor's Lucky Mountaineer ex Ch. Fleeting Fancy of the Nile)

Ch. Kstar's Adonis of Anubis — 1981
(Ch. Trotwood's Hercules of Anubis ex Fatima of Ango)

Ch. Thackery Toast Reveille — 1982–1983
(Ch. Reveille Do Be Sirius ex Ch. Rose of Caucasia)

Ch. Aleika-Absinthe Rajah's JR — 1983
(Ch. Absinthe The Rose's Gimlet ex Khajah's Gay Reflection)

Ch. Hai Aari Tshiluba — 1983
(Ch. Shadowbye's Mitty ex Hai Aari Devil May Care)

Ch. Rameses Golden Phoenix, F. Ch. — 1984
(Ch. Asari's Ti-Jii ex Rameses Gold Masterpiece)

Ch. Jen-Nell's Kris Kringle — 1985
(Ch. Mata Hauri Hai Karate ex Wimowey's Pirate Jenny)

Ch. Arabrac's Evening in Paris — 1986
(Ch. Arabrac's Mountain Mamba ex Ch. Arabrac's Peaches N' Cream)

Ch. Reliant Inferno — 1986
(Ch. Arabrac's Mountain Mamba ex Ch. Reliant Cinnamon)

Ch. Anasazi's Whidbey Osiris — 1986
(Ch. Cambria's Zartuu ex Ch. Tennji's Anasazi Foxfire)

Ch. Music City Serengeti Jazzman — 1985–1988
(Am./Can. Ch. Shantara's Gentaa Snowflurry ex Ch. Serengeti Brazen Bantu)
Held breed record of 20 Bests in Show until 1993

Ch. Kazor's Intrepid Icebreaker — 1988
(Ch. Asari's Envoy ex Ch. Kazor's Xenia)

Ch. Arubmec's The Victor — 1988
(Ch. Asari's Envoy ex Ch. Pero's Cayenne of N'Gi)

Best of Breed Winners
Basenji Club of America National Specialty
(Since Restarted in 1979)

1979
Ch. Absin' Bublin' Brown Sugar Lihu

Judge: Michelle Billings
Owner-Handler: Diane Coleman

1980
Ch. Khajah's Gay Jessica

Judge: Mrs. Judith Fellton
Owner-handler: Susan Coe

1981
Pendragon's Little Bit

Judge: Elspet Ford
Owner-handler: Andrea Paysinger

1982 & 1983
Ch. Aleika-Absinthe Rajah's JR

Judges: Mrs. Barbara K. Camp and Dr. Gerda Marie Kennedy
Handler: Michael Work
Owners: Dr. and Mrs. James Wessman

1984
Ch. Arabrac's Mountain Mamba

Judge: Mrs. Melody Russell
Handler: Carlos Jimenez
Owners: Barbara and Carlos Jimenez

1985

Ch. Kenset's Wayfarer From Asbah, F.Ch.

Judge: Mrs. Thelma Brown
Handler: Ted Hagemoser
Owner: Mary Lou Kenworthy

1986
Ch. Arubmec's The Victor

Judge: Mrs. James E. Clark
Handler: Michael Work
Owner: Pat Cembura

1987
Ch. Akuaba's Saturday Strut

Judge: Mrs. Michelle Billings
Owner-handler: Susan Coe

1988
Meri-O Beausoleil D'Orion

Judge: Russell Hendren
Handler: Renee Meriaux Harris
Owners: L. Charles Harris and Renee Meriaux Harris

1990's

The 1990's produced a whole new crop of top winners. The lovely red-and-white bitch Ch. Vikentor's Country Rose was Number One in 1990 with two Best in Show wins. For the following three years the Number One spot in all the tallies was taken by Ch. Sonbar's Celestial Wizard, who set new records for the breed. This red-an- white dog was an exuberant showman for professional handlers Michael and Nina Work. Bravo racked up a record 24 all-breed best- in-show victories. His 14 best-in-show wins in 1993 is by far the most bests won by a Basenji in a single year.

The following are Best of Show winners for the 1990's through this writing:

Ch. Vikentor's Country Rose — 1990
(Ch. Changa's Gala Celebration ex Ch. Vikentor"s Aligator of Darp)

Ch. Beacham-Bryn-of-Orion — 1990
(Am. Bra. Can. Ch. Jen-Nell's Kris Kringle ex Ch. Winart's Po Tolo of Daze-Dun)

Ch. Serengeti Reveille Larkspur — 1990-1991
(Ch. Termay's Dial Reveille ex Ch. Serengeti Hollyhock)

Ch. Sonbar's Celestial Wizard — 1991-1993
(Ch. Arubmec's The Victor ex Ch. Sonbar's Celestial Lalande)
Now holds breed record of 24 Bests in Show

Ch. Akuaba's Tornado, JC — 1992-1994
(Ch. Changa's Gala Celebration ex Am. Guat. Ch. Young-Kwanza Over the Rainbow)

Ch. Calaz Executive of Embasi — 1993
(Ch. Reveille Season No Ka Oi ex Ch. Calaz Ever Redi)

Ch. Changa's Dan Patch — 1994
(Changa's Hold That Tiger ex Flurry's Xmass Angel)

Ch. Sukari's Raider of the Lost Bark — 1994
(Ch. Orion's Bold Adventure x Ch. Sukari's Mindiana Jones, CD)

National Specialty Winners

1989
Am. Can. Ch. Conamore's Sun and Jasmine
Judge: Mrs. Jeraldeeen R. Crandall
Owner-Handler: Cheryl Myers Egerton

1990
Ch. Serengeti Reveille Larkspur
Judge: Mr. Forrest Dye
Handler: Damara Bolte
Owner: Mrs. James H. Symington

1991 and 1993
Ch. Sonbar's Celestial Wizard
1991 Judge: Mr. Robert Stein
1993 Judge: Mrs. James E. Clark
Handlers: Michael and Nina Work
Owners: Michael and Karen Burnside

1992
The 50th Anniversary of the Basenji Club of America
Ch. Candu's Light My Fire
Judge: Mr. Robert Cole
Owner-Handler: L. Jane Williams

Ch. Sonbar's Celestial Wizard set a new breed record by winning 21 Bests in Show. His final show and final best was in February 1994 at the Marion Kennel Club in Marion, Indiana.

1989 BCOA Specialty - Am. Can. Ch. Conamore's Sun and Jasmine.

1990 BCOA Specialty - Ch. Serengeti Reveille Larkspur.

1992 BCOA Specialty - Ch. Candu's Light My Fire.

Canada

With the help of Marnie Lang

Canadian Basenjis have many show ring firsts to brag about. Can. Ch. Kwillo of the Congo, bred by Veronica Tudor-Williams and owned by Dr. Andrew Richmond, was the first Basenji champion in the world. He accomplished this historic feat on September 7, 1943. The Progressive Kennel Club show, Toronto, 1951, was the venue for the first Group-winning Basenji in Canada, Ch. Abakaru of the Blue Nile. American bred by Mary McWain but owned by Canadian Roberta Jenkins, Baka was also the first American and Canadian champion. He completed his American championship, in 1953, in four shows with two Group placements and was Best of Breed at the Basenji Club of America Specialty along the way. Mrs. Jenkins reported that Basenjis were placing well in the groups in Canada during the 1950's, with many Best Puppy and Group Brace and Best Brace in Show awards.

One of the breed's pioneers was Sheila Anderson, who was influential in a number of historical events. In 1949, the Andersons moved to Hong Kong taking Magician of the Congo and Lotus of the Congo from England to the Orient. Lotus was in whelp with the interesting result that the litter was bred in England but whelped in Hong Kong. They kept a pup from this litter who, upon their return to Canada, became Can. Ch. Joss of Glenairley, Can. C.D., the first conformation and obedience-titled dog in Canada. Mrs. Anderson also owned English and Canadian Champion Orange Fizz of the Congo, the first Basenji to obtain both titles. Not to be outdone by his parents Joss and Fizz, Am./Can. Ch. Glenairley's Black Trellis assured himself a place in the record books by being the first tri-color to win a Group First in Canada.

One of the most famous Basenjis in Canadian history was Am./Can. Ch. Dainty Dancer of Glenairley. She was born on December 12, 1956, and breeder Margot Bowden promised her to Margaret Robertson, Merlea Basenjis, at the tender age of five weeks. Mrs. Robertson had already found Dainty to be a standout! Dainty was the first Basenji to take a Best in Show in Canada on September 6, 1957, at the ripe old age of nine months. She completed her championship with 3 Group Firsts and 2 Bests in Show. Her overall show record is remarkable. In a little over a year she won a total of 7 Bests in Show in Canada and the U.S. In 1958, Dainty competed 24 times. She had 23 Breed wins with a Group placement each time, including 18 Group Firsts! She received the Ken-L-Ration award for the top-winning Western Zone Dog (all breeds), the Canadian Kennel Club medal for top-winning Canadian-bred dog, and at the breed level the Basenji Club of America Best in Show trophy and the Bettina Belmont Ward trophy for the most Group placements by a Basenji. Dainty's descendants have also done well. Merlea Dancing Redwing and Am./Can. Ch. Merlea Sun Dancer sired over 20 champions each.

Another famous Glenairley dog was Ch. Glenairley Black Merlin,

Am./Can. Ch. Dainty Dancer of Glenairley was important to the history of Basenjis in both the U.S.A. and Canada.

Am./Can. C.D. Owner Margaret Robertson handled him to a record-breaking obedience score in Bremerton, Washington, in 1957. His tally of 199 points out of a possible 200 is enviable.

In 1964, Am./Can. Ch. Feliji of the Zande was both #1 Basenji and #10 Hound. The triple-champion, Eng./Am./Can. Ch. Hadrian of Basenlake was #3 Basenji in 1965, and #1 Canadian Basenji in 1966.

The Basenji Club of Canada was organized in the Vancouver home of

Ch. Hadrian of Basenlake was Number 1 in 1966.

breeder John Fenney, in 1964. The first Canadian Basenji Specialty was held in St. John, New Brunswick in August, 1967. The winner was a tri-color puppy, Benji Tricop Ebony Kayunga, bred by well-known Basenji figure Malcolm McDonald.

The year 1968 found another triple champion American, Canadian and Bermudian Champion Zambesi Sparkle, owned by Donna Spencer and Mr. Vix, as #1 Basenji and #4 among all the Hounds. American, Canadian and Bermudian Champion Pyramid's Zulu, owned by Harvey and Vi Lazarenko, Zanzu Kennels, Ontario, was an outstanding winner as well. One of his most impressive wins was Best of Breed from the Puppy Class at the 1969 Basenji Club of Canada Specialty over an entry of 61—43 in the classes plus 18 champions. He became the #1 Basenji in 1970, with 28 Breed wins and 9 Group placements plus another specialty win. Zulu was also a top-producing stud with over 20 champion get to his credit.

After a 14 year drought of Best in Show wins for Canadian Basenjis, Dainty Dancer's great-granddaughter, Can./Ber. Ch. Spearwood Tirzah made judges sit up and take notice once more. She captured a Best at nine months of age on September 15, 1973. Owned and handled by Cheryl (Myers) Egerton of New Brunswick, Tirzah went on to finish as #3 Basenji in 1973, and #2 in 1974. Perhaps her greatest contribution to the breed was in the whelping box. She produced many champions with the most notable being Ch. Conamore's Follow T'Sun. "Sun-Sun" was owned by Marilyn Corbett and Mildred Sniderman. Campaigned during 1976 and 1977, he racked up a record of 136

Am./Can./Bda. Ch. Pyramid's Zulu—1968's Number 1 Basenji.

Can./Ber. Ch. Spearwood Tirzah at 8 months old with owner-handler Cheryl Myers and judge Margaret Thomas.

Ch. Conamore's Follow T'Sun at 10 months old winning a Best Puppy ι. Show with owner-handler Marillyn Corbett.

Breed wins and 50 Group placements for 3,280 points and was #1 Basenji both years. Additionally, he was #4 in the Hound Group in 1976, and #5 in 1977. Mrs. Egerton currently holds the honor of having owned the most Best in Show winners in Canada. In addition to Tirzah, she owned Ch. Spearwood Questt O'Bushongo, Best in Show in 1975, and is the breeder-owner of Am./Can. Ch. Conamore's Sun and Jasmine. In 1988, Jasmine became the only Basenji other than Dainty Dancer to capture more than one Best in Show in Canada.

Am./Can. Ch. Conamore's Sun and Jasmine is handled by breeder-owner Cheryl Egerton.

Another interesting Canadian Best in Show winner was Ch. Mzuri Shamba of Albion, owned by Anne (Mander) Smith, Madhara Basenjis. She was a special in 1975, when she accumulated 1 Best in Show, 2 Canadian-bred Bests and several other Group placements to end the year #3 Basenji and #1 bitch. Shamba also produced a total of 16 pups in three litters with 14 of them becoming champions.

Can./Ber. Ch. Mzuri Shamba of Albion produced fourteen Canadian champions.

The years 1978 and 1979 belonged to Am./Can. Ch. Nordayl's Daily Double, bred by Daylene (Heenan) Neveu and owned by Larry Kunz. Originally sold as a pet, his breeder once again saw him at 10 months of age and whisked him into the show ring where he speedily attained his Canadian title in two weekends with a Group Second from the classes. "Charles" went on to

Am./Can. Ch. Nordayl's Daily Double is handled here by Daylene Neveu with judge Mary Nelson Stephenson.

capture the Basenji Club of Canada Specialty later that year and took a Group First the following day at the Toronto Metropolitan Show in an entry of 284 Hounds. He followed that up with a string of Group placements and a Best in Show to become the #1 Basenji and #9 Hound in 1978. He repeated as #1 Basenji in 1979 achieving a lifetime Canadian record of 61 Breed wins with 35 Group placements including 7 Group Firsts and 1 Best in Show. In 1980, Charles continued his triumphs south of the border. He was #5 Basenji in the U.S. with 23 Breeds and 11 Group placements for 1,665 points.

Canada's first Group-winning black and white is believed to be Am./Can.

Ch. Shantara's Blactamb Solar Scene. Owned by breeder Marnie Lang, Shantara Kennels, Winnipeg, "Cryssie" captured Group First on September 6, 1980, and was the top Basenji female in 1980 and 1981. Shantara also produced the red and white Group First winner, Am./Can. Ch. Shantara's Gentaa Snowdancer, C.D., who sired the first non-red Canadian Best in Show winner, Ch. Shantara's Dalaf Thunderbolt. "Thunderbolt," a tri-color, was also a grandson of Solar Scene. The three dogs combined bring Miss Lang the distinction of being the breeder-owner-handler of Group-winning Basenjis in all three recognized colors.

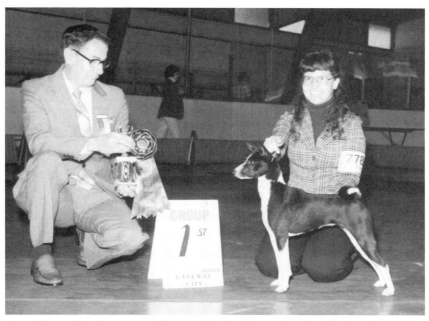

Am./Can. Ch. Shantara's Blactamb Solar Scene, handled by breeder-owner Marnie Lang, being awarded a Group win by judge Stan Whitmore.

Some additional recent winners have been Ch. Kurush Kel Khalil Ben Kala, owned by George and Beth Bujea and bred by Pam and Ray Roy, Kurush Kennels. He was top Basenji in 1983 and 1984 and accumulated a total of 2,593 points over a six-year period. Ch. Tagati Chimo's Brigadoon Bride, owned by breeder Nancy Kneen, Tagati Kennels, Quebec, was the top bitch from 1984 to 1986, and was #1 Basenji in 1985 and 1986. She retired with a lifetime total of 2,703 points earned from 129 Breed wins and 49 Group placements. Ch. Conamore's Sun and Jasmine was the #1 Basenji in 1987. She has a lifetime total of 97 Breed wins with 62 Group placements including 17

Ch. Shantara's Dalaf Thunderbolt is shown with judge Hilda Pugh and handled by Marnie Lang.

Group Firsts and 2 Bests in Show for 1,878 points through 1987 . . . and still counting.

Only one Basenji in Canada is known to have earned a Utility Dog title in obedience. In 1985, this new title plus a field title was added to the impressive list of credits taken by Ch. Kaduna's The Cat's Miaow, F.Ch., U.D.! This multi-purpose Basenji is owned and handled by Peter Mitchell.

Canadian Kennel Club All-Breed Best in Show Winners
1950's

Am./Can. Ch. Dainty Dancer of Glenairley — 1957–1959
(Drumadoon Ducat ex Glenairley Melodious)
Six Canadian Bests in Show.

1970's

Can./Bda. Ch. Spearwood Tirzah — 1973
(Ch. Ber-Vic's Centurion of DFW ex Ch. Spearwood Bedazzle of Bakuba)
Can. Ch. Jarina's Christmas Star — 1974
(Wazimba's Benboli ex Ch. Cango Caves Carina)
Can. Ch. Spearwood Questt O'Bushongo — 1975
(Ch. Questt O' A-Talisman ex Spearwood's Questt O'Blaquena)
Can./Bda. Ch. Mzuri Shamba of Albion — 1975
(Killer The Bushwacker of Albion ex Budjala's Rafiki Tamu)
Can. Ch. Iyindi's Ballerina — 1976
(Khajah's Gay Chieftan ex Ch. Merlea Aurora Dancer)
Am./Can. Ch. Nordayl's Daily Double — 1978
(Am./Can. Ch. Mata Hauri Super Sheik ex Nordayl's Automation)

1980's

Am./Can. Ch. Burgundy Wine Sir Gay of Linlo — 1980
(Kadee's Kenya Benji Sen ex Shajo's Sweet Burgundy Wine)
Can. Ch. Heshima's Prancer — 1980
(Can. Ch. Madhara's Chukuma ex Can. Ch. Madhara's Kanee Heshima)
Can. Ch. Sphinx Christmas Unity — 1980
(Merlea Dancing Redwing ex Jarina's December Dream)
Can. Ch. Sphinx Christmas Star — 1982
(Merlea Dancing Redwing ex Jarina's December Dream)
Am./Can. Ch. Conamore's Sun and Jasmine — 1986 & 1988
(Am./Can. Ch. Tagati's Shadow of a Memory ex Conamore's Sun Chantza)
Can. Ch. Shantara's Dalaf of Thunderbolt — 1986
(Am./Can. Ch. Shantara's Gentaa Snowdancer, C.D. ex
 Am./Can. Ch. Shantara's Denee Fireflash)
Am./Can. Ch. Anasazi's Whidbey Osiris — 1986
(Ch. Cambria's Zartuu ex Ch. Tennji's Anasazi Foxfire)
Am./Can. Ch. Valor's Daktari of Abydos — 1987
(Ch. Mikado of Anubis ex Abydos Butter)

SECTION V
A Look At The Standard

- *My Interpretation:*
     The Standard
- *Form Follows Function*

The Basenji's African roots as an all-purpose hunting dog should not be forgotten while studying the standard.

CHAPTER 19

My Interpretation: The Standard

The standard of every breed tries to paint a word picture of the features of the perfect specimen of that breed. Every breeder, judge or ringside fancier interprets the words a bit differently and, for a variety of reasons, places special emphasis on certain features he feels are most important. Each judge's placements and breeder's line of dogs will reflect his ideas and interpretations of the standard.

When you are starting to learn about a new breed of dogs there is a natural tendency to like what you happen to have, to be influenced by current winning dogs, or to rely heavily on a breeder who may or may not have the experience to know what he is talking about. My husband and I were lucky, really, that when we started out in Basenjis we lived in Alberta, Canada. Since there were not very many Basenjis or Basenji breeders, we were forced to learn by reading, traveling and the study of home movies of dogs and a variety of books about dog conformation. We trained ourselves to think independently while assimilating advice from a variety of more experienced people. We were also lucky to be rather tucked away when we went through the common phase of thinking we knew everything about the breed! By the time we moved back to a more populated area in the U.S.A., we had begun to realize that one never knows everything about a breed of dog. An open mind is the surest way to develop a kennel of champions.

An effort to understand the standard is essential to breeding and showing Basenjis. A balanced view of the total standard must be considered in the evaluation of your own dog or dogs if you wish to breed toward the ideal Basenji.

An interesting way to begin to understand the standard is to read the old standards going back to the one first published in England in 1939. Robert Cole's book, *The Basenji Illustrated*, has them all through 1954. A bit more detailed description was added each time the standard was reworked. For example, the 1939 Standard's only reference to gait is "very like that of a thoroughbred horse." The 1990 Standard has an entire paragraph on the subject. The 1939 Standard was prepared very shortly after the first imports arrived from Africa, and those early dogs were small. The Standard called for: "Dogs approximately 16 inches, Bitches approximately 15 inches." No weights were given. The dogs reached their more natural potential size with better feeding and veterinary care, so the 1942 Standard was altered to read: "Approximately 16 inches bitches, 17 inches dogs." The approximate weight also appears in 1942 and has not changed.

The American Kennel Club recently decided that all the quaint old standards should be replaced with more modern versions that cover each part of the animal thoroughly. The AKC established an outline for each national breed club to follow as a means of making all the standards more uniform. The terminology used in the new standards comply with the language given in Harold R. Spira's book, *Canine Terminology*. The AKC wanted a standard that would be easy for newcomers to learn and for judges to understand. Some of the national clubs were displeased that their old standards were no longer considered adequate.

When the members of the Basenji Club of America voted to add the brindle-and-white color to the standard, there was no question that the standard would have to be altered to fit the new AKC format because no other format would be accepted allowing any changes, even the addition of one color. A great deal of effort went into reworking the standard to fit the terminology and format without changing the intent of the 1954 Standard.

What follows are quotes from the 1990 Standard with my interpretation and comments:

GENERAL APPEARANCE: The Basenji is a small, short-haired hunting dog from Africa. It is short backed and lightly built, appearing high on the leg compared to its length. The wrinkled head is proudly carried on a well arched neck and the tail is set high and curled. Elegant and graceful, the whole demeanor is one of poise and inquiring alertness. The balanced structure and smooth musculature enables it to move with ease and agility. The Basenji hunts by both sight and scent. Characteristics: The Basenji should not bark but is not mute. The wrinkled forehead, tightly curled tail and effortless gait (resembling a racehorse trotting full out) are typical of the breed.

The intent of this first paragraph is to paint an overall picture of the breed. These are the primary characteristics which distinguish the Basenji from all other breeds and make the dog recognizable even from a distance. In the past, the standards have compared the Basenji to either an antelope or a gazelle. That picture has not changed, especially in the distant view. Imagine seeing a dog in the distance (see photo). The noticeable features are the smooth coat, the square proportions, the legginess and the proud carriage of both head and body, showing grace, poise and alertness. As the dog begins to move, its easy movement with a free, long stride becomes noticeable. The dog moves closer and the wrinkled expression and curly tail ends all question as to what breed of dog you have found.

In the distance...

Free, long stride...

The wrinkled expression...

Judging the attitude of a dog in the confines of the show ring has significant disadvantages. How many times have you heard: "If the judge could only see my dog in the backyard, waiting his turn in the coursing field of chasing squirrels in the park!" The skill of the trainer and handler can be a great influence here since the trainer must have taught the desired lessons without killing the dog's interest by overwork or harsh correction. The handler must keep the dog both happy and under control. Work to make your dog all he can be in the show ring if you intend to show him. As you can see from this description, the correct Basenji is more than a properly assembled collection of parts. It is also a personality.

While a Basenji who barks is not correct, other typical dog vocalizations are quite acceptable. The happy "yodel" is a pleasant trait in the breed. (Barklessness was covered in detail in a previous chapter.)

> **Faults:** Any departure from the following points must be considered a fault, and the seriousness with which the fault is regarded is to be in exact proportion to its degree.

A great deal of discussion regarding how to revise the standard centered on how to handle faults. The increase in listed major faults was interesting when we reviewed the old standards. Each time a standard was revised another fault that had been bothering breeders was added to the list. Deciding which faults were serious enough to be listed posed a very difficult issue this time. Finally, the decision was made to use this general statement to establish, for example, that if the dog is not square, it may be a bit long and slightly faulty or very long and seriously at fault.

> **SIZE, PROPORTION, SUBSTANCE:** Ideal height for dogs is 17 inches and bitches 16 inches. Dogs 17 inches and bitches 16 inches from front of chest to point of buttocks. Approximate weight for dogs, 24 pounds, and bitches, 22 pounds. Lightly built within this height-to-weight ratio.

This little paragraph is more important than its length might suggest. Here we have not only the correct height for the breed but also the correct length. A dog of the correct height who is several inches longer than tall is just as faulty as the dog who is too tall for the standard. The proportions for Basenjis are clearly stated here. While the truly square Basenji may be relatively rare, the closer the dog comes to these proportions as well as to the stated dimensions, the more correct it is. We can't consider just height when talking about correct size in Basenjis.

Also remember that these are the heights, lengths and weights for adults. It is not unusual for young Basenjis to be entered in the open classes at dog shows because they are often well coordinated for their age. This does not make the judge's job any easier. One judge explained to me that my puppy was "very nice but I do not like to give puppies the points," as he handed me the reserve ribbon on my puppy class entry. Unbeknownst to him, he had just given the points as well as first, second and fourth in the open class to puppies. Many Basenjis complete their championships before they are mature, and it is the breeder's bob to be aware of how they finally mature. Judges may be fooled by an immature dog who is about the right weight and substance for an adult, but if you are interested in the quality of the Basenjis you produce you will be prouder of the four-year-old dog who maintains his trim figure than the dog who rushed through to his championship as a youngster never to be seen again.

HEAD: The head is proudly carried. **Eyes**—dark hazel to dark brown, almond shaped, obliquely set and farseeing, rims dark. **Ears**—small, erect, and slightly hooded, of fine texture and set well forward on top of head. The skull is flat, well chiseled and of medium width, tapering toward the eyes. The foreface tapers from eye to muzzle with a perceptible stop. Muzzle shorter than skull, neither course nor snippy, but with rounded cushions. Wrinkles appear upon the forehead when the ears are erect, and are fine and profuse. Side wrinkles are desirable, but should never be exaggerated into dewlap. Wrinkles are most noticeable in puppies, and because of lack of shadowing, less noticeable in blacks, tricolors and brindles. **Nose**—black greatly desired. **Teeth**—Evenly aligned with a scissors bite.

I have gathered several photographs of what I feel are good Basenji heads with proper proportions, taper, width and chiseling. This collection is used to build an overall impression. Some are modern Basenjis and some are dogs from past generations. (See photos.)

The Basenji's wrinkles appear on his forehead when his ears are pricked up and forward. There should not be such an abundance of skin that wrinkles develop whether or not the ears are up. Nor should the wrinkle be so heavy that the shape of the head is changed. The wrinkle should be relatively fine.

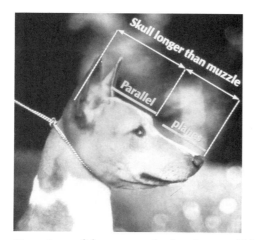 

Two views of the same male showing parallel planes of muzzle and skull and correct proportion of skull length to muzzle. Courtesy of the American Kennel Club.

Correct ear size and placement. Note: "Muzzle, neither coarse nor snipy with rounded cushions."

—222 —

Here the eyes are exceptionally good—
"Dark hazel, almond shaped, oblique-
ly set and far seeing." Courtesy of the
American Kennel Club.

Long time breed expert Veronica
Tudor-Williams chose this photo to
represent "a practically perfect head"
in her 1976 book. Courtesy of Veronica
Tudor-Williams.

This Basenji was whelped in 1953, more
than 40 years ago. Photo by E. Shafer.

Some Basenjis seem to figure out how desperate you are to have them display their wrinkles in the show ring and are exceedingly clever at hiding them. One dog comes to mind who regularly put his ears up in the show ring but purposely turned them out just enough to hide the beautiful wrinkle he carried when the ears were swiveled around to the front. Most Basenjis put their ears partially down in deference when the judge's hands are on them or when the judge talks to them. The judge, interested in seeing the best expression from each dog, should stand back a bit and make a small noise to attract the dog's interest.

The quality of the wrinkle is not determined by how much time the dog remains alerted with the wrinkle showing but by the standard's request of

A pleasant male head with the correct amount of side wrinkle. Courtesy of Carlos Jimenez.

This Basenji has an exceptional head shape with clean jaw line and absence of cheekiness. The dog also has hooded ears, beautiful eyes and the desirable black nose.

"fine and profuse." The wrinkle is difficult to see on the black and tricolor Basenjis, especially if the light is poor, because the defining shadows are lost. The brindle Basenji's wrinkle may be hidden or confused with the black stripes on his face. The unbiased observer will learn to detect the wrinkle regardless of coat color.

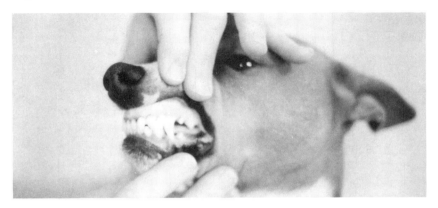

The correct bite has the front upper teeth just outside of a lapping the lower front teeth.

NECK, TOPLINE, BODY: Neck of good length, well crested and slightly full at base of throat. Well set into shoulders. **Topline**—back level. **Body**—balanced with a short back, short coupled and ending in a definite waist. Ribs moderately sprung, deep to elbows and oval. Slight forechest in front of point of shoulder. Chest of medium width. **Tail**—set high on topline, bends acutely forward and lies well curled over either side.

The accompanying photo clearly shows desirable length of neck, with proper arch and good set into correct shoulders. We see too many Basenjis in the show ring today with short necks and no smooth line of transition into the body. These short, graceless necks are often associated with straighter undesirable shoulders.

The standard calls for a short body with a strong, level back and a short coupling or loin. The ribs should have spring to allow plenty of room for heart and lungs rather than being flat or slab-sided. A barrel or very rounded rib cage will interfere with good movement and may actually throw the elbows away from the body so far that the feet twist and are weakened. We once had a favorite bitch with beautiful proportions and a lovely head, but her two worst faults were a barrel chest and out-bending elbows. We later learned that the two faults were related. Breeding to correct that shape of the rib cage may also have solved the elbow problem. When you begin to breed, it can be very helpful to know the source of the basic fault.

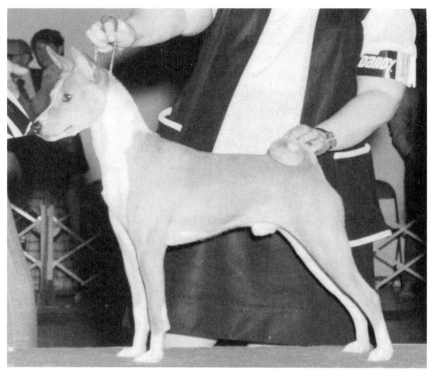

A lovely outline—light build, leggy, short back, strong topline, long neck with smooth transition through shoulders and the desired high-set tail.

The body: Note the strong topline, chest depth, compact body with short coupling and the tuck up.

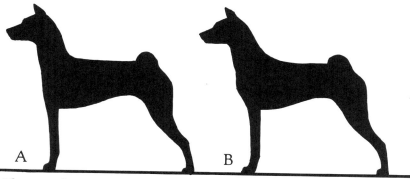

These two dogs are identical except "A" has a very straight front which makes the space under the body a long rectangle while the set on of the neck makes the back longer. Both these faults make the dog appear longer.

When a third dog, "C" (who is a well-constructed square dog) is added to the line up, the differences in outline become even more striking.

Going back to the "general appearance" paragraph at the beginning of the standard, remember the phrase "short backed and lightly built, appearing high on the leg compared to its length?" The smooth neck-to-shoulder transition, the short back, short coupling and definite waist or tuck up as well as the high-set tail called for in this body section are part of the leggy appearance. Leggy does not mean just long legs.

The shape of the space under the dog, defined by the front and rear legs and the underline of the body, also has a significant impact on the leggy impression. Given two dogs with identical overall height and length of leg, the dog with a square or vertical rectangle under his body will look leggier. When the rectangle defined on the sides by the dog's front and back legs becomes horizontal or long, the dog no longer looks leggy. The dog that appears leggy from having a very short upper arm or who lacks depth of chest is not correct.

The leggy, light and short-backed dog with a definite waist will have great agility and is probably better for quick change of direction than overall speed in the hunting and coursing fields. These are features of a versatile hound who should be able to course or scent on any terrain in all types of cover. The call of the coursing field should not lead one to breed for exceedingly light dogs with very narrow waists. Yes, they would be more agile and flexible at the gallop than a thicker-waisted dog, but they would begin to resemble whippets. The whippet is a running specialist, while the Basenji should remain an all-purpose hound.

The emphasis is on the set of the tail rather than the curl in old books on the breed. A high-set tail usually goes along with the angle desired in the pelvis. A low-set tail goes along with a steep pelvis that does not work as well when the dog moves. The early Basenjis exported from Africa tended to have rather loosely curled tails. The single-curled tail is quite adequate, but I think the tighter curl adds to the clean finished look of the best Basenjis. Judges should not try to straighten the Basenji's tail because some have such tight hurls that it is quite uncomfortable to have them straightened. The correct tail lays on one hip or the other rather than on top of the back.

> **FOREQUARTERS:** Shoulders moderately laid back. Shoulder blade and upper arm of approximately equal length. Elbows tucked firmly against brisket. Legs straight with clean fine bone, long forearm and well-defined sinews. Pasterns of good length, strong and flexible. **Feet —** small, oval and compact, with thick pads and well-arched toes. Dewclaws are usually removed.

Here we see a good example of why it is so hard to write a standard. The difficulty comes in explaining each separate part, when some of the emphasis should be on how the parts fit together. The accompanying drawing shows good muscling and shoulder layback. The photo shows the long arched neck blending into the shoulder as well as upper-arm angulation. The smooth line of neck blending cleanly into the topline is usually associated with good

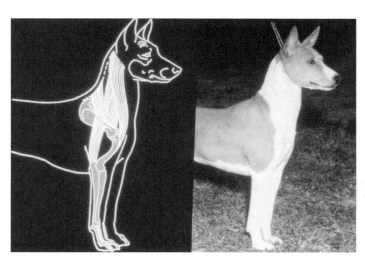

Courtesy of The American Kennel Club.

shoulders. Bulky wrinkles often appear over the withers when the shoulders are steep. An upper arm that comes straight down from the forward point of the shoulder instead of being tucked under the body will not function well in movement. The upper arm will almost look as though it were tacked to the front of the body as an afterthought, and the space under the dog will become the longer rectangle that detracts from the leggy appearance. You'll need to lay your hands on the dog to discover the shoulder layback. You will need to put your hands on many dogs to learn the range of layback angles that exist. After you lay your hands on the shoulders and note the length and layback of the upper arm, you should watch the dog move from the side. Dogs with correctly angulated shoulders and upper arms will move freely and easily. If the angles and muscling are correct, the movement should be correct.

This bitch's clean, straight legs are tucked under her body. The body width is good and the chest is well filled in between her legs. The feet are slightly wider than her legs.

The front legs should be tucked under the body when viewed from the front. The legs should be straight, not bowed. They should come straight down from the body with long bones without bulky joints at the pasterns. The leg should flow cleanly into feet just wider than the leg. The pastern should be strong with very little slope.

The small, tight, narrow feet of the Basenji not only look nice on a very tidy little dog but are important to his function in the field. A flat or splayed foot is very week and cannot hold up. Send several dogs out in rough terrain and those with poor feet will become bruised or sprained or may pick up spines or splinters. They will stop long before their strong-footed companions.

Good topline with tail set right on top. Tail is well curled and lays over on the hip. There is a nice amount of hip bone beyond the root of the tail. The upper and lower thighs are a good length and an equal length with short (low) hocks.

HINDQUARTERS: Medium width, strong and muscular, hocks well let down and turned neither in nor out, with long second thighs and moderately bent stifles. **Feet**—same as in "Forequarters."

As requested in the forequarters, the rear quarters should be straight, clean, strong columns of support when viewed from the rear. A narrow rear lacking good muscling is not made correctly, nor is a dog standing with hocks either in, out or very close together.

Starting at the top, the high tail set and flat hip bone (about 30 degrees from the horizontal) are often associated. There should be plenty of hip bone projecting behind the tail for the leg muscle attachment. The long second thigh should be about equal in length to the upper thigh, with a distinct bend at the stifle joint. The low or short hock is often associated with endurance.

Small, tight feet with well arched toes are very important.

We see too many Basenjis with little or no bend of stifle and long hocks. These dogs are often, but not always, high in the rear when standing naturally, with the hock straight up and down. I feel the exceedingly straight stifles can lead to problems with the stifle joint. Too much bend of stifle or bones too long with a rear rather like a German shepherd is not seen as often but would be equally incorrect for a Basenji.

One point not covered in the standard is the need for the angulation in the forequarters to match the angulation in the hindquarters. The dog with a straighter front and a well angulated rear, or the opposite, will not move in smooth, balanced manner. We are seeking smooth, easy and efficient movement so the dog can endure in his work in the field. There are a number of faults that can be seen on dogs that lack balance. It is better to have a straighter dog with less reach and drive on both ends than a dog with mismatched angulation.

Three of the accepted color combinations (from the left): Black, tan and white (tricolor); red and white, and pure black and white. Courtesy of the American Kennel Club.

COAT AND COLOR: Coat short and fine. Skin very pliant. **Color—** chestnut red; pure black; tricolor (pure black and chestnut red); or brindle (black stripes on a background of chestnut red), all with white feet, chest and tail tip. White legs, blaze and collar optional. The amount of white should never predominate over primary color. Color and markings should be rich, clear and well defined, with a distinct line of demarcation between the black and red of tricolors and the stripes on brindles.

This section is clear as written. The pliant skin is a bonus for the hunting dog who will lose a bit of skin rather than muscle if he is working in rough brush or comes too close to difficult game. Judges should not test the pliancy of the skin by rough handling. The feel of the skin can be assessed by simple stroking.

The coat color is simply stated. The clear bright colors are most attractive. Black hairs intermixed with the red (or vise versa) are not desirable. Black hair on the face forming or beginning to form a mask is not typical. However, it is very common for red and white Basenjis who carry the recessive gene for tricolor coats to have a sprinkling of black hair on the back of the ears and/or on the top of the tail inside the curl.

The imports from the 1987 and 1988 Africa trips reintroduced the western world to brindle and white Basenjis. The best brindle coats have a strong red overlaid with clear black stripes. The amount of brindling varies from very little to a pattern that appears to be black with red stripes. These variations are all considered brindles, as described in the standard.

This half-African puppy shows off his brindle stripes as he twists to perform helping chores in the kitchen.

These new imports also brought us a few color problems: the openfaced or "capped" tricolor, the red or brindle carrying a black saddle, and the tricolor with brindle replacing the red, sometimes called a brindle-pointed tricolor. All are not desired. Sables, creams and other off colors were listed in previous standards as faults to be heavily penalized. Creams were listed as banned in the British standard between 1942 and 1954. Some in the fancy would like to see all off colors as disqualifying faults even now. I feel such an emphasis on a single element of the standard is a mistake. We are working with a very small gene pool and should not limit the possibilities for the future. Breeders tend to eliminate these undesirable colors without such stringent rulings. Saddled tricolors did not become a problem even though Ch. Haku's Black Icicle finished his title in 1951. For a time in the 1980s it was not unusual to see reds with strong black masks, but now black on the face is less prevalent. Breeders have selected away from it without the standard ever being touched.

Beyond the required white feet, chest and tail tip, the amount of white the Basenji carries is a matter of personal preference. Markings can at times cause optical illusions when the dog is standing or moving (see photos). One must

Markings can cause optical illusions. Two photos of the same bitch illustrate the difference in apparent length of the hock when only the foot is white on the one side and the leg has white above the hock on the other side.

Breeders should be aware that it is possible to produce pups with too much white.

learn to look carefully when there is more or less than the ordinary amount of white or if the dog has an unusual marking. Some people put great emphasis on flashy markings, while others prefer plain, minimal markings. There are no correct show markings other than the minimum white requested in the standard. The Basenji should appeared to be a colored dog with white markings rather than a white dog with color added.

> **GAIT:** Swift, tireless trot. Stride is long, smooth, effortless and the topline remains level. Coming and going, the straight column of bones from shoulder joint to foot and from hip joint to pad remains unbroken, converging toward the centerline under the body. The faster the trot, the greater the convergence.

Let's return again to the "general appearance" paragraph for the initial description of Basenji movement. The phrase "resembling a racehorse" is interesting. Early dog people were horsemen and frequently drew parallels with horses when trying to describe their dogs. Many of us no longer have the background to understand what is being sought when it is stated in horse terms. The difference between the anatomy of a horse and a dog is often suggested as an argument against equine terminology, but I feel there is still a great deal to be learned from even a brief study of a trotting race horse.

We traced the series of accompanying illustrations from stop–action movie film. The horse was racing at a small track in Washington state. These frames fail to convey the smoothness and ease of the trot exhibited by this particular horse. They do show his level topline and the period of suspension using natural momentum to propel the horse forward effortlessly, saving energy in the process. The horse is off the ground and gliding just over 40 percent

Drawn from a movie film of a race horse at a track in Washington state. Note: suspension, balance, reach, drive, head carriage and topline.

of the time. The good reach under the body with the rear leg, coupled with its flex and drive behind with the hock extended can clearly be seen. The front assembly is working in its entirety with the shoulder and upper arm rotating to their maximum extension. The front and rear seem in balance,

Three dogs from different kennels demonstrate good side movement.

Super head carriage and length of neck.
Courtesy of the American Kennel Club.

Front reach using the entire front assembly —shoulder and upper arm as well as leg.
Courtesy of the American Kennel Club.

Exceptional topline. Note all four feet are off the ground in energy-saving glide.
Courtesy of Nancy Swanson.

with the length of the front and rear strides about the same. The front and rear hooves leave and return to the ground at the same time, equally dividing the stress of impact. The head is carried up but slightly forward.

The accompanying photos of some of our champion Basenjis demonstrate many of these same characteristics of movement—reach, drive, balance, level topline, glide and head carriage.

This dog moves "high behind" with a clearly sloping topline. His front and rear legs are interfering under his body.

Correct movement as viewed from the front.

If you are new to dogs, it may take some study to become aware of good side gait in the brief time allowed in the show ring. The use of movies or videos at various speeds might help you make the transition from frame-to-frame to full-speed evaluation. The level, smooth topline is easy to find at any speed. Some of the best trotting dogs have such a board-flat topline and such smooth movement that you might think they could balance glasses of water on their backs without spilling a drop. A dog with a long suspension will appear to freeze briefly in the extended position while he keeps his legs almost still to avoid disturbing his glide. Do not confuse this with the dog who pauses only with the front, creating a goose step or hackney gait, to compensate for an over-powerful rear. The better mover isn't always the dog who appears to be really putting himself out to travel around the ring at a good speed. The

Correct movement viewed from the rear. Courtesy of The American Kennel Club.

dog that seems to be moving without effort but is not falling behind his showy competitors is the one who could trot all day in the field.

Movement should be clean coming and going. There should be no elbows popping out, pasterns flipping or other deterrents to the front moving efficiently. The front should not work to one side of the rear. This is called sidewinding and usually indicates a lack of balance between front and rear or a very steep pelvis. Sometimes it is easy to see the front movement faults from the rear as the dog moves away. You should not be able to see the front legs as the dog moves away. If you do, you are observing a movement fault. The rear should also move cleanly with no leaning of the hocks in or out. A line could be drawn from the joint of the hip down the center of the rear leg to indicate the line the physical forces take. As the dog moves faster, the legs tend to converge under the body, but the clean column of support remains.

TEMPERAMENT: An intelligent, independent, but affectionate and alert breed. Can be aloof with strangers.

Summarizing the wonderful special temperament of the Basenji in so few words must have been a very difficult chore. However, I think the words "intelligent, independent, affectionate and alert" are as good a summation as one can make. Most breeders make an effort to obtain a friendly disposition in their dogs so that one day perhaps the term "aloof with strangers" can be deleted from the standard.

CHAPTER 20

Form Follows Function

Laurie Montgomery.

That form follows function is very important for you, as a breeder, to know. In many ways that is a way to tell the differences in many breeds. A Cocker Spaniel with its long neck—allowing the nose to be close to the ground so its long ears can help waft the scent of game is a good example. The galloping, hunting hound, because of its function, has a unique physical form (flexible spine, arched loin with somewhat sloping croup and low tailset and flat ribs) follows the function which is the speed to run down game and/or kill or hold for the hunter. Or the Dachshund, whose function is to go to ground after game (up to and including the dangerous badger), has the form to perform such work—long, low body, heavy bone and digging feet, and a long, powerful head and jaw.

If you have ever designed anything with functional parts, you know that structural design implies more than bare bones of anatomy. A good design takes into account all factors that will help the structure serve its purpose. Similarly, the structural design of a dog must provide for all the needs of its owner.

In keeping with the principles of good architectural design, body and head structure must take into account the specific properties the animal uses in his work. These materials must be able to withstand the stresses implicit in the design. Therefore, no breeder of a dog designed to herd flocks would think of placing a thin unprotected skin where a tough layer of subcutaneous muscle and bristly coat should go. Here again, the interrelationship of structure and function is obvious—the two go together. One of the most important things in designing and working with any breed is to always keep in mind the inseparability of structure and function. That is, the form of the animal must be designed for the function for which it has been originally bred.

To go along with function we have established breed types. That is a physical form which allows the dog to perform its function and around which we can weave an artistic word description. The definition of breed is type. The division of animals into groups of their species, according to differences in physical type, is the basis of breeds. A definite recognizable type must be common to all members of the group. For, without BREED type there is no breed. A BREED is the highest form of a species, that over a number of generations of controlled breeding, has developed definite physical characteristics that, taken together, are the consistent type of that species.

Organic Engineering

You can get a better understanding of the functional aspects of a breed of dog if you think of them in terms of engineering. Consider, for example, the role of the early breeders in England. They had two kinds of jobs. First, they tried to design a useful product: a dog who could go after upland birds, stay close to the hunter, have a good nose, be steady and have the ability to go all day long in the field. Originally these hunting dogs had to put food on the table, only later were they hunted for sport. Then these early breeders had to find a way to manufacture these products. In bringing a new product into being, an engineer first lays out a method of operation. He might even design and build a new tool just for making this one product. With the breeder, he might bring in another breed and cross it and re-cross it and introduce others until he got the correct mixture. The breeder might have to go through dozens of developmental stages before turning out a satisfactory replica of the designed product. But no matter how many steps you must take, a good product engineer (breeder) never departs from the intent of the basic design. He recognizes that the design has a special purpose which his efforts must serve. The farmer in England, who had to protect his livestock and fowl against the incursion of foxes who holed up in dens in rocky lairs, invented a sturdy little dog to take care of that problem. This dog had to get along with the pack of hounds who were to be used to run the fox to ground. Added to the design was the necessity of having a skull and rib cage that were flat enough to allow him to squeeze into any crevice the fox could. Finally, to have punishing jaws to dispatch the fox and haul him out. This little dog was called the Lakeland Terrier. He is about the same size as the Basenji but certainly built for an expressly different function.

But whether we are talking about a dog breeder or an engineer, they both design their products or devise techniques to make use of certain basic designs. For example, an engineer must use only those geometrical figures that would yield desired structural strength. He must also use shapes that will conserve on materials and yet provide for the greatest efficiency. Futhermore, he must also concern himself with simplicity of design. Therefore, whenever possible he must construct simple machines (levers, pulleys, and inclined planes) rather than intricate combinations of these machines.

Obviously, a dog—or any living organism—is its own engineer. Throughout its life, it constantly refers to a basic design and manufactures the product it needs. In so doing, it makes use of the same principles of design that men use in building machines and other conveniences. The dog also makes use of the same mechanical principles that underline the operation of man-made devices. Consider, for example, the transmission of force. When an animal moves its movable parts, it transmits force in much the same way that machines do. In so doing, the animal uses its built-in, simple machines. You can see this quite clearly in locomotor structures and that is why judging the gait of a dog in terms of its ability to perform its function is so very important in the overall approach to judging dogs.

Movement

For many years vast majority of dog people, and even physiologists, believed that animals running at higher speeds would exact a higher "cost" in terms of energy burned—it didn't turn out that way! Recent studies have shown that animals use up energy at a uniform, predictable rate as the speed of movement increases.

As if that shattering piece of information wasn't enough—they found out that for any given animal, the amount of energy expended in getting from point A to point B was the same regardless of how fast the trip was taken. A Cheetah running 100 yards at a top speed of 60 mph, uses the same amount of energy as it would *walking* the same distance. The running is more exhausting because the calories are used up more quickly.

Size, however, does make a difference. Small dogs require much more energy per unit of weight to run at top speed than a Great Dane would. Small dogs appear to have higher "idling" speeds. The cost of maintaining muscular tension and of stretching and shortening the muscles are higher in small animals.

These same series of studies suggest that as much as 77 percent of the energy used in walking comes, not from the operation of the muscles themselves, but from a continual interplay between gravity and kinetic energy. From an engineering standpoint it seems that the body tends to rotate about a center of mass, somewhat like an egg rolling end on end or the swing of an inverted pendulum. The 30 percent of effort supplied by the muscles is imparted through the limbs to the ground to keep the animal's center of mass moving forward.

At faster speeds, four-footed animals appear to be capable of calling into use a work-saving scheme that relies upon the elastic storage of energy in muscles and tendons. Some are better at it than others. Some are capable of storing more energy per stride than others.

During running or trotting the built-in springs for propulsion are the muscles and tendons of the limbs. When the animal has need to move even faster, he has the ability to use an even bigger spring. As the dog shifts from the fast trot to a gallop they tend to use their bodies as a large spring to store more energy. They do *not* change the frequency of their strides, rather they increase the length of them.

Simple Bio-Machines

Let us now consider how the dog compares with man-made machines. The dog can be compared to combinations of simple machines and other mechanical systems you might find in any factory. A few familar examples will quickly clarify this analogy. The dog's legs for example. You could diagram them as levers. The appendages of all animals in fact, serve as levers. If laid out side by side, they would present a rather special array of "machines." As we have certainly seen dogs—from the Chihuahua to the Great Dane—present a wide variety of angles and levers.

Of course you would expect this, for their owners have widely different ways of life. Modifications in such bio-levers reflect the animal's way of life. So you would expect the Saluki's leg to be the kind of lever that gives the advantage of speed and distance. By the same token, you would expect the design of the front legs of the Basset, "a burrowing animal," to provide for the multiplication of force, rather than the advantage of distance or speed.

Another simple machine that is easy to detect in nature is the pulley. You will find the living counterpart of the pulley wherever you find a muscle-tendon joint apparatus. Whenever a tendon moves over a joint, it behaves like a pulley. Such mechanisms enable the dog to change the direction of force. A notable example of an application of the pulley principle is the action of the tendons and muscles in the dog's neck. When the handler "strings the dog up" on a tight lead, the ability of the dog to use that pulley correctly is gone. What you have looks like a spastic alligator moving.

Inclined planes are prevalent in all living things, but their presence is not always obvious. They frequently appear as wedges, which are made up of two inclined planes arranged back-to-back. The incisors of the dog, for example, are wedges. The cutting action of these teeth is an application of the wedge principle in nature. The terrier-type of mouth is vastly different from that of the sporting dog. The sporting dog mouth is designed to hold a bird gently without crushing it. Therefore, its construction does not allow for great force to be generated. In contrast, the terrier jaws are punishing and can generate enough force to kill game. Another illustration is when a standard calls for a sloping topline in movement. The sloping plane from withers to tail is designed to harness the thrust or drive from the rear quarters and move the dog along a straight line with power.

Hydraulics and Life

Any person who has tried to dam up a creek, or in some other way tried to manage moving water, has had experience with hydraulics. It involves the application of energy to practical uses. Frequently, therefore, hydraulics deals with the transfer of mechanical energy of moving fluids to the powering of machinery. It also deals with the the use of pressure created by fluids (hydraulic pressure). All this, of course, finds an application in biology, wherein fluid is of paramount importance. Applications of hydraulic pressure are evident in dogs. Certainly the pumping action of the heart (as being responsible for the movement of blood through the circulatory system) is an appropriate example. A standard asking for a deep chest and the front wide enough for adequate heart and lung space is telling us we need room for a pump big enough to keep the dog going under pressure all day long. This pump exerts pressure, directly or indirectly, on all body fluids. As you know, when the heart is in need of repair or is worn out, the blood pressure of the animal varies abnormally. When this happens, the animal finds it hard to maintain a proper fluid balance of its tissues and organs. The final result is interference with the movement of the materials of life. Death can occur if the equipment designed to maintain hydraulic pressure fails in its function. As you may recall from your school studies of anatomy, it takes more than the pumping of the heart to maintain normal fluid pressure in an animal. The condition of the arteries and the veins is equally important. If these circulatory structures do not have the proper strength or elasticity, this condition could cause abnormal variation in the hydraulic pressure of the body. The arteries and veins are fluid conduits. Therefore, they must have a structural design that will enable them to withstand and adjust to sudden changes in hydraulic pressure.

From your studies, you may recall how effectively the design met the need. The walls of the arteries are designed to have heavier muscular construction than the veins. That's because the blood being pumped under great pressure from the heart goes out through the arteries and returns under less pressure through the veins. Thus, the arteries can withstand greater pressure than the veins can tolerate. The arteries tend to be more elastic than the veins so they can react more quickly to changes in pressure and so regulate the movement of fluid to compensate for the change in the situation.

Organic Architecture (Type)

The shape of a building usually reflects its function. The design of its various parts (roof, doors, ventilators) also relates to special functions. So it is with the shape of the dog. In a large dog, the design often calls for a shape that will provide the necessary strength, compactness and capability to perform certain functions. For example, dogs such as the Malamute were used to haul heavy loads. They were designed with a shoulder construction and balanced size that would enable them to perform this function. On the other hand, for example, a long and slender shape characterizes the coursing type of dog (Afghan, Greyhound, Borzoi and Saluki). This shape facilitates the faster movement of energy from place to place. A Basenji, on the other hand, is designed with a balanced shape to be neither a hauler or speed demon, but to go at a moderate pace for a sustained period of time.

In all cases we need to consider how we recognize the shape we are dealing with. First we must consider outline. Outline encompasses every aspect of the individual animal, making it immediately clear as to what breed or species it belongs.

Structure, Shape and Symmetry

As we have noted, overall body shape has a definite relationship to a dog's way of life. It relates, for example, to the use of energy. It also has to do with the animal's ability to relate to its environment and to perform the function for which it was originally bred. As you continue to study dogs, you will see more and more how the shape of things facilitates their function. Take the opportunity to see how the smooth functioning of an animal or of its parts, relates to its function.

A major identifying characteristic of a breed is its head. The head and expression is the very essence of a dog. Without proper breed type, an individual is just a dog, not a Basenji, a Springer or even a Great Dane.

Balance is also very important. No part should be longer, shorter, larger or smaller than is compatible with the whole. Everything must fit together to form a pleasing picture of "rightness."

Most breed standards call for a short back. Rightly so, for this is where the strength is. However, a short back is not synonymous with a short dog. The back is actually that small portion of the topline which lies between the the base of the withers and the loin. A dog with a long sloping shoulder and a long hip may give the impression of a longer dog. A dog which gives the impression of being taller than it is long, is a dog badly out of balance. This dog is quite likely to have such a short croup that it appears to have none at all. A short steep croup will straighten the leg bones and leads to a highly ineffective and inefficient rear movement. A dog properly angulated at one end, but not on the other, is in even worse balance.

The too-upright shoulder is probably the worst imbalance of all because it affects every other part of the body. It puts great stress on a moving dog, making it pound its front feet into the ground, or crab sidewise to avoid interference with its hind feet.

As you look at your dog in the yard at home, in the show ring or out in the field working birds, look for the features of its design that might account for its survival and popularity. Look for the relationship of structural design to vital functions. Ask yourself: "How is this shape most suitable for the function of this structure?" "How is the body shape of this animal related to the environment in which it has to live?" In searching for answers, go beyond the obvious facts and look for subtle relationships. Look for special problems. For example, in reading many of the breed magazines today, we find breeders bewailing the promiscuous breedings and the terrible things that have happened to their breed. They often point out their breed is no longer able to perform its primary function because of straight shoulders, over-angulated rears or incorrect coat. Their claim is the breed is no longer functional. FORM NO LONGER FOLLOWS FUNCTION! . . . What are the breeders of today going to do about it?

SECTION VI

The Basis of Heredity

- *Basic Genetics*
- *Coat Color in Basenjis*

CHAPTER 21

Basic Genetics

Consistent breeding of show-quality dogs should be considered an art. To some breeders it comes naturally, others have to learn this art. Still others will never achieve success in this vital and important facet of pure-bred dogs.

To some breeders "having an eye for a dog" is second nature. Breeders lacking this natural talent can become self-taught provided they have the intelligence and motivation to discern between the good and poor examples set before them.

Consistent breeding of show-quality specimens depends on important factors besides the natural or acquired talents of the breeder. The breeding stock itself is of prime importance and should be the very best the breeder can obtain. Many breeders still operate under the illusion that second best will produce as well as the choice specimen, pedigrees being equal. This will hold true in isolated instances, of course, but it will not hold true consistently.

Another important element contributing to the success or failure of any given breeding program is that of chance. Everything else being equal, sex distribution, puppy mortality, timing, transmission of the best factors (or the poorest), etc., all depends to a great extent on chance.

There is no shortcut to breed improvement—no miraculous or secret formula which can put Mother Nature out of business and place the breeder in full control. There are, however, many do's and don'ts which can be used as a formula of sorts to minimize the chances of failure and to encourage the chances of success. These do's and don'ts are axioms of our breed, yet there are breeders who ignore and bypass them.

The first step in your breeding program is to decide what is ideal. Until a breeder knows what kind of specimen he wants, he is stopped cold and can neither select the best nor discard the worst. This is where the breeder's capabilities and talents come into play. For this is the basis of selective breeding, and the backbone of any breeding program.

Characteristics such as height and coat color are known as inherited traits. They are traits which an offspring "inherits" or receives from his parents. Every living thing has an inheritance, or "heredity." Inherited traits are passed along from generation to generation. As a result of heredity, each generation is linked to older generations and to past generations. For example, a dog may resemble his parents with respect to height, head shape, and coat color. His grandsire or great grandsire may have also possessed the same identifying features.

A whole science known as genetics has grown up around the study of heredity. Specifically, the science of genetics is the study of how the reproduction process determines the characteristics of an offspring and how these characteristics are distributed.

According to Anthony Smith, writing in *The Human Pedigree*:

Gregor Mendel, a 19th-century monk living in Czechoslovakia, is credited as the founder of genetics. Basically, Mendel's work had proved that traits can be passed from one generation to the next, both with mathematical precision and in separate packets. Before this time, it had been assumed that inheritance was always the result of being colored water of a weaker hue. Mendel foresaw genes, the differing units of inheritance (that are named, incidentally, after the Greek for race). Genes remain distinct entities. They do not blend, like that of colored water. They produce, to continue the analogy, either plain water, or colored water or a mixture between the two. Moreover, assuming no other genes are involved to complicate the story, they continue to create three kinds of product in generation after generation. The packets remained distinct.

The mathematics also has a pleasing simplicity at least in the early stages. The human blue-eye/brown-eye situation is a good elementary example. There are genes for brown and genes for blue, everybody receives one of each from each parent. To receive two browns is to be brown-eyed. To receive two blues is to be blue-eyed. To receive one of each is also to be brown-eyed because the brown has the effect of masking the relative transparency of the blue.

This also signifies that brown is dominant over blue and will always cover over the recessive blue color. Blue will only be expressed when it, as a recessive, is inherited from both parents.

The clarity of Mendel's vision certainly helped science. It was assumed that all of inheritance was equally clear cut, with a ratio of 3:1, or his equally famous ratio of 9:3:1 (involving two characteristics) explaining all of our genetic fortunes. So they do (in a sense) but the real situation is *much* more complex. Only a *few* aspects of inheritance are controlled by a single pair of genes. Only a few more are controlled by two pairs. A feature like height, for example, or coat color may be organized by twenty or so pair of genes. Each pair is working in a Mendelian manner, but the cumulative effect of all of them working together is a bewilderment. The mathematics still have the same precision, but it is only for mathematicians, not for the rest of us. As for a feature like intelligence, with the brain differentiated to fill a tremendous range of different tasks, its inheritance cannot be thought of in a simple ratio of any kind.

There are literally thousands and thousands of paired genes within each animal. There are enough of them, and enough possible variations, to ensure that each specimen is unique. Never in history has there been a duplicate of any specimen. Never in all of future history will there be another one just like it again. Each dog is a combination that is entirely individual and yet his/her genes are common to the population they live in. There is nothing unique about them.

Piggybacking now upon Mendel's work and that of later scientists, let us look at how breeders can use this knowledge and breed better dogs.

Each dog contains a pair of genes in each of its cells for each trait (characteristic) that it inherits. One of the genes is contributed by the sire and the other by the dam. For example, let's take a generic breed: When a black dog is bred to a buff one, all the first-generation offspring will be black. Each parent contributed one gene for color to each offspring. Since they were different colors, the offspring were hybrid. One parent, contributed a "factor" for black color while the other parent passed along a "factor" for buff coat color. Why, then, were all the hybrid offspring black? Because in our generic breed, black is *dominant* over buff.

The recessive characteristic (buff) was the hidden or masked one that did not appear in the hybrid offspring. A dog can show a recessive trait such as a buff coat, only when both factors (genes) are recessive in one individual (remember the blue-eye/brown-eye example?). The dominant trait will appear when one or both genes are present.

When a dog is dominant for a trait it is called homozygous for that trait. When it carries recessive genes for that trait *i.e.*, "plush head," it is called heterozygous.

To clarify the matter a bit, let's see what happens when an all black hybrid specimen is crossed with another just like it. Every hybrid can pass on to each of its offspring either the black or buff characteristics. Therefore, buff and black has a 50/50 chance of being transmitted to the offspring. These hybrids have a black (dominant) gene and a buff (recessive) gene. Let's symbolize them B-Dominant, b-Recessive. Since the combination is random, the ways in which these can be combined in a hybrid × hybrid cross are shown in Figure VI-1. As shown, it is possible to predict not only the possible combinations of factors, but also the probability for each of the combinations.

Chance plays a part in both the biological and physical worlds. By "chance," it is meant events that happen at random. Mendel was aware of this and knew something of the laws of probability. He used these in explaining his results. These laws say: "Be wary of interpreting the occurrence of a single random event." However, it goes on to postulate that if large numbers of occurrences of the same event take place at random, there is a kind of order in the result, in spite of the uncertainty of the occurrence of a single event.

By moving from the inheritance of a single trait to the inheritance of two traits simultaneously, life gets a bit more complex. Start by breeding a homozygous (pure) black dog that is tall (also homozygous) to a short buff specimen that is also homozygous for its traits. Naturally enough, the breeding produces tall black offspring, since those traits are dominant. They look exactly like the black parent. Take these hybrid (heterozygous) offspring which are hybrid-tall, hybrid-black and mate them with like spec-

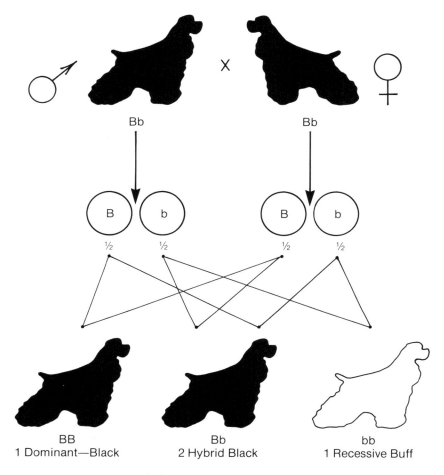

BB
1 Dominant—Black

Bb
2 Hybrid Black

bb
1 Recessive Buff

Figure VI-1. Genetic probability of a single trait—in this case exemplifying the dominance of black over the recessive buff color in Cocker Spaniels.

imens. The resultant types can be quite interesting. There might be four different types produced. There could be a small black type and a tall buff one. These types are new combinations of the two traits.

Continuing in this vein, and for all other traits as well, the distribution ratio turns out to be just about 9:3:3:1. This means for every nine tall, black dogs in a hybrid × hybrid mating there should be three tall dogs with buff coats, three small dogs with black coats and one short, buff specimen.

A quick glance at the above will show twelve tall dogs to four short ones and twelve blacks to four buffs. Both demonstrate the 3:1 ratio already established for the inheritance of a single trait in which segregation occurs.

For example, Mendel and later researchers also uncovered the fact that tallness is independent of color. This is called the "law of independent assortment" and is supported by numerous experiments. The probability of two or more related events is calculated by multiplying the individual probabilities. Thus, if the probability of one event occurring is ¼ and the probability of a simultaneous event is also ¼, then the probability of the two occuring together is ¼ × ¼, or ¹/₁₆. That is, one in every sixteen.

In breeding for color in dogs, we find that the majority of factors which determine coat color appear to be "single factors," inherited according to Mendel's laws. However, many of these color factors are influenced by other genes which have the ability to modify the expression of the "key" gene in numerous ways and thus account for considerable variation in the finished product. As an example, while a dog may possess the "key" genes which have the ability to create the black and tan pattern, independent modifying genes may alter its appearance by restricting or allowing full expression to the tan pigment in its coat, so that it looks like a black dog or a tan dog.

Though the color of a dog's coat may be determined by a single gene or by a pair of genes, the skeletal structure of a dog is determined by the interaction of a large number of genes. It should be easy to understand why something as highly complex as the structure of a dog's head or body is controlled by the actions of multiple hereditary factors.

Movement is a good example. No one gene labeled "gait" has the ability to determine whether an individual puppy will move properly or improperly. Rather, there are countless genes, working in concert which determine these facts.

What factors enable an individual dog to move in a way which has been designated as correct for its particular breed? Every breed has a characteristic gait, which is determined by its structure; not the structure of the legs, or the feet, or the hips, or the shoulders, but the structure of all the parts working in concert for this breed. Thus, the Chow Chow moves with short steps and stilted action, the Pekingese and Bulldog "roll" along, the Miniature Pinscher has its hackney gait and the German Shepherd Dog covers ground rapidly with far-reaching steps and a smooth action. These differences in gait are the result of differences in structure—the manner in which all the body parts are assembled in an individual.

Whether a stifle is straight or short, or whether a foreface is deeply chiseled or built up is not determined, in all probability, by hereditary factors alone. When breeders seek to determine the manner in which any part of an animal's skeletal structure is inherited, they are not dealing with single-factor inheritance, but with multiple-factor inheritance.

Any attempt to explain multiple-factor inheritance fully would prove to be a real puzzle, for most dog breeders have no formal training in advanced genetics. However, the following facts may serve to give a better understanding of this complex subject:

1. What is seen and described as a single character (a leg, a foot, a tail, etc.) is often affected and influenced in its development by a large number of different and unrelated genes which are capable of independent assortment.
2. It is extremely difficult to sort out the various genes which influence a particular characteristic and to determine the specific effect each has on that characteristic. In other words, just how important is a given gene in the development of a particular characteristic?
3. Some genes have a direct, complete influence on the development of a character (dominant genes). Some have only a partial effect, being neutralized to some extent by the action of the opposing member of the pair of which it is one (incompletely dominant genes). Some genes are completely masked and have no effect unless such genes comprise both members of a given pair (recessive genes).
4. The combination of multiple gene effects together with environmental influences, is the rule rather than the exception in such characteristics as body length, height, weight, head and muzzle development, tooth characteristics, foot size and shape, muscle and bone development, and such recognized faults as loose shoulders, flat ribs, cowhocks, weak pasterns and splay feet. As an example, body size depends upon some genes that affect all the tissue and upon others that influence only certain regions, such as the legs, neck, head or tail. In addition, diet, exercise and other environmental influences determine the degree to which genes are able to stimulate and produce growth of the different tissues, organs and body parts.

There are some 130 breeds eligible for registration with the American Kennel Club. None of the breeds is "pure bred" in the true genetic sense of the word. All of them are subject to variations of form and type which may account for considerable differences in appearance between specimens of the same breed. Unlike certain strains of laboratory mice, which have been standardized by inbreeding and selection, and which are like peas in a pod, no breed of dog exists which duplicates its own kind without variation.

Major differences between breeds are probably due to independent genes which may be found in one breed and not in another. Therefore, the manner in which the multiple hereditary factors responsible for the construction of a Greyhound's body are inherited, may differ from the manner in which countless genes which build a Chihuahua's body are inherited. To understand the manner in which complex parts such as the body, legs, head, and other structural parts are inherited, the following will be necessary:

1. Observations of a large number of animals, resulting in careful and accurate records of the differences in structure which exist within the breed.

2. Accurately recording breeding tests between the animals of contrasting structural types, and recording observations of their resultant offspring. This may well require the crossing of breeds at one or more genetic research laboratories (as was done in the controlled experiments done by Dr. C.C. Little at the Jackson Memorial Laboratory of Bar Harbor, Maine). In this way, extreme types can be compared and the inheritance of marked differences in structure can be studied.

3. The making available of these records to scientists who are qualified to analyze them. The task of breeding and raising a large enough number of animals representing different breeds, the recording of observations of their structural types and the types of their offspring is beyond the finances and ability of any one person or any one institution. However, such data could be collected by breeders at no additional expense and a small amount of additional work. Each breeder's records could be sent to a central laboratory for analysis and any resulting conclusions could, in turn, be made available to breeders.

What kind of questions pertaining to inheritance in dogs can geneticists answer right now? Information pertaining to a great variety of subjects is available, including: color differences found in the coat, eyes, and skin of most breeds of dog; differences in the length, quantity, texture and distribution of hair; various reproductive problems such as fertility, fecundity, the production of stillborn or non-viable young, and such conditions as monorchidism; various abnormalities of the eye; malformations resulting from arrested development such as harelip, cleft palate, cleft abdomen, etc.; such diseases as hemophilia and night blindness; differences in ear, eye, nose, jaw, foot and tail characteristics; differences in head size and shape; and numerous physiological differences resulting in characteristic patterns of behavior.

Many of the characteristics in the above list are influenced by multiple genes and/or are affected in varying degrees by environmental factors. Therefore, the available information pertaining to most of these subjects is incomplete; though in some breeds and for some characteristics it is surprisingly extensive. New information is being added daily, as geneticists all over the world make their contributions available.

Many breeders have practiced linebreeding (grandfather to granddaughter, etc.) but have only skirted around the edges of inbreeding (brother to sister, father to daughter, and mother to son matings) shying away from carrying it to its full potential. As a means of finding out which animals have the best genes, inbreeding deserves more use than it has received. Not only does it uncover recessives more surely than any other method, but also, it increases the relationship between the inbred animal and its parents and other relatives so that the animal's pedigree and the merits of the family to which it belongs become more dependable as indicators of its own genes.

Considerable inbreeding is necessary if family selection is to be very effective. The gene is the unit of inheritance, but, for our purposes, the animal is the smallest unit which can be chosen or rejected for breeding purposes. To breed exclusively to one or two of the best specimens available would tend to fix their qualities, both good and bad. In fact, that is the essence of what happens under extreme inbreeding. Moreover, the breeder will make at least a few mistakes in estimating which animals have the very best inheritance. Hence, in a practical program, the breeder will hesitate to use even a very good stud too extensively.

The breeder also is far from having final authority, to decide how many offspring each of his bitches will produce. Some of his basic stock may die or prove to be sterile or will be prevented by a wide variety of factors from having as many get as the breeder wants. Bitches from which he wants a top stud dog may persist in producing only females for several litters. Consequently, he must work with what he has because he did not get what he wanted from more desirable specimens.

The ideal plan for the most rapid improvement of the breed may differ from the plan of the individual breeder chiefly in that he dare not risk quite so much inbreeding deterioration. If the object were to improve the breed with little regard for immediate show prospects, then it would be a different story. This is an important point and deserves more attention.

Inbreeding refers to the mating of two closely-related individuals. Most breeders practice inbreeding to a limited extent, even though they may call it "close line breeding." Actually, the breeding of half brother × half sister, as well as niece × uncle or nephew × aunt is a limited form of inbreeding. For purposes of this discussion, however, inbreeding will refer to the mating of full brother × full sister, father × daughter, and son × mother. Most breeders probably consider these three categories as representative of true inbreeding.

It is not the purpose of this chapter to advocate or condemn the practice of inbreeding, but rather to ascertain what it can and cannot accomplish. It will also be the objective to present known facts and dispel some common fallacies.

It would certainly be interesting to know exactly what percentage of inbreeding takes place in various breeds and what results are obtained. Speaking in generalities, it would probably be safe to say that only one or two percent of all champions finishing within the past ten years were the products of inbreeding. On this basis, it would be reasonable to conclude that the practice of close inbreeding on these terms is relatively rare.

In the breeding of domestic animals, such as cattle, chickens, etc., as well as plant breeding, inbreeding is regarded as a most valuable tool to fix a desired type and purify a strain. This raises the question as to why inbreeding has not gained more widespread acceptance among dog breeders. By combining inbreeding with the selection of those individuals most nearly ideal in appearance and temperament, the desired stability of the stock is quickly obtained.

Breeding the offspring of the father × daughter or son × mother mating back to a parent is called "backcrossing." To illustrate this, suppose an outstanding male specimen is produced and the breeder's thought is to obtain more of the same type: the male is bred back to his dam, and the breeder retains the best bitch puppies in the resulting litter. By breeding these back to the excellent male (backcrossing), there is a good chance that some of the puppies produced as a result of this backcross will greatly resemble the outstanding sire. In backcrossing to a superior male, one may find some inbreeding degeneration in the offspring, but this is improbable according to Dr. Ojvind Winge in his book, *Inheritance in Dogs*.

The mating of brothers × sisters is far more likely to produce inbreeding degeneration. This is because a brother × sister mating is the most intense form of inbreeding. Studies show that those breeders who have attempted to cross full brothers and sisters, for the purpose of fixing good characteristics in their stock, give very contradictory reports of their results. It has been found that the mating of brother × sister results in somewhat decreased vitality and robustness in the offspring.

It may happen that abnormal or stillborn individuals are segregated out in the litter if special genes are carried in the stock. Everything depends upon the hereditary nature of the animals concerned. Inbreeding degeneration is of such a peculiar nature that it may be totally abolished by a single crossing with unrelated or distantly related animals. However, if it had made its appearance, the breeder should know it was present in the hereditary make-up of his stock.

Most of the studies on inbreeding are in agreement with one another. The decline in vigor, including the extinction of certain lines, follows largely the regrouping and fixing (making alike) of *recessive* genes which are, on the whole, injurious to the breed. However, along with the fixing of such recessives, there is also a fixing of gene pairs which are beneficial and desirable. It is a matter of chance as to what combination gene pairs a family finally comes to possess, except that selection is always at work weeding out combinations that are not well adapted to the conditions of life. There is a common belief that inbreeding causes the production of monstrosities and defects. Seemingly reliable evidence indicates that inbreeding itself has no specific connection with the production of monstrosities. Inbreeding seems merely to have brought to light genetic traits in the original stock. Inbreeding does not *create* problems or virtues, it *uncovers* them.

One of the most interesting and extensive investigations of inbreeding in animals was done by the U.S. Department of Agriculture. Thirty-five healthy and vigorous females were selected from general breeding stock and mated with a like number of similarly selected males. The matings were numbered and the offspring of each mating were kept separate and mated exclusively brother × sister. Only the best two of each generation were selected to carry on the succeeding generations.

Two striking results followed this close inbreeding. First, each family became more like itself. While this was going on, there was a gradual elimination of sub-branches. Second, there was a decline in vigor during the first nine years, covering about 12 generations. This decline applied to weight, fertility and vitality in the young.

During the second nine years of inbreeding, there was no further decline in vigor of the inbred animals as a group. This stability was taken to mean that after 12 generations, the families had become essentially pure-bred—that is, no longer different with respect to many genes.

What does all this mean in relation to breeding good dogs? From the foregoing data, several conclusions come to mind. Inbreeding coupled with selection can be utilized to "fix" traits in breeding stock at a rapid rate. These traits may be good or they may be undesirable, depending entirely upon the individual's hereditary nature. Inbreeding creates nothing new—it merely intensifies what is already present. If the hereditary nature of an individual already contains undesirable traits, these will naturally be manifested when the recessive genes become grouped and fixed. This applies to the desirable traits as well.

The term "genotype" refers to the complete genetic make-up of an individual, in contrast to the outward appearance of the individual, which is called "phenotype." In selecting puppies to retain for breeding stock, breeders must rely on phenotype because they have no way of knowing an unproven individual's genotype. Inbreeding can reduce genotype and phenotype to one common denominator.

Suppose that an outstanding specimen appears as the product of inbreeding. What would this mean in terms of breeding? It would mean that this specimen has a greater chance of passing on his visible traits rather than possible hidden ones. Prepotent dogs and bitches are usually those that are pure for many of their outstanding characteristics. Since such a limited amount of inbreeding has been carried on in most breeds, prepotent specimens have become pure for certain traits more or less by chance, for they have appeared in most breeds as products of outcrossing, as well as by line breeding. Since line breeding, and especially close line breeding, is a limited form of inbreeding, the same good and bad points apply to line breeding, but in a much more modified degree. The practice of inbreeding appears to be extremely limited in dogs, so one must assume that breeders are willing to trade slower progress for a lower element of risk with respect to degeneration.

Now to review present conclusions insofar as a breeding program is concerned. Assume that you have selected a given bitch to be either line bred or outcrossed and the proper stud dog which compliments her has been chosen. The breeding has been made, the puppies are tenderly watched over, and have begun to grow up. Hopefully, it will be a good breeding and the results will yield several good prospects, all carrying the dam's good traits but showing great improvement in the areas where she needed help. But what if it doesn't turn out this way? What if the breeding results in general disappointment with none of the puppies showing much improvement? You might well ask how this can possibly happen when all the proper aspects were taken into consideration in planning this breeding.

Remember the concept of "dominance"? Test breeding is the only true way of determining whether a dog or bitch is especially dominant. Here again, line breeding comes into play, for the closely line-bred dog or bitch has a *much* better chance of being dominant by virtue of a concentrated bloodline than the dog or bitch that is not line bred. When selecting a stud to compliment your bitch, it is important to take into consideration the qualities of his parents as well. For example, suppose a stud is sought to improve the bitch in head. Obviously, a dog with a beautiful head is chosen, but it is also important that his parents had beautiful heads. Then the stud can be considered "homozygous" for this trait. If the dog selected does not have parents with beautiful heads, or only one parent has a beautiful head, he is said to be "heterozygous" for this characteristic and his chances of reproducing it are diminished. Dominant dogs and bitches are homozygous for more of their traits, while less dominant dogs and bitches are primarily heterozygous in their genetic make-up.

The great majority of dogs and bitches are probably dominant for some of their traits and not especially dominant for others. It is up to the breeder to attempt to match the proper combination of dominant traits, which is why the dog and bitch should compliment each other—that being the best practical way of attempting to come up with the right combinations. There are some dogs and bitches that are completely non-dominant in their genetic make-up when bred to a dominant partner, so good things result provided that their partner is of top quality. In this fashion, a number of dogs and bitches in a breed have "produced" top-quality offspring when they themselves were of lesser quality. When a non-dominant bitch is bred to a non-dominant stud, the resulting litter is bound to be a disappointment. When a dominant bitch is bred to a dominant stud it is possible that the resulting litter will be a failure. This explains why some "dream breedings" result in puppies which do not approach the quality of either parent.

There are some dominant sires which pass on their ability to produce to their sons which, in turn, pass on their producing ability to their sons, etc. Likewise, there are dominant bitches which pass on their producing ability to their daughters, granddaughters, great granddaughters, etc. Thus, some lines are noted for their outstanding producing sires and/or bitches. Such a line is a true "producing bloodline." A producing bitch, usually with a heritage of producing bitches behind her, bred to a proven stud dog will usually come through with those sought-after champions. To this, only one additional qualification need be added—that the breeder exercise some degree of intelligence.

Much discussion between breeders has centered on the subject of which parent contributes the most, the sire or the dam. As we have seen, each contribute 50% of their genetic heritage; but by so doing, their respective factors of dominance and recessiveness are brought into play. Thus, in reality, there is not an equal contribution. If there were, there would be no outstanding producers.

The producing bitch is a very special entity unto herself. Those fortunate enough to own or to have owned one will surely attest to this. When a bitch has produced champion offspring she is singled out for recognition, and well she should be. Depending upon his popularity, the stud dog's production is unlimited; this is not true in the case of the bitch. Many stud dogs, in achieving a producing record, have sired hundreds and hundreds of puppies. The average bitch will produce between 20 and 30 offspring in her lifetime, which drastically limits her chances of producing champions in any great numbers. Taking this limitation into account, it becomes quite obvious that those bitches which produce quality in any amount must possess an attribute different from the average. That attribute is dominance.

The producing bitch may or may not contribute the qualities she herself possesses. Her puppies will, however, bear a resemblence to one another and to subsequent puppies she will produce, regardless of the sire. Whether closely line bred or outcrossed, whether bred to a sire of note or to a comparative unknown, the consistency of quality and type will be apparent in the offspring.

There is no foolproof way to determine in advance those bitches destined to become "producers." The odds will have it, though, that their dams were producers and their granddams and even their great-granddams. Chances are, they will come from a line noted for the producing ability of its bitches.

Occasionally a bitch will come along with little or no producing heritage close behind her, yet she will be a standout in producing ability. It can only be assumed that such a specimen inherited a genetic make-up "different" from that of her immediate ancestors, or else the potential was always there, but remained untapped until some enterprising breeder parlayed it to advantage. There are known instances when specific bitches will produce only with one particular dog and not with others. In such cases, the desired results are achieved through an ideal "blending" rather than by virtue of dominance. It might be well to mention the fact that some bitches are extremely negative. Such a bitch bred to a prepotent sire will necessarily produce only as a result of the stud's dominance.

The availability of a true producing bitch is necessarily limited. Whereas all are free to breed to the outstanding sires of the breed, few have access to the producing bitches. Their offspring can and should command top prices; demand always exceeds supply. Their bitch puppies especially are highly valued, for it is primarily through them that continuity is achieved.

The producing bitch imparts something extra special to her offspring. Though all but impossible to define, this "something extra" is determined genetically, as well as the more obvious physical traits which are handed down. She is also a good mother, conscientious but not fanatical, calm, and possessing an even temperament.

In summary a basic knowledge of genetics will allow the breeding of better specimens and thus improve the breed. It is not possible to be a successful breeder by hit and miss breedings. Hoping that Dame Fortune will smile on you is trusting to chance; not scientific principles. Utilizing the contents of this chapter and other parts of this section will enable a conscientious breeder to score and score well in the winners circle.

Champions in all four of the accepted colors:

Tricolor, Ch. Cambria's Ti-Mungai (right); red and white, Eng. Ch. Fulafuture of the Congo (below); brindle and white, Ch. Changa's Dan Patch (center right), and black and white, Ch. Black Silk-N-Silver of Woz (lower right).

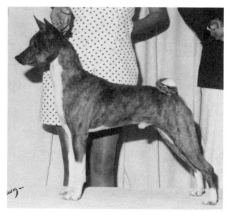

CHAPTER 22

Coat Color in Basenjis

The earliest descriptions of Basenjis in Africa mentioned only red and white dogs. Additionally, there were occasionally photos of tri-color Basenjis.

Olivia Burn founded the Blean Kennel in England and had the earliest Basenjis to survive in England. About 1930, Mrs. Burn joined her husband in his lengthy travels in Africa. Writing in 1937, she described the color of the dogs she had seen in the Congo: "The majority of the dogs are chestnut with white points . . . A small percentage are black, while others are cream, or pale sand colored." Many early writers used "black" to describe our common tri-colors so these could be either black and whites or tri-colors. Correspondence between other breed pioneers as well as writings of early observers of the breed in Africa seem to indicate the same colors being common. The first Basenjis imported from Africa were all red and white. In 1947, the first tri-colors that were not born in Africa appeared and were from a breeding of two red and whites.

Creams were determined to be an undesirable color because they lacked pigment, having light noses and eye rims. (In other breeds, this type of dilute is often sensitive to light, and may be deaf.) One English breeder who found the creams attractive also developed a "blue" variety which

The cream-colored Basenjis lack pigment on the nose and eye rims.

were like a tri but had light eye rims and noses and cream color in place of the tan markings. A dilute tri was also mentioned with tan, cream and white, another recessive lacking dark pigment.

Another color pattern which has since been bred away from was a tri-color marked liked a Beagle. This is a red and white dog with a black blanket. The best known Basenji of this color was Ch. Haku Black Icicle

Ch. Haku Black Icicle was the best known saddle-marked tri-color.

owned and bred by Mary McWain. Black Icicle's championship was won in 1951, and he was Best of Breed at the Westminster Kennel Club show in 1952. This color was generally not well accepted by breeders. It is difficult to follow early correspondence regarding color as there was little clarification of terms. Early tri-colors were often referred to as blacks. One did not quite know what type of markings were being discussed but recessive and dominant blacks and whites did not show up until much later.

The majority of the dogs seen by Veronica Tudor-Williams on her 1959 expedition were some shade of red with the normal white markings. She wrote:

> . . . about one quarter of the dogs were typical tri-colors of black, tan and white clearly defined. We saw only one black and white, without any tan on it. The most surprising of all was the fact that about one-fifth of the dogs were true tiger-striped brindle, bright red with black stripes—a color I had not known to exist . . . We saw only two dogs, an adult and a puppy, of the unattractive coloring which we have called in England shaded reds . . . or blanketed tri-colors, which is really a mixture of red and tri-color black hairs being sprinkled through the red.

The tiger-stripe brindle color was discovered in Africa in 1959. The red should be bright, not tan, and the black stripes should be distinct. Michael Work.

In an article published in 1979, Veronica Tudor-Williams describes some additional colors which had been found in Africa. A bitch named Nyanabiem was bred in the South Sudan by Captain Richards, a great Basenji expert of that time, 1928–1938. She was dark mahogany, tan and white. There were tan hairs mixed with the mahogany making spectacles around her eyes. Another Basenji exported to England, who died in quarantine, was described originally as black and white, but on arrival was found to have pale yellow melon pips but no tan on the cheeks. Simolo of the Congo, exported from Uganda, had different markings. This male was tri-color but had tan spectacles. It appeared that the tan mask on the face had merged with the tan pips. He was used very little at stud because his puppies were large, coarse and heavily coated. He is not counted among the foundation stock as his line died out.

Recessive black and whites turned up in the mid 1960's. These early recessive black and whites appeared to be pure black and white but were from red and white parents. Recessive blacks (also called "Fula" blacks) usually develop tan hairs in their black coats as they mature. Most breeders feel that this intermingling of hair colors is undesirable since our standard calls for pure black and goes on to say that shaded or off-colors should be heavily penalized. Dominant black and whites maintain pure black color.

The "Fula" tri does not have clear markings as tan hairs are mixed in the black portions of the coat. The first indication that you have a "Fula" tri is often seen as the youngsters lose their first puppy coat at just a few weeks of age. At this time, a black bar is sometimes noted running across the tan cheek markings. Not all "Fula" tris have this mark, but most do. As the puppy matures, other intermingling of hair color begins to show up. Each dog is a bit different and some have quite a clear coat while others become very muddy colored. One commonly finds "Fula" tris with tan hairs mixed in with the black around the eyes making "spectacles." Others have a cap of mixed color on the top of their heads. Sometimes the black seems to be a bit of a dull color when compared to a clear tri color. In other cases there is obvious mixing of the tan hairs throughout the black coat. On some dogs the shafts of hair are tan at the base and black at the tips.

The genetics of breeding the Basenji colors is beyond this simple descriptive discourse, but let's cover a few simple points. Breeding of reds and tri-colors seems to run true as a simple recessive with the red being genetically dominant to tri-color. A red Basenji must carry tri-color as a recessive to produce tri-color pups and it must be mated to another which is either tri-color or carries tri-color as a recessive to produce both colors in a litter. A tri-color bred to a tri-color produces a litter of all tri-colors. I would like to point out that litters can contain all three colors, dominant black, red and tri-color, in several instances. A black carrying tri-color bred to a red carrying tri-color can produce a litter of all three colors. However, the

Left is a "Fula" tri showing the typical black bar across the tan cheek marking and right are the face markings on a clear tri-color. Courtesy of The American Kennel Club.

These three puppies of the three accepted colors came from a breeding of a red and white male to a black and white female. Note the black hairs on the red puppy's tail indicating she carries the recessive gene for tri-color. Terri Gavaletz.

black appears to be more complex genetically than the reds and tris and some blacks produce litters with all three colors even though they have been bred to a tri color. The books *Breeding and Genetics of the Dog* by Anne Fitzgerald Paramoure and *The Inheritance of Coat Color in Dogs*, by C.C. Little have been recommended to me as good sources describing the different genetic series for color in such a way as to explain what happens in our breed. Some blacks, like some reds, carry "Fula" tri while others carry clear tri-color as a recessive. Recessive blacks, although unusual, could turn up in any combination—red to red, red to tri, tri to tri or black to any color. It can turn up whenever the recessive genes for it are lurking behind the parents.

Another color pattern has been showing up quite a bit in the past few years. This is a red with quite a bit of black hair on the face creating a masked effect. (The only African export reported to have black hair on the muzzle was Wau of the Congo. It was not considered a desirable feature.) Sometimes there is a lot of black hair near the eyes as if a woman had smeared her mascara. Dark hair should not be confused with dark pigment

Black hair on this dog's muzzle and around his eyes begins to form the undesirable mask. *Courtesy of The American Kennel Club.*

which refers to the color of the skin. One needs to look closely to see whether the dog has black hair or a thin coat with very dark skin pigment. Some of these shaded dogs actually have light pigment and lack the desirable black nose color. This masking is not the black and tan called for in the standard. In fact, the tri-colors with this fault often have quite a bit of black hair on the tan masks. The shaded red dogs usually have quite dark coats. Perhaps that is why some breeders have been forgiving of the obviously shaded markings even though the standard states they should be heavily penalized. Some of the Basenjis seen many years ago were a very light color, often referred to as a "paper bag brown." When the standard requested a deep color of red, the intent was to try to eliminate the "paper bag brown," but not to introduce deep red colors at the expense of adding black shading. The bright red colors are as attractive as deep reds.

Another form of shading, or sabling, sometimes shows up when a red dog is found to have some black hair mixed into the red along the topline. This is sometimes very slight and sometimes rather severe. Red Basenji puppies are usually a gray shade when they are born. Some have black hairs mixed in their coats at that time and some do not. The black hairs should completely disappear when the dog matures. If your dogs have a tendency to keep the black hair until they are close to a year old, you should probably be careful in your breeding to avoid getting mature dogs with coats that always have black hairs mixed in.

This five-month old puppy has black shading on her side, neck and along her topline. As she matured, the black hair disappeared except on top over her shoulders.

Red dogs who carry tri-color as a recessive often have some black hair on the top (inside) of the tail near the root or a few black hairs on the back of the ears. This should not be penalized.

After the 1987 trip made to Africa, participant Jon Curby wrote of the colors of dogs they saw:

> . . . About one-third were brindle . . . The degree of brindle varies. A dog could have very few black marks or be red with a covering of uniformly spaced lines. Others were predominately black on the dorsal area with red between the stripes on the sides and head. There was no evidence that brindle dogs being a part of the population had any effect on the quality of color in red and tri dogs. Over the entire trip, we saw only three dogs that could have been pure black and white, and two other black and whites that had red hair scattered in the black. We saw several examples of two rather unusual colors. One is a tri-color dog with a tan mask covering the face just over the eyes creating a look similar to that of a Malamute. The other color was what Veronica Tudor-Williams described as a "mahogany tri," a tri-color dog with dark red replacing what is usually black. The tan and white colors appear in the same places they usually do.

While all the visitors to Africa over the years did not go to the same areas and villages, the differences in the described colors is a bit of a mystery. It is very interesting to note the general change in the color of the population as described over the years. Why did the earliest observers in the 1920's and 30's, and even earlier, never mention tiger-striped dogs? Was there some outside influence or is it a genetic drift? Did the early explorers just not come across this color? It would seem that the brindles are on the rise in Africa as indicated by the early lack of mention of the color to an increase of from one-fifth to one-third seen in 1959 and 1987.

The first American-born puppies resulting from breedings of the brindles brought from Africa in 1987 and 1988 were born in 1988. There were three matings made with these results: pure-for-red American male bred to an African brindle bitch produced four red and white offspring; African brindle dog bred to an African red bitch (who had had tri-litter mates) produced two red and one brindle offspring; and the same African brindle male bred to a pure-for-red American bitch produced one red and five brindle offspring. There were a total of thirteen offspring with six brindles.

The new imports brought us several color problems. The saddle tricolor returned, and the saddle also appeared on some brindles. Slight sabling, a continuing nuisance, was seen more strongly in some descendants of the new dogs. Brindle can replace the red on tricolors. This was true with a new pattern called a capped tricolor in which the marking is more open on the face like a Siberian husky. Occasionally, a puppy with have a faded looking muzzle, with the faded area like the mask on the tricolor with the suggestion of pips in the pale lemon color as well. Over time, breeders should be able to work through these problems as did the earliest breeders.

The brindle color was accepted by the BCOA in 1987 and by the AKC in the new standard of 1990. No other colors or patterns were added.

The brindle pattern is shown here.

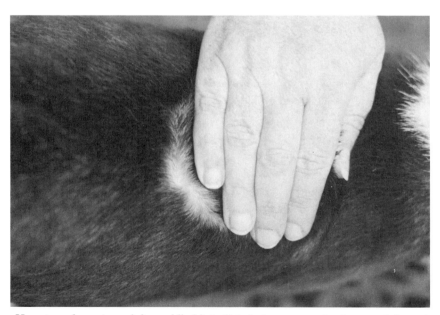

Here is a close view of the saddled brindle's hair pattern. At the top of the ruffled hair, you can see a dark stripe of skin which is found under the darker hair in the brindle pattern. You can also see that the black color in the saddle does not go down to the skin on the shafts of hair.

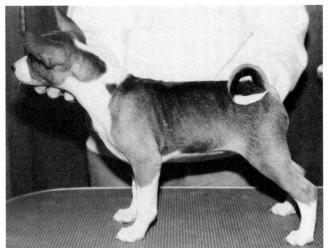

Here is a nicely put together half-African puppy with an unfortunate mix of black hair in her red coat.

Here is a capped tricolor at seven months. When capped pups are born, it is very difficult to distinguish them from regular tricolors. As the pup matures, the black starts to fade and the pattern emerges.

SECTION VII
Becoming A Breeder

- *The Stud Dog*
- *The Bitch and Her Puppies*
- *Nutrition for Puppies and Adults*
- *Problems of Early Puppyhood*
- *Choosing the Best Puppies*
- *Frozen and Extended Semen*

Jon Coe

CHAPTER 23

The Stud Dog

The dog you select to stand at stud should have certain things going for him. First, he should be masculine in appearance and, to at least your appraisal, conform closely to the breed standard. A major mistake made by breeders is to keep a dog that is overdone in some features in the hope he can overcome a bitch with deficiencies in these areas. It doesn't work that way! Breeding an oversize dog to a small bitch in the hope of getting average size puppies is a futile effort. The hallmark of a good breeder, one who understands basic genetics, is breeding to dogs who conform to the standard. Extremes should be avoided like the plague. They only add complications to a breeding program down the road.

Second, it is extremely important that the stud dog come from an unbroken line of producers on both his sire's and dam's side. By unbroken it is meant that at least his sire, grandfather and great grandfather should have produced ten or more champions each. If his sire is still young he may not have hit that mark, but from reading the magazines and seeing his offspring an intelligent breeder can tell if he is going to make it. This unbroken line helps to ensure that he is likely to be homozygous for his good traits. An unbroken producing bitch line is frosting on the cake. It's usually more difficult to find because bitches have fewer offspring. So, when a dog is found that has unbroken producing lines for three generations on his sire's and dam's side, there is an excellent chance of having a prepotent stud.

Third, is appearance. Let's face it, if the male is not constructed right or if his color is not quite right, he is not going to be a great show dog. While the dog doesn't have to be a great show winner to attract the bitches, it helps. Believe me, it helps. Of course there are outstanding examples of non-titled dogs being excellent studs. However, they are few and far between.

There is more to breeding than just dropping a bitch in season into the stud dog's pen and hoping for the best.

First off, let's talk about a subject that never seems to be addressed in the literature about stud dogs, the psyche of the dog. Young stud dogs need to be brought along slowly. If he is a show dog to begin with, he is most likely outgoing and the "gung ho" type. If he is not, please do not think about using him at stud. Behavior traits such as shyness and lack of aggressiveness are transmitted to the next generation just as beautiful necks or slipped stifles are.

He should be taught to get along with other male dogs. Do *not* put him in with an older male too early on. If you do, there is a good likelihood that he will be intimidated and it may harm his prospects of being a good stud. Good stud dogs have to be aggressive in the breeding box. Dogs who have been intimidated early seldom shape up. However, running, playing and even puppy fighting with littermates or slightly older puppies doesn't seem to have a detrimental effect.

The young male, until he is old enough to stand up for himself, should be quartered first with puppies his own age and then introduced to older bitches as kennel mates. It's not a good idea to keep him in a pen by himself. Socialization is extremely important. Time for play as a puppy and a companion to keep him from boredom helps his growth and development.

His quarters and food should present no special problems. Serious breeders all feed their dogs a nourishing and balanced diet. Study after study in colleges of veterinary medicine and by nutritionists at major dog food companies, have shown that the major brands of dry dog food come as close to meeting the total needs of the dog as any elaborately concocted breeder's formula. Each of you has probably learned to add three drops of this and two teaspoons of that, but honestly, a good dry food does the trick. Many breeders spice up the basic diet with their own version of goodies, including table scraps, to break up the monotony or to stimulate a finicky eater. However, for the most part, this is more cosmetic than nutritional. If it makes you feel better, feed him those extra goodies. Supplements will be discussed in the chapter on Nutrition For Puppies and Adults. Do not get him fat and out of condition. That could do terrible things to his libido.

A very important aspect of being the owner of a stud dog is to make sure he can produce puppies. Therefore, at around 11–12 months of age it's a good idea to trundle him off to the vet's for a check on his sperm count. This will tell you if he is producing enough viable sperm cells to make sure he can fertilize eggs in the ovum of a bitch. Sometimes it is found that while a stud produces spermatozoa, they are not active. The chances of this dog being able to fertilize an egg is markedly reduced. While this problem is usually found in older dogs, it happens often enough in young animals to be of concern. Thus the sperm count exam is important, and should be done yearly.

Since we are dealing with the breeding of a warm-blooded mammal, there is need to be concerned with his general health. Sexual contact with a variety of bitches exposes the dog to a wide variety of minor infections and some major ones. Some, if not promptly identified and treated, can lead to sterility—and there goes the farm! Other non-sexual infections and illnesses, such as urinary infections, stones, etc., can also reduce a dog's ability to sire puppies. Since it is not desirable for any of these things to happen stud dog owners need to watch their young Romeos like a hawk.

It's a good idea to have your vet check all incoming bitches. While checking them for obvious signs of infection, especially brucellosis, he can also run a smear to see when they are ready to breed. The dog should also be checked frequently to see if there is any type of discharge from his penis. A dog at regular stud should not have a discharge. Usually he will lick himself frequently to keep the area clean. After breeding it is also a good idea to rinse off the area with a clean saline solution. Your vet may also advise flushing out the penile area after breeding using a special solution.

The testicles and penis are the male organs of reproduction. Testicles are housed in a sac called the scrotum. The AKC will not allow dogs who are cryptorchids (neither testicle descended) nor monorchids (a dog that has only one testicle descended) to be shown.

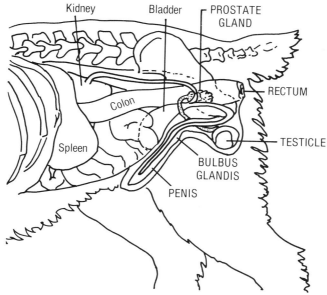

Figure VII-1. Left side of dog showing genital organs and related parts.

The male's testicles are outside the body because the internal heat of the body would curtail the production of sperm. There is a special muscle that keeps them close to the body for warmth in cold weather and relaxes and lets them down to get air cooled in hot weather.

In the male fetus the gonads, or sex organs, develop in the abdominal cavity—migrating during gestation toward their eventual position. Shortly before birth they hover over an opening in the muscular structure of the pubic area through which they will descend to reach the scrotal sac. This external position is vital to the fertility of the animal, for production of live sperm can only proceed at a temperature several degrees cooler than normal body temperature. The glandular tissue of the testes are nourished and supported by arteries, veins, nerves, connective tissue and duct work, collectively known as the spermatic cord. The scrotum acts as a thermostat. As noted above, there are many involuntary muscle fibers within it that are stimulated to contract with the environmental temperature pulling the testes closer to the body for warmth. Contraction also occurs as a result of any stimulus which might be interpreted by the dog as a threat of physical harm—sight of a strange dog, being picked up, etc. This contraction does not force the testicles back up into the abdominal cavity of the adult dog because the inguinal rings have tightened and will not allow them to be drawn back up. The tightening of the rings usually occurs at about ten months of age.

There are a number of reasons why a dog may be a monorchid or cryptorchid. For example the size of the opening through the muscles may be too small to allow for easy passage of the testes, or the spermatic cord may not be long enough for the testes to remain in the scrotum most of the time, and as the proportions of the inguinal ring and testes change in the growing puppy, the time comes when the testes may be trapped above the ring as they grow at different rates. Also, there exists a fibrous muscular band which attaches both to the testes and scrotal wall, gradually shortening and actually guiding the testes in their descent. Possibly this structure could be at fault.

The important thing about all of this is to help the prospective stud dog owner learn about the anatomy of the reproduction organs of the dog. From the foregoing, is it any wonder that many puppies are described as being down one day and up the next?

Next time you place that favorite male puppy up on the grooming table be wary when probing for all of his standard equipment. The scrotal muscles may contract and the still generous inguinal rings may allow the disappearance of the parts sought.

Great luck, a youngster has been found that has "IT" and it is decided to let the world share in the good fortune of owning him. It's a good idea to get him started on the right foot with a cooperative, experienced bitch, one of your own preferably. By introducing the young and inexperienced stud to a "woman of the world," his first experience will result in an easy and successful breeding. Like all males, his ego will soar as a result. This is important. He needs to have the feeling of accomplishment and success. A feisty, difficult bitch the first time around could very well frustrate the youngster and, as a result, he may not be too enthusiastic about future breedings. Remember, we want a confident and aggressive stud dog in the breeding box. There will be difficult bitches to come so it's best to bring him along slow and easy until he will be a match for these fearsome females.

When the bitch is ready to breed (as your stud gains experience he will not pay too much attention to her until she is really ready) both animals should be allowed to exercise and relieve themselves just before being brought together. It's also a good idea not to feed them before mating. Bring the bitch in first. The place should be quiet and away from noise and other dogs. Spend a few minutes petting her and telling her how wonderful she is. Then bring the dog in on a lead. Do not allow him to come lunging in and make a frustrated leap at her. This can cause her to panic and bite him out of fear.

After a few minutes of pirouetting around together—she throwing her vulva in his face and he, with his ears curled on top of his head, trying to lick fore and aft—take off the lead. Allow them to court for a few minutes. She should tell you she is ready by being coquettish and continually backing into the dog.

Now comes the important time for the future success of the young stud. The dog needs to learn the owner is there to help and should not back away from breeding the bitch just because someone is holding her.

Having planned ahead, there will be a large non-skid rug on the floor. Place the bitch on the rug, add a little vaseline around the vulva and face her rump toward the dog. Pat her on the fanny to encourage the dog to come ahead. Generally speaking, he will. As a rule he will lick her again around the vulva. Some dogs are truly considerate lovers, they will go around to the front and gently lick at the bitches eyes and ears. These are true gentlemen. However, this will get him nowhere, so again encourage him to come around to where the action is. If he is unsure of himself, lift the bitch's rear and dangle it in front of the dog's nose.

By now, encouraged and emboldened, the male will mount the bitch from the rear and begin to slowly probe for the opening to the vagina. Once he discovers it, he will begin to move more rapidly. This is a critical time. Some young dogs are so far off the target they never get near the right opening. It's time to gently reposition the bitch so he can have a better angle. This may occur any number of times. He may get frustrated and back off. Don't get worried, this is normal in a young dog. He may even get so excited and confused that he swings around and tries to breed her from the front. This approach never ends successfully.

If he is getting all hot and bothered and not having much success; take a break. Put the dog back by himself for a couple of hours. Don't let him wear himself out. This lack of success can make him lose interest. Pet him and tell him how great he is. At the end of that time, try again. The approach should be the same. If it happens a second time the bitch may not be ready. And if after 20 minutes of fruitless endeavor you do not have a tie, there is always tomorrow. Do not work the young dog to the point of exhaustion. When the next day rolls around you can begin again, giving him maximum encouragement. Don't let him fool around again or he will learn bad habits and think that he has to perform these antics before breeding the bitch.

Get him back on track. Show him the business end again, and encourage him to proceed. By now you have noticed a red, bone-like protuberance sticking out from the penis sheath. This, of course, is the penis itself. When, as a dog continues to probe and finds the opening, he will begin to move frenetically. As he moves in this fashion, a section just behind the pointed penis bone begins to swell. It is capable of great enlargement. This enlargement of the bulbous takes place due to its filling with blood, and it becomes some three times larger than the rest of the penis. In this way the dog, once having made penetrance, is "tied" to the bitch; it is entirely due to the male, the bitch having no part in the initial tying.

When a tie has occurred the semen is pumped in spurts into the vagina. The bitch then helps to keep the penis enlarged as she begins to have a series of pulsating waves which cause a slight tightening and relaxing of the vagina. Some males will stay tied for up to sixty minutes and others as little as five. A five minute successful tie is just as satisfactory as a longer one, because the semen has moved up through the uterus and fallopian tubes to the ovarian capsules by the end of five minutes.

Once the dog and bitch are successfully tied, the male characteristically tries to lift his rear leg over the bitch to keep the tie in a back-to-back position. Some dogs merely slide off the back of a bitch and maintain a tie facing in the same direction. One thing you can count on, they will not stay in one position for any length of time. If someone were to chart the moves of a dog and a bitch during a thirty minute tie, it would look like break dancing at its best. Because of this it's a good idea to have two people involved at this point. One at the bitch's head and one at the male's.

Every now and then a fractious bitch will be sent for breeding. She can be frightened about being shipped, or just plain spooked by a variety of things. Certainly one doesn't want the dog to be bitten by a frightened bitch, nor to have one's fingers lacerated. The easiest solution to this problem is to tie her jaws loosely with wide gauze. This muzzle should tie behind her ears to make sure it doesn't slide off. Pet her, reassure her, but hold her firmly during the breeding so she doesn't lunge at the dog.

After the tie has been broken, there sometimes will be a rush of fluid from the bitch. Don't worry about it, the sperm is well on its way up the fallopian tubes. Gently move the bitch to a quiet pen, apart from other dogs, and give her fresh water and an opportunity to relieve herself. The dog should be petted and told how well he has done. This is also a good time to flush out his sheath, and if your vet has recommended any medication, apply it now. Then, he too should be put in a separate quiet pen with fresh water. It is not a good idea to put him back with a group of male dogs. The opportunity for a serious fight is greatest at this time. The other dogs smell him and get quite upset that it wasn't their turn.

How often can the dog be used at stud? If the dog is in good condition he should be able to be used every day for a week. Some serious breeders who, when faced with many bitches to be bred to a popular stud, have used the dog in the morning and the evening for at least three days. If a dog is used regularly he can be used from day-to-day for a long time. However, if a dog is seldom used, he should not be expected to be able to service day-after-day for any great length of time.

Nature is most generous with sperm. In one good mating a dog may discharge millions, and by and large, a copious amount of sperm is produced in dogs who are used regularly. Dr. Leon Whitney in his book, *This is the Cocker Spaniel*, describes a stud left with a bitch who copulated five times with her, and remained tied at least 18 minutes each time.

All this Olympian activity may be possible for a short time, but for good health and good management, three times a week in normal use seems about right. Of course most breeders would give their eye teeth for such a popular stud. An individual bitch should be serviced twice—once every other day—for the best chance of conception.

For some breeders to breed to a stud of their choice is often difficult, especially in countries that have quarantine restrictions. In the U.S., the basic cost of shipping, the possibility of the dog being booked, the chance of making connections with a popular stud who is out on a circuit being campaigned, etc., are some of the problems that can produce a great deal of frustration. The use of frozen sperm opens up many new possibilities. Owners of popular stud dogs should definitely look into it. At the time of this writing, there are a number of AKC-sanctioned collection stations. There should be many more in the near future.

Collecting sperm from dogs is not like collecting from cattle. One collection from the latter produces enough to inseminate over 100 cows. The largest amount collected, at one time, over the many years of research in dogs was 22 vials. Usually two to three vials are used to breed a bitch on two to three occasions while she is in season.

The estimated time to store enough semen to inseminate 30 bitches differs by age, health, and sperm quantity and quality. Estimate approximately a month for a young dog, approximately three months for a dog of eight or nine years of age or older. Collection is still time consuming.

It doesn't take one long to recognize that, in the early stages, those males of outstanding quality will make up the main reservoir of the sperm bank. It is suggested by the collection centers that collection be done at a young age—three to five years.

Limitations in quality and quantity due to old age lengthen the period necessary to store enough sperm for even a few bitches. In addition, the daily routine of a dog's life may limit freezability: The settling down in a new environment, changes in diet/water, minor health problems, etc. It is also not uncommon to get poor freeze results from a stud dog that has not been used for a month or longer. For the dog, once he settles down, the process of collection is a pleasant experience. The chapter on Frozen and Extended Semen goes into greater depth on the subject.

Up to now the discussion has touched only on the "easy" part of being a stud dog owner. Next is a look into the day-by-day tasks of the business. Trying to plan a schedule is virtually impossible. Even though some bitch owners say they plan to breed to your dog at the bitch's next season, that can be three to seven months away. Certainly knowing the exact week, let alone the day, is clearly impossible. The bitch's owner will call and say the bitch is on the way. (My God, I've got three unanticipated bitches here now!) Mother Nature does not keep an exact schedule. Unless the bitch's owner has actually sent a deposit to hold a stud service for June of 19__ (this is so rare it would come as a shock), a breeder can only approximate the arrival of his dog's fan club. That's why it is important to keep the stud in top condition . . . he may need to perform yeoman service on short notice.

Okay, now it's known the bitch will be arriving on Tiddlewink Airlines, flight #111, at 1:05 a.m., and has to be picked up at the airport. Those living in a metropolis where there are dog delivery services available that provide for both pickup and delivery are most fortunate. However, these services are expensive. Therefore, being a typical small breeder, it means trudging off to the airport giving up a good night's sleep in the process. When a bitch is shipped air freight or air express, the airlines seem to have a conspiracy as to how long to make you wait to pick up live cargo.

The plane arrives and gets unloaded. No dog! It seems they wait until all the baggage is unloaded to take off the livestock and then they transport them to the air freight building at the other end of the field. This means that 1:05 a.m. has now stretched to close to 3:00 a.m. before they release the bitch. After letting her relieve herself, putting her back in the crate, driving home and then putting her safely in an isolation pen (hopefully you have planned ahead and provided a special quiet run) we're talking 5:00 a.m. before you get to sleep. Now that's fun!

A good stud dog owner will have found out that various dog food companies, and others, print standard stud contracts. These usually provide for payment in advance and a guaranteed return service if the bitch misses. Both of these stipulations are well advised. As well meaning as most breeders are, many stud fees are either late or not paid at all. Some breeders even wait until they are sure the bitch is pregnant before taking pen in hand. Be firm, no check, no service. This is an expensive hobby, you deserve to be paid for breeding, feeding, picking up and delivering the bitch to and from the airport. By the way, it is a good idea to call the owner collect when the bitch has arrived and also when the bitch is being returned.

What if the dog is either standing at stud at his handler's or being actively campaigned? This can get tricky. If the handler is taking care of the breeding, he expects to be paid for his services. So . . . expect very little from the stud fee unless the dog is so famous as a *prepotent* stud that the stud fees allow you to drive a Mercedes. Expect the handler to ask for 50% or more of the stud fee. Don't complain, they work hard for their money. When the dog is at home, all of the fee can go into the piggy bank. Of course, someone has to perform 100% of the work connected with it.

A real problem can occur when you try to get the in-season bitch together with an actively campaigned dog. Airline schedules and the phone become your steady companion. You arrange for the bitch to be shipped to Toonerville and to arrive at 3:30 in the afternoon. This looks like good planning, because there is a show in Slyville the same day and your handler has to drive through Toonerville on his way to Lizard Butte where the third show on the circuit is being held the following day.

Lucky you, your dog goes Best in Show at Slyville! After the pictures and the congratulations, your handler feeds his string of dogs, cleans up, packs his motorhome and looks at his watch, it's 6:45 p.m. He needs to get going for he has to be in Lizard Butte by 10:00 p.m. to hold his reserved overnight parking at the show grounds. He also needs to pick up that bitch at the Toonerville airport and then find a decent place to eat. He also must call and tell you that your dog went "all the way" that day, before you plow a furrow in the rug pacing around waiting for the news.

Now, are you ready for this? When he arrives at the airport he finds the air freight office is closed—not to open until 7:00 a.m. Don't laugh, it happens! Small airports don't stay open all night. So, what does the handler do? He's showing his client's Beagles at 8:00 a.m. the next morning! The purpose of this commentary is not to try to solve this particular problem, but to allow some insight into the problems of breeding to a dog being actively campaigned.

Now, for a most important item: How much should be charged for the dog's services? A good rule of thumb says that for a young unproven stud, charge 65%-75% of the average being charged. Don't include the Mr. Big's who have already sired 20 or more champions in your calculations. Their fees are elevated based upon accomplishment. You are charging a fee based upon hope and good bloodlines. After the dog has sired at least five champions boost his fee to the average being charged. If he should prove to be a *prepotent* stud and sires some 115 champion offspring, a price more commensurate with his siring abilities should be set. Don't be afraid to ask a price above the average. The average breeder, like the average buyer of goods, equates a good price with a good product.

There are four major things to consider when you decide to promote a stud dog: How often to advertise? How big should the advertisement be? How to use words and pictures to get people to do what you want them to do? And, where to place the advertising to get the best results?

A cardinal rule of advertising is repetition. It has been found that no matter how good the advertisement is, it won't sell unless it is repeated often. The more often an ad is seen, the more likely it will be remembered.

On average, both readership and responses increase as the size of the advertisement increases. However, a full page will not get twice as much attention as a half page. A half-page advertisement will usually be noticed by such a high percentage of readers that it would be impossible to double the readership. On the other hand, a single column ad—a couple of inches deep—will attract the attention of such a small percentage of readers that doubling its size is likely to double its readership. Advertising experts say that nearly everyone involved with print advertising would like their ad to be larger than it should be.

Get their attention. Try to prove that you have a better stud dog for their bitch than anyone else. The more physical the better. Push—better puppies, better puppy sales, etc., and you need to back it up with logic and proof. Cite examples. The magic formula could be stated, "to get what you *want*, do what I want." By citing all the famous and near famous breeders who have bred to your dog, you get them to identify—"if I do the same thing as those famous people did, I will be right in line with those big shots and get champions to boot." This type of identification advertising is highly successful, because it appeals to the need to belong to a group and it unifies people.

First promote his winning look to all-breed magazines and newspapers to catch the eye of both the all-rounders and specialty judges and to help his career along. Then, after his winning record is established, turn greater emphasis to the breed magazines to promote his offspring.

When promoting the dog both as a show dog and as a stud, you have a chicken-and-egg situation. The early advertisements should emphasize his winning record and his winning (producing) ancestors. Later, as the bitches come in, is the time to stress the numbers of bitches being bred to him. Finally, as he produces, trumpet the achievements of his offspring and the history of the producers behind him.

CHAPTER 24

The Bitch and Her Puppies

G. Quitslund

It has been said that a good bitch is worth her weight in gold. I don't know what gold is selling for today but it's a good bet a really good bitch is worth it. "Really good" doesn't necessarily mean one who will win Westminster. However, she should be a solid bitch who is good enough to finish—or come mighty close—and who comes from a top-producing bloodline. In the chapter, The Stud Dog, emphasis was placed on the continuous, unbroken line of champion ancestors. This holds true in bitches as well, although it is somewhat harder to obtain because of the limited number of puppies they produce when compared to the male.

To begin, assume you have been fortunate and have procured the best bitch that is affordable and she comes from producing bloodlines. Now all that has to be done is sit back and count the champions in each litter. Right? Wrong! There are many extraneous factors to deal with before that can even be a possibility.

It's best to start at the beginning. When thinking about breeding that good bitch, first make sure she is in good condition. Take her to the veterinarian to have her thoroughly checked out. This should include checking for heartworm and other parasites and to make sure she is not carrying a sexually-transmitted disease like brucellosis, which can cause sterility and abortions. All this should be done at least a couple of months before she is due in season.

If there are any problems they can be taken care of early. It is important that she be parasite free. Check for this once again just before she is to be bred. Parasites can be quite debilitating to the puppies. The bitch needs to be in tip-top shape.

Her diet should continue along normal lines with plenty of exercise and fresh water. Be sure she is lean and hard. A fat bitch spells trouble in the whelping box.

Once she has been bred, there is nothing special to do for the first few weeks. She should have good nourishment, fresh water and normal exercise. Be sure her diet is well balanced. Most of the good commercial dry foods provide this. After the third week increase her intake to twice what she has been eating. Feed her twice a day to make digestion easier. After week seven has gone by, feed at the same level but spread it over three feedings. All this time she should be getting regular exercise. In the last three weeks cut out any hard-to-digest foods and walk her briskly on lead, but don't let her overextend herself physically. The week before she is due to whelp, modify her diet by making it more liquid—to assist her to eliminate easily. Within three days of whelping give her a teaspoon full of milk of magnesia daily.

The average whelping time is 63 days after conception. No two bitches are alike, and whelping can occur from the 59th day to the 65th day just as easily. Remember the Boy Scout motto—"Be Prepared!"

There are a number of things that can be done to prepare for the arrival

Table VII-1. Sixty-Three Day Whelping Table

Date Bred JANUARY	Puppies Due MARCH	Date Bred FEBRUARY	Puppies Due APRIL	Date Bred MARCH	Puppies Due MAY	Date Bred APRIL	Puppies Due JUNE	Date Bred MAY	Puppies Due JULY	Date Bred JUNE	Puppies Due AUGUST	Date Bred JULY	Puppies Due SEPTEMBER	Date Bred AUGUST	Puppies Due OCTOBER	Date Bred SEPTEMBER	Puppies Due NOVEMBER	Date Bred OCTOBER	Puppies Due DECEMBER	Date Bred NOVEMBER	Puppies Due JANUARY	Date Bred DECEMBER	Puppies Due FEBRUARY
1	5	1	5	1	3	1	3	1	3	1	3	1	2	1	3	1	3	1	3	1	3	1	2
2	6	2	6	2	4	2	4	2	4	2	4	2	3	2	4	2	4	2	4	2	4	2	3
3	7	3	7	3	5	3	5	3	5	3	5	3	4	3	5	3	5	3	5	3	5	3	4
4	8	4	8	4	6	4	6	4	6	4	6	4	5	4	6	4	6	4	6	4	6	4	5
5	9	5	9	5	7	5	7	5	7	5	7	5	6	5	7	5	7	5	7	5	7	5	6
6	10	6	10	6	8	6	8	6	8	6	8	6	7	6	8	6	8	6	8	6	8	6	7
7	11	7	11	7	9	7	9	7	9	7	9	7	8	7	9	7	9	7	9	7	9	7	8
8	12	8	12	8	10	8	10	8	10	8	10	8	9	8	10	8	10	8	10	8	10	8	9
9	13	9	13	9	11	9	11	9	11	9	11	9	10	9	11	9	11	9	11	9	11	9	10
10	14	10	14	10	12	10	12	10	12	10	12	10	11	10	12	10	12	10	12	10	12	10	11
11	15	11	15	11	13	11	13	11	13	11	13	11	12	11	13	11	13	11	13	11	13	11	12
12	16	12	16	12	14	12	14	12	14	12	14	12	13	12	14	12	14	12	14	12	14	12	13
13	17	13	17	13	15	13	15	13	15	13	15	13	14	13	15	13	15	13	15	13	15	13	14
14	18	14	18	14	16	14	16	14	16	14	16	14	15	14	16	14	16	14	16	14	16	14	15
15	19	15	19	15	17	15	17	15	17	15	17	15	16	15	17	15	17	15	17	15	17	15	16
16	20	16	20	16	18	16	18	16	18	16	18	16	17	16	18	16	18	16	18	16	18	16	17
17	21	17	21	17	19	17	19	17	19	17	19	17	18	17	19	17	19	17	19	17	19	17	18
18	22	18	22	18	20	18	20	18	20	18	20	18	19	18	20	18	20	18	20	18	20	18	19
19	23	19	23	19	21	19	21	19	21	19	21	19	20	19	21	19	21	19	21	19	21	19	20
20	24	20	24	20	22	20	22	20	22	20	22	20	21	20	22	20	22	20	22	20	22	20	21
21	25	21	25	21	23	21	23	21	23	21	23	21	22	21	23	21	23	21	23	21	23	21	22
22	26	22	26	22	24	22	24	22	24	22	24	22	23	22	24	22	24	22	24	22	24	22	23
23	27	23	27	23	25	23	25	23	25	23	25	23	24	23	25	23	25	23	25	23	25	23	24
24	28	24	28	24	26	24	26	24	26	24	26	24	25	24	26	24	26	24	26	24	26	24	25
25	29	25	29	25	27	25	27	25	27	25	27	25	26	25	27	25	27	25	27	25	27	25	26
26	30	26	30	26	28	26	28	26	28	26	28	26	27	26	28	26	28	26	28	26	28	26	27
27	31	27	1 (May)	27	29	27	29	27	29	27	29	27	28	27	29	27	29	27	29	27	29	27	28
28	1 (Apr)	28	2	28	30	28	30	28	30	28	29	28	29	28	30	28	30 (Dec)	28	30	28	30	28	1 (Mar)
29	2			29	31	29	1 (Jul)	29	31	29	30	29	30	29	31	29	1	29	31	29	31	29	2
30	3			30	1 (Jun)	30	2	30	1 (Aug)	30	1 (Sep)	30	1 (Oct)	30	1 (Nov)	30	2	30	1 (Jan)	30	1 (Feb)	30	3
31	4			31	2			31	2			31	2	31	2			31	2			31	4

of the puppies. First, prepare a comfortable, quiet place for the bitch to whelp. This is not time for a block party, so set-up to keep vistors out. Either make or buy a whelping box. This box should sit above the floor (a minimum of 2″) to be out of drafts. It should have enough room for the dam to lie just outside an area where the puppies will snuggle but allow her some respite from them when she needs it. Of course, the bigger the bitch, the larger the box. It should have a lip to keep the puppies in. It should also have enough room for her to whelp the puppies without feeling crowded and allow you room to assist her if you need to. The whelping area should have a good supply of newspaper for sterilization reasons (newsprint is antiseptic) and to allow the bitch in labor to dig as she tries to nest. The floor itself should be covered with a rough surface like indoor/outdoor carpeting, to allow the puppies to gain traction while they are nursing. After a couple of weeks, cover this over with newspaper since the mother will probably no longer clean up after them and it can get messy.

It's also a good idea to have a "pig rail" (a protective barrier) around the inside flooring. This rail can be constructed from large broom handles. Its purpose is to protect the puppy that may crawl behind his mother and be trapped or crushed before she can see, smell or hear him. This is more prone to happen when there is a large litter. There should be an outside heating source (either under the flooring or just above) to make sure the puppies don't get chilled. Newborn puppies are unable to generate enough body heat to insulate themselves. It's imperative to supply that warmth externally. Listen for crying, this indicates something is wrong and it's often lack of warmth. Puppies will pile on one another to help keep warm. After about ten days their internal "furnace" can stoke up enough body heat to protect themselves. If the puppies are scattered around the box and not heaped together, the heat is too high.

There are some other supplies that are needed. Since the puppies usually don't come all at once, a place is needed to keep the puppies that have arrived in sight of the mother but out of the way as she whelps the next one. Most people use a small cardboard box with high sides. (Get a *clean* one from your supermarket.) At the bottom of this box put a heating pad or a hot water bottle. Cover it with a rough towel. Make sure it doesn't get too warm. After the dam has cleaned up each puppy, roughly licking it with her tongue and drying it off, she may wish to nurse it. Let her try. But most of the time Mother Nature is telling her to prepare for the next whelp. If the bitch starts to dig at the papers on the floor of the box, remove the puppy and place it in the cardboard box. You may wish to leave the box in the corner of the whelping box. However, if the bitch starts to whirl around while whelping, get the box out of there and up on some surface where it won't be knocked down. Be sure the bitch can see it at all times.

Clean, sharp scissors, alcohol and string should also be present. The scissors—which along with the string—should be sitting in the alcohol, are to cut the umbilical cord if necessary. Cut it at least 2″ from the puppy. Later, when the puppy is in the cardboard box, tie off the cord with the string. Disposable towels, washcloths, cotton swabs, toenail clipper, garbage pail and pans for warm and cold water are among the other supplies that you should have on hand.

Harking back to the "Be Prepared" motto, there should also be on hand a small syringe with a rubber bulb on it. These can be found in most drug stores and are called "aspirators." They are like the kind used for basting, only smaller. If you can't find the proper tool, use your basting syringe. The purpose of this device is to clear the puppies nostrils and lungs of excess fluid. Some puppies are born sputtering because fluid has accumulated in their nostrils or lungs during their trip through the birth canal. Try to suck the fluid from the nostrils first. Listen for a wheezing sound, this means there is still fluid. The puppy will also cough or choke. If all the fluid is still not out and the puppy is still sputtering, take the next step. Wrap the pup in the rough washcloth and—grasping it under the chest and hindquarters—raise it above head level and then swing it down between your legs to try and give centrifugal force a chance to expel the fluid. Hold the puppy face down during this maneuver. Be firm but gentle—never do this violently. Repeat two or three times. This should do the trick. The heat in the bottom of the cardboard box should dry out any excess fluid.

As the time of whelping approaches, the bitch will have been giving all sorts of signs. In the last ten days her shape begins to change as the puppies drop down lower. She now begins to look like a stuffed sausage. As the fateful day approaches, she will seem restless and be unable to settle down for any length of time. She acts as though she can't get comfortable. She will also want to keep you in her sight. She may or may not show an interest in the whelping box. Some bitches go to it, sniff around and walk away, while others lie in it and occasionally dig it up. Take her temperature on a regular basis as she grows more restless. A reading of 101.5 is normal for a dog. Just before whelping she can take a sudden drop to about 98 degrees. Unless the temperature drops, it's pretty sure there will be no immediate action. Oh yes, just so there is no misunderstanding, this may not be a piece of cake. Most bitches whelp at night. There are exceptions to these rules—but, "Be Prepared." It's a good idea for someone to stay close by the whelping box to keep an eye on things. You can take turns as the time draws near.

The most important sign to look for after her temperature starts to drop is the breaking of the water sac. There will suddenly be a small pool of water around her. This is often referred to as "the water breaking." This means that real action is close at hand, at least in a matter of hours.

When her temperature goes down, alert the vet that a whelping is imminent and request that he stand by if any problems come up. Of course, being a well-prepared person, the vet was alerted at least a month ago that you might need his help. He was alerted, wasn't he?

If this is the bitch's first litter she may be a bit confused and frightened by all this. Pet her and tell her how wonderful she is. Get her over to the whelping box and make her comfortable. She may pace, she may dig or she may settle down. But, rest assured, she will probably do all three. She will also make everyone nervous. Allow things to proceed on their own. Don't panic! Let her go four or five hours *if she seems in no distress.* HOWEVER, if she goes into hard labor and has not delivered a puppy in a few hour's time, check with your vet. "Hard labor" means digging up papers, heavy panting, obvious straining followed by short rest periods. She may also issue large groans as she bears down. All this is normal if it is followed by the birth of a puppy.

As she bears down, sometimes standing in a defecating position, sometimes lying on her side, a blob will appear issuing from her vagina and with one big push, she will force it out. Usually she will reach back and break the sac, cut the umbilical cord with her teeth, and start to lick the puppy to stimulate a cry. If she does not do so immediately or if she seems confused you need to step in, cut the cord, and take the puppy out of the sac. Then clear its lungs and nose and give it back to its dam to stimulate.

Many dams will eat the afterbirth (the blueish/black blob attached to the sac the puppy came in). Let her eat a couple. It stimulates delivery of the next puppies. If she makes no move to do so, remove it and put it into a garbage pail. *Keep track of the afterbirths*—make sure they are all accounted for. A retained afterbirth can cause great harm to the bitch. In fact, once she has finished whelping, be sure to take her to the vet—to check her over and to make sure no afterbirths have been retained. The vet may give her a shot of pituitrin or a similar drug to induce the uterus to force out anything that's been retained.

Puppies may come one right after the other or there can be hours between deliveries. Remember, as long as she does not seem in distress, any pattern can be considered normal. If labor persists for a prolonged time and no puppies are forthcoming, call the vet even though she has already whelped one or more puppies. You *may* have a problem. (For more detailed information on whelping, read *The Great American Dog Show Game,* by Alvin Grossman, published by Doral Publishing).

The vet will probably advise bringing her to the clinic where he can examine her to determine her problem. In most cases, it is usually only a sluggish uterus and he will give her a shot to speed things along and send her home to whelp the rest of the puppies. On occasion, there is a problem and he might opt to do a Caesarean section—that is, to take the rest of the puppies surgically. Usually he will perform this surgery immediately. Some bitches have a problem and cannot even push the puppies down into the birthing canal. The vet may take these puppies by C-section without having her try to go into serious labor. It's a good idea to have another small box, with a hot-water bottle in it, when you go to the vet so any puppies delivered there can be taken care of.

Mary Donnelly, writing in the March 1987 issue of The *Min Pin Monthly* also says to take a crate along to bring the bitch home if she has to have a Caesarean.

If you feel the trip from the vet will take an hour or more, you may consider giving the puppies the opportunity to nurse before you leave the office. This will also help you see if you will have any problems introducing them to nursing. You can take a supply of formula with you in the event you have to feed or supplement them.

Once home, the dam should be your first concern. Position her on her side with her back flush against the side of the whelping box. Don't worry, she won't be going anywhere for several hours. With the pan of warm cleaning water, dip your disposable towel and clean any blood from her incision or vaginal area. Because she has had a C-section, she will bleed a bit more than she would from a normal birth. (In a normal birth, the bitch will have a blackish discharge at first turning to bright red shortly thereafter.) Those little pups won't take long learning to explore the dam so you must keep her clean until she can take over. If you will notice, her tongue is probably hanging from the side of her mouth. Take a bowl of clean water and dip a cloth in, squeeze most of the excess water back into the bowl and just moisten her tongue and mouth. Never put water into her mouth at this point. She could choke because her natural reflexes are on vacation because of the anesthetic.

Don't leave the puppies alone for too long a period. They will get cold and hungry. There are a number of things that need to be done promptly. Begin with the smallest ones. Use a toenail clipper and take the tips off their nails to preclude their causing problems with the stitches. Eliminate as much discomfort for the dam as possible. Once this is done, introduce the puppy to his dam. Let it sniff and try on its own to fit a teat to nurse. If the pup needs help, gently open its mouth and squeeze a bit of milk on the pup's tongue. (Even without a C-section some pups have to be shown how to nurse and others just dig right in.) If the puppy won't cooperate, go ahead and give it a bit of formula. Continue this process until all the puppies have had their toenails cut and have been fed.

It is important to remember *you* must do everything for the puppies. The bitch may be "out of it" anywhere from 6 to 12 hours . . . or more. This is normal. During the time she is helpless, someone must carefully watch her and care for the puppies at the same time. Hopefully there will be help and shifts can be rotated. If not, roll up your sleeves.

As soon as the puppies are fed and the bitch has been cleaned up again, help the pups to eliminate their waste. Dip a cotton ball in warm water, squeeze out most of the excess and gently rub it on their genitalia. This should produce urination. Do the same around the anal area for a bowel movement. (This doesn't always work for there is a "plug" in there that is a bit hard to intially dislodge.) If there is not initial success in getting a bowel movement, be patient and try tickling the anal area with a swab. If that doesn't work, don't be too alarmed for the dam will soon be awake and will take care of this.

Generally, most puppies are worn out by now and ready to curl up next to their dam and go to sleep . . . but you can count on one or two little brats to be obnoxious and climb on her or try to see what's on the other side of the box. Let them explore but try to convince them to stay in the heated area. The dam is not going to grab them and cuddle them, so you want to keep them warm. They expected life to be different and are finding out that their mother isn't doing her job. Go ahead and clean the bitch again while they explore and you cast longing eyes at the bed nearby. NO!! you can't go to sleep yet!

Try and moisten the bitch's mouth again. While taking care of business, be aware if the bitch feels cold to the touch. Once all the puppies have settled down for a nap, you can drape a light sheet over the dam and the puppies. (Do not attempt to do this with a dam who has not had a C-section.) Now it's possible to lay down. There is a specific way to lay down. (Why should this be easy?) Stretch out, but be sure you are close enough to the box so a hand can rest against the bitch. It is not advisable to fall asleep but since you are exhausted, it will happen anyway. The bitch will undoubtedly wait until you have just fallen asleep to wake up. (Just like she had her emergency C-section at 3:00 a.m.) Hopefully, you will feel her stir and awaken.

Just because she starts to stir does not mean she is anywhere close to being left alone. Do not let her stand on her own right away. She is not in control. She may think she is but she could fall and injure herself and/or her puppies.

Usually the first time she stirs she will not need to relieve herself. She may, or may not, be interested in her litter. In most cases, she is going to be convinced to go back to sleep. Offer her a bit of water but not too much. Too much water at this time can cause nausea. Just about five good laps is all she needs. Be assured she needs cleaning again and the pups have been awakened and want to eat. So take care of this all over again.

Some dams will shake as they come awake. More often than not, this is caused by the anesthetic. This shaking can be slight or strong. In the event she shakes to the extent it could cause injury to the puppies, calm her by petting and covering the puppies a bit away from her. If at any time the shaking is too much, or there is a concern for any reason, call the veterinarian.

When the bitch really becomes restless she won't be talked into going back to sleep. Try to judge by the control she exhibits as to how stable she is. Take her outside when she becomes too restless. On her first trip, carry her. Place her in a safe area and be ready to assist her should she fall.

The rest of the recovery consists of your attention to the dam and the safety of her and her litter. If you are patient and see her through her "time of need," she will eventually ease you right out of a job.

Now, whether the puppies have arrived normally or by C-section, they are pursuing normal puppy behavior. Their primary concerns are keeping warm and being fed. A healthy dam will be able to take care of those needs. Be sure to keep a keen eye on both the dam and the puppies; watch for signs of distress . . . crying, being unable to settle down, and/or looking bloated—all portend trouble for the puppies. Call the vet. Watch the bitch to see if her discharge turns from a blackish color to bright red. See if she has milk and if the puppies can nurse from her. It is *extremely* important to stay vigilant for the next three weeks. It's a critical time.

There are times, however, when you may be faced with either losing the dam through complications from whelping or she cannot nurse her puppies due to a variety of reasons. YOU are now the mother and must deal with these orphaned puppies. Times like these test the mettle of any dog breeder. R.K. Mohrman, Director of the Pet Nutrition and Care Center at the Ralston Purina Company has some sage advice when you find yourself in this predicament.

Several critical problems must be addressed in caring for orphan puppies. Among these are chilling, dehydration and hypoglycemia. These problems are interrelated and may exist concurrently. Close observation and prompt attention if any of these problems develop are essential to survival. Of course, proper feeding of the orphan puppies is extremely important. A veterinarian should examine the puppies to determine if special therapy is needed.

Chilling

Chilling in newborn puppies (as described in the chapter Problems of Early Puppyhood) can lead to significant mortality. A puppy will dissipate far more body heat per pound of body weight than an adult dog. The normal newborn puppy depends on radiant heat from the bitch to help maintain its body temperature. In the absence of the bitch, various methods of providing heat can be used, such as: incubators, heating pads, heat lamps or hot water bottles.

Rectal temperatures in a newborn puppy range from 95 to 99°F (Fahrenheit) for the first week, 97 to 100°F for the second and third weeks, and reach the normal temperature of an adult dog (100.5 to 102.5°F) by the fourth week.

When the rectal temperature drops below 94°F, the accompanying metabolic alterations are life-threatning. Therefore, immediate action is necessary to provide the warmth the puppy needs to survive. A healthy newborn can survive chilling if warmed slowly.

During the first four days of its life, the orphan puppy should be maintained in an environmental temperature of 85 to 90°F. The temperature may gradually be decreased to 80°F by the seventh to tenth day and to 72°F by the end of the fourth week. If the litter is large, the temperature need not be as high. As puppies huddle together, their body heat provides additional warmth.

CAUTION: *Too rapid warming of a chilled puppy may result in its death.*

Dehydration

The lack of regular liquid intake or the exposure of the puppy to a low humidity environment can easily result in dehydration. The inefficiency of the digestion and metabolism of a chilled puppy may also lead to dehydration and other serious changes.

Experienced breeders can detect dehydration by the sense of touch. Two signs of dehydration are the loss of elasticity in the skin and dry and sticky mucous membranes in the mouth. If dehydration is severe or persistent, a veterinarian should be contacted immediately

An environmental relative humidity of 55 to 65 percent is adequate to prevent drying of the skin in a normal newborn puppy. However, a relative humidity of 85 to 90 percent is more effective in maintaining puppies if they are small and weak.

CAUTION: *The environmental temperature should not exceed 90°F when high humidity is provided. A temperature of 95°F coupled with relative humidity of 95 percent can lead to respiratory distress.*

Feeding

Total nutrition for the newborn orphans must be supplied by a bitch-milk replacer until the pups are about three weeks of age. At this age, the pups are ready to start nibbling moistened solid food.

Bitch-milk replacers are:
1. Commercial bitch-milk replacers, *e.g.* Esbilac, Vetalac, etc.
2. Emergency home-formulated bitch-milk replacer:
   1 cup milk
   1 tablespoon corn oil
   Salt (a pinch)
   1 drop high-quality oral multiple vitamins for dogs
   3 egg yolks (albumin)
   Blend mixture uniformly
3. Purina Puppy Chow brand dog food: 20 grams (2/3 oz. by weight) or 1/4-cup (8 oz. measure). Water: 80 grams (2-2/3 ounces by weight) or 1/4-cup (8 ounce measure). Blend into a soft gruel. Other formulas are to be found in the chapter Nutrition for Puppies and Adults.

Food Temperature

Since the newborn may have trouble generating enough heat to maintain its body temperature, the milk replacer should be warmed to 95-100°F for the best results. As the puppies grow older, the replacer can be fed at room temperature.

Feeding Methods

Spoon-feeding is slow and requires great patience. Each spoonful must be slowly "poured" into the puppy's mouth to prevent liquid from entering the lungs. The pup's head must not be elevated, or the lungs may fill with fluids. Newborn pups usually do not have a "gag" reflex to signal this.

Dropper-feeding accomplishes the same result as spoon-feeding but it is somewhat cleaner and generally speedier.

Baby bottles with premature infant-size nipples can be used for some puppies. Some doll-size bottles with high-quality rubber nipples are even better. Bottle-feeding is preferable to spoon or dropper-feeding but is less satisfactory than tube-feeding. Tube-feeding is the easiest, cleanest and most efficient way of hand-feeding.

The following equipment is needed for tube-feeding:

Syringe: 10 to 50 ml., preferably plastic

Tubing: No. 10 catheter or small, semi-rigid tube that can easily be passed into the puppy's stomach. (Consult your veterinarian.)

Adhesive tape: To mark the depth of the tube in the puppy's stomach.

Disinfectant: To flush tube and syringe after each feeding. (Be sure to rinse thoroughly after disinfecting.)

1. Mark the tube. The feeding tube should extend into the puppy's stomach but not far enough to cause either pressure or perforation. Measure the tube alongside the puppy's body on the outside. (Tube should extend almost to the far end of the ribcage.) Place tape on the tube to mark the correct distance of the insertion. As the puppy grows, the tape can be moved so the tube can be inserted further.
2. Fill the syringe and expell all the air.
3. Hold the puppy horizontally, with the head extended but not raised, so the tube will slide into the esophagus. This helps keep fluids from entering the lungs.
4. Moisten the tube with a few drops of milk replacer for lubrication. Insert the tube gently through the mouth, throat and esophagus into the stomach. If the puppy struggles, withdraw the tube and try again. Do not force it.
5. Gently inject syringe contents into the stomach. If a slight resistance is met, the stomach is probably full. Withdraw the tube.
6. Massage the genital and anal area with a moist cotton cloth to stimulate excretion. Stimulating the pups following each feeding teaches the pup to defecate.

Amount To Feed

Puppies being fed by spoon, dropper or bottle reject food when they are full. When tube-feeding, care must be taken not to overfeed, since fluid can be drawn into the pup's lungs. When adequate liquid has been injected into the pup the syringe plunger will become more difficult to push as resistance to flow increases.

In establishing the amount to feed a newborn puppy check the recommendations in the chapter on Nutrition for Puppies and Adults. Basically, a one pound puppy (when fed four times a day) should consume 21 cc per feeding.

Some puppies, during their first feedings, cannot handle the determined amount per feeding. More than the scheduled four feedings may be necessary for the appropriate caloric intake.

Monitor the pup's weight and continue to adjust the pup's intake proportionally throughout the use of milk replacer formula.

CAUTION: *Diarrhea is a common digestive disorder in very young puppies. Consult your veterinarian if diarrhea develops, as alterations in the feeding program may be necessary.*

Feeding Schedule

Three meals, equally spaced during a 24-hour period are ample for feeding puppies when adequate nutrients are provided. Four or more daily feedings may be necessary if the puppies are small. Tube- and hand-feeding can generally be ended by the third week and certainly by the fourth. By this time, the puppy can consume food, free-choice, from a dish.

Cleaning Puppies

As has been stated earlier in this chapter and elsewhere, the puppy's genital and anal areas must be stimulated after feeding to effect urination. Use a moist cloth or a piece of cotton to do this. This cleaning should continue for the first two weeks. If you do not do this, the puppy may suffer from constipation.

Bowl Feeding

By two-and-one-half to three weeks, the puppies can start to eat food from the dish along with the bitch-milk replacer.

A gruel can be made by thoroughly moistening dry puppy food with water to reach the consistency of a thick milkshake. The mixture must *not* be sloppy, or the puppies will not consume very much. As the consumption of supplemental food increases, the amount of water can be decreased.

By four weeks, orphaned puppies can consume enough moistened solid food to meet their needs.

It is better to avoid starting puppies on a meat-milk-baby food regimen. This creates extra work and can also create finicky eaters. Many times such foods will not meet the nutritional needs of growing puppies.

Size and Sex of a Litter

It is helpful to understand how the size and sex of a litter is determined. One of the most informative and entertaining articles written on the subject was by Patricia Gail Burnham, a Greyhound breeder from Sacramento, California. Her article "Breeding, Litter Size and Gender" appeared in an issue of the *American Cocker Review* and I will paraphrase the information so that it is most applicable.

The number of puppies in a litter at whelping time is determined by several different factors. The order in which they occur, are:
1. The number of ova (gametes) produced by the dam;
2. The number of ova that are successfully fertilized and implanted in the uterus;
3. The prenatal mortality rate among the embryos while they are developing.

It is not possible to end up with more puppies than the number of ova that the bitch produces. As a bitch ages, the number of ova will often decrease. Bitches don't manufacture ova on demand the way a male dog can manufacture sperm. All the ova a bitch will ever have are stored in her ovaries.

In each season some of them will be shed (ovulated) into her uterus for a chance at fertilization. Elderly bitches quite commonly produce two or three puppy litters. Sometimes, just living hard can have the same effect on a bitch as old age.

If a bitch does produce a large number of ova, what happens next? The ova need to be fertilized. If they are not fertilized, or if they are fertilized and not implanted, they will perish. If a bitch ovulates over an extended period of time and she is bred late in her season, then the ova which were produced early may have died unfertilized before the sperm could reach them, and the result can be a small litter.

Sometimes there is a noticeable difference in birth weight. It is a good idea not to consider the small ones runts. They may have been conceived a few days later than their larger litter mates and may grow up to be average-sized adults.

All the puppies in a litter are never conceived simultaneously, since all the ova are not released at once. Ovulation takes place over an extended period, so at birth some of the puppies may be 59 days old while others may be 64 days old. A few days' difference in puppies of this age can create noticeable differences in size.

The mature size of a dog is determined by its heredity and its nutrition. Its size at birth is determined by the size of its dam, the number of puppies in the litter, and their individual dates of conception. The small puppies could just be more refined than the others and could always be smaller. Only time will tell.

The sire is always responsible for the sex of the offspring. The rule applies equally to people and dogs. While dams are often blamed for not producing males, they have nothing to do with the sex of their offspring. If the bitch determined the sex of the offspring, then all the puppies would be bitches, because the only chromosomes that a bitch can contribute to her offspring are those that she and every female has, homozygous (XX) sex chromosomes.

What's the difference between boys and girls? It's not sugar and spice and puppy dog's tails. It's the makeup of their sex chromosomes. All of the chromosome pairs are matched to each other with the exception of one pair. Dogs (and people) each have one pair of chromosomes that may or may not match. This is the chromosome pair that determines sex. Sex chromosomes may be either X chromosomes (which are named for their shape) or X chromosomes that are missing one leg, which makes them Y chromosomes (again named for their shape).

All females have two homozygous X chromosomes. They are XX genetically. All males are heterozygous (unmatched). They have one X and one Y chromosome to be XY genetically.

In each breeding, all ova contain an X chromosome, which is all a female can donate, while the sperm can contain either an X or a Y chromosome. If the X-carrying ovum is fertilized by an X-carrying sperm, then the result is female (XX). If the X-carrying ovum is fertilized by a Y-carrying sperm, then the result is a male (XY).

What influences whether an X- or a Y-carrying sperm reaches the ovum to fertilize it? The Y chromosome is smaller and lighter weight than the X chromosome. This enables the Y chromosome-carrying (male) sperm to swim faster than the heavier X-carrying (female) sperm. This gives the males an edge in the upstream sprint to reach the ovum that is waiting to be fertilized.

As a result, slightly more than 50% of the fertilized ova are male. More males are conceived than females. However, things even up, because males have a higher mortality rate than females, both in the womb and later.

What if ova are not ready and waiting when the sperm arrive? If sperm have to wait in the uterus or fallopian tubes for an ovum to arrive, then the odds change. Female sperm live longer than male ones. As the wait increases, the males die off and leave the female sperm waiting when the ovum arrives.

This is the reason that some breeders advise breeding as early as the bitch will stand to maximize the chance for female puppies. The idea is to breed—if she will allow it—before the bitch ovulates. This allows the male sperm time to die off and leaves the female sperm waiting when the ova arrive. Whether this has a basis in fact is not known.

What can influence the number of males and females in a litter other than the time of the breeding? The age of the sire can influence the gender of the puppies. As a stud dog ages, all his sperm slow down. Instead of a sprint, the race to fertilize the ova becomes an endurance race in which the female sperm's greater lifespan and hardiness can offset the male sperm's early speed advantage. When they are both slowed down, then the male sperm's higher mortality rate gives the female sperm the advantage.

CHAPTER 25

Nutrition for Puppies and Adults

Alex Lewin

Nutrition of dogs can be maintained at a high level through the use of good commercial diets. It is not necessary for the owner to be an expert in nutrition, but some background in this science is helpful in understanding the problems that may be encountered in the normal care of your dog.

Dog food is generally prepared in one of two ways; dry and canned. Dry food is usually cooked cereal and meat blended together. The cereal grains need to be cooked or heated to improve digestibility. Fats are added to increase calories; vitamins and minerals are added as needed. Dry foods contain about 10% moisture.

A subject frequently discussed among "dog people" is the addition of supplements to commercially prepared dog foods. But supplements are usually unneccessary because major dog food manufacturers incorporate into their products all the protein, vitamins, minerals, and other nutrients dogs are known to need. The diet may be specific for a particular life stage such as adult maintenance or growth, or it may be shown as complete and balanced for all stages of life. When it is fed to normal dogs of any breed, no additional supplementation in the forms of vitamins, minerals, meats or other additives is needed.

Dry meals are usually pelleted, sprayed with oil and crumbled. Biscuit and kibbled foods are baked on sheets and then kibbled or broken into small bits. Expanded foods are mixed, cooked and forced through a die to make nuggets which are then expanded with steam, dried and coated with oil. Food to be expanded must be at least 40% carbohydrates or the expansion process will not work.

Soft-moist foods, which are considered dry foods, contain about 25% moisture. They can be stored in cellophane without refrigeration due to the added preservatives.

Canned foods come in four types:

1. "Ration" types are usually the cheapest and are a mix of cereals, meat products, fats, etc. to make a complete diet containing 50–70% water.
2. All animal tissue may be beef, chicken, horsemeat, etc. Generally this type is not balanced although some may add supplements. These are sometimes used to improve palatability of dry foods.
3. "Chunk" style has meat by-products ground and extruded into pellets or chunks. Some of the cheaper ones have vegetable matter mixed in. A gravy or juice is added.
4. "Stews" are meat or chunks mixed with vegetables.

Nutritional Requirements

The exact nutritional requirements of any dog are complicated by the wide variation in size, hair coat, activity, etc. Diets can be suggested based on body weight, but the final determination must be based on how the individual responds to the diet. Gain or loss in weight, change in activity, etc. must be observed and some adjustments made.

WHEN TO SUPPLEMENT. There are generally two exceptions to the rule that supplementation is not necessary when dogs receive a complete and balanced commercial diet. These instances are: (1) to correct a specific deficiency due to the dog's inability to utilize the normal level of a particular nutrient, and (2) to stimulate food intake, particularly during periods of hard work or heavy lactation. This includes hard-working dogs such as bird dogs or sled dogs and bitches with large litters that require a high level of milk production. The addition of 10% to 20% meat or meat by-products to the diet will normally increase food acceptance and as a result will increase food intake. At this level of supplementation, the nutritional balance of the commercial product would not be affected.

WATER. Fresh and clean water should be available at all times. The amount of water needed is dependent upon the type of food provided (dry, canned, semi-soft, etc.), but generally a dog gets 25% of its total water requirements from drinking.

PROTEIN. Ten of the approximately twenty amino acids that make up protein are essential for the dog. The dog must receive adequate amounts of these ten proteins for good nutrition. The natural sources containing these ten are milk, eggs, meat and soybeans. Sources such as gelatin, flour and wheat are incomplete.

Also important is the ratio of nitrogen retained to the amount of nitrogen taken into the body. In this respect, eggs, muscle meat and organ meat are all good. Some legumes such as soybeans are only fair. Most other vegetative proteins are poor. As dogs get older, this vegetative type of food tends to overwork the kidneys. This is especially important with chronic kidney disease in old dogs. More dog food companies produce products for each stage in a dogs life—from puppyhood to old age and including special diets for lactating bitches.

Another important aspect of protein is digestibility. A good quality dry ration has about 75% digestibility, while canned foods are up to 95%. Some typical figures for digestibility are:

Horsemeat	91%	Meat scraps	75–86%
Fishmeal	99%	Soybean meal	86%
Liver meal	88%	Linseed meal	81%

The dog's utilization of protein is dependent upon both the biological value and the digestibility. The digestibility of protein in the dog is related to the temperature to which the protein is subjected during processing. Some dog foods that seem to have proper ingredients at the time they are mixed, can give disappointing results. This may well be due to the processing at high temperatures or heating for long periods of time.

It is generally recommended that the dietary crude protein for adult dogs be 18 to 25% on a dry basis. For example, if a canned food is 12% protein and has a 50% moisture content then it is really 24% protein on a "dry basis." If the protein is of high quality, such as from milk, eggs, and meat, the total needed would be less than if it contains substantial amounts of the vegetative proteins.

FAT. Fats and oils have an important effect on palatability. A small increase in fat in a diet may greatly increase its acceptability to the dog. Fats supply essential fatty acids, particularly linolenic and arachidonic acids. Pork fat is an excellent source of these essential fatty acids. Other sources are animal fats, corn oil, olive oil, and raw linseed oil. A dietary deficiency of the essential fatty acids leads to defective growth, dry hair, scaly skin, and susceptibility to skin infections.

The absorption of vitamins A, D, E, and K is associated with the absorption of fats. Rancid fat destroys vitamins A and E. Extended use of rancid fats can cause hair loss, rash, loss of appetite, constipation progressing to diarrhea and even death. Commercial dog foods must therefore use an antioxidant to retard rancidity.

The principal danger of excess fat in the diet is that it contains more energy than is needed and leads to storage of fat and obesity.

CARBOHYDRATES. Requirements for carbohydrates in the dog are not known. The dog can utilize as much as 65 to 70% in his diet. Since this is the cheapest source of energy, it composes the major part of commercial foods. Carbohydrates are well utilized if properly prepared. Potatoes, oats and corn are poorly utilized unless cooked. High levels of uncooked starch can cause diarrhea. Milk can upset some dogs as some do not have the lactase enzyme needed to digest lactose, the milk sugar. Fresh cow's milk is 50% lactose. In some dogs, a ration with as much as 10% dried skim milk may cause diarrhea.

FIBER. Fiber is also a part of the carbohydrate portion of the ration. It is only slightly digested. Some fibers absorb water and produce a more voluminous stool. This can help stimulate intestinal action, especially in old or inactive animals. Fiber aids in the prevention of constipation and other intestinal problems. Most foods have 1 to 8% fiber. Reducing diets may have as much as 32% fiber. Sources of fiber are cellulose, bran, beet pulp, and string beans.

GROSS ENERGY. Dogs expend energy in every form of body activity. This energy comes from food or from destruction of body sources. Carbohydrates and fats provide the main source of energy for dogs. Caloric requirements are greater per pound of body weight for small dogs than for large dogs. From Table VII-2, determine the number of calories per pound of body weight a puppy requires for his age. For example, a ten-week old puppy weighing 10 lbs. would require 650 calories per day. At twelve weeks and weighing 15 lbs. he would need 840 calories daily. Divide the number of calories contained in one pound of feed into the number of calories required by the puppy on a daily basis to determine how much to offer the puppy initially. Using the example: At ten weeks, he requires 650

Weeks	1	2	3	4	5	10	15	20	25	30	40	50	60	70
5	100	200	300	400	500	1000	1500							
6	90	180	270	360	450	900	1350							
7	80	160	240	320	400	800	1200							
8	75	150	225	300	375	750	1125	1500						
9	70	140	210	280	350	700	1050	1400						
10		130	195	260	325	650	975	1300	1625					
11			180	240	300	600	900	1200	1500	1680				
12				224	280	560	840	1128	1400	1560				
13				208	260	520	780	1040	1300	1440	1920			
14					240	480	720	960	1200	1350	1800			
15						450	675	900	1125	1260	1680	2100		
16						420	630	840	1050	1170	1560	1950		
17							585	780	975	1080	1440	1800	2160	
18								720	900	990	1320	1650	1980	
19									825	900	1280	1500	1800	2100

Table VII-2. Daily Caloric Needs of Puppies

To determine the number of calories needed by a particular puppy, find the dog's weight in the top row of numbers and move downward until you come to the line corresponding to the dog's age. The figure in the spot where the two lines intersect is the number of calories that puppy needs during a 24-hour period.

calories per day. Divide this by 690 (the number of calories in one pound of a popular dry puppy food) and the answer is approximately 1.0 lbs.

There are various theories on how often to feed a dog. The *Gaines Basic Guide To Canine Nutrition* establishes this schedule: Up to 5 months feed 3 times daily; from 5 to 12 months feed twice daily; over 12 months feed twice daily for the rest of the dog's life.

Divide the amount of food needed each day into the appropriate number of feedings to determine the amount of food to give the puppy at each feeding. For example: For a twelve-week old pup, the appropriate number of feedings per day is three. Divide the puppy's 1 lb of food into 3 servings of 1/3 lb. each.

Russell V. Brown writing in the February 1987 issue of *The Basenji*, points out "While caloric needs vary with age and activity, a rule of thumb is that for dogs of 5 to 65 lbs. the need is $S(33\text{-}1/4\ X) = kcal/day.$* In this case "X" is the body weight in pounds. A 20-lb. dog would work out as $20(33\text{-}20/4) = 20(28) = 560$ kcals per day. For dogs over 65 lbs., the formula is $18X = kcal/day$. The following adjustments are recommended:

   a. Age adjustments
      1. add 10% for dogs 1 year of age
      2. add 30% for dogs 6 months of age
      3. add 60% for dogs 3 months of age

   b. Activity variable
      1. add 25% for moderate activity
      2. add 60% for heavy activity (hunting or coursing)

   c. Pregnancy and lactation
      1. from conception to whelping—increase 20%
      2. at whelping—increase 25%
      3. 2nd week of lactation—increase 50%
      4. 3rd week of lactation—increase 75%
      5. 4th week of lactation—increase 100%

   ***Authors Note:** "Kcal" is the scientific term for what laymen call calorie."*

Some find that the portion-control methods such as the feeding schedule listed above is inconvenient. They opt for the self-feeding method which is also called the free-choice method. Free choice ensures that the puppy's food consumption correlates with his rate of growth. The idea behind free-choice feeding is that it provides reasonable assurance that the puppy is obtaining all he needs for growth, even though these needs are essentially changing.

Free-choice advocates believe that dogs generally know quite accurately what their needs are and eat accordingly. (This is generally true.) Free-choice works especially well for the pup who dawdles over his food for hours. A slight variation on the free-choice scheme is to feed the pup all he can eat in a specified time period, usually 20 minutes. The pup would be fed for those time periods a certain number of times a day. This timed method may not be suitable for the slow or picky eater (or the glutton) for that matter. Studies have indicated that free-choice eaters tend to turn out heavier by some 23% and that these weight differences were principally in body fat.

Other controlled studies have proven that overfeeding can cause skeletal problems. When overfed, puppies may develop hip dysplasia (a disintegration of the ball and socket joint) more often, earlier, and more severely, than littermates who were fed less. Breeds larger in size are particularly vulnerable to these skeletal defects.

If in doubt on how much to feed, slight underfeeding is preferable to overfeeding. Studies have shown no serious effects from slight underfeeding. On the contrary, when obesity develops through overfeeding, the number of fat cells increase in the puppy. Facts prove that the chance of a dog being obese as an adult has its roots in overfeeding as a puppy.

Regardless of the feeding method used, food should be served lukewarm or at room temperature. If the food is prepared with an ingredient that can spoil quickly, such as meat or milk, be sure to serve fresh food only.

Estimating Caloric Content

In determining how much to feed a dog, use the following:

    a. Dry food usually contains about 1360 calories per pound.
    b. Canned food can be estimated at 475 calories per pound.

MINERALS. Calcium and phosphorus are needed in a ratio of 1.2 parts calcium to 1 part phosphorous. A deficiency causes rickets and other less serious diseases. Young and old dogs need additional calcium. Common sources are bone meal, skim milk, and alfalfa leaf meal. Sources of phosphorous are bone meal and meat scraps. Vitamin D is necessary for proper utilization of the calcium and phosphorous.

Magnesium is needed for bones and teeth—bone meal is a good source. Sodium chloride should be in the diet as 1% salt. Sulphur and potassium are needed, and are usually in the foods dogs eat. Iron's best sources are liver and eggs. A strict vegetarian diet will cause iron deficiency. Trace minerals (copper, cobalt, manganese, zinc, and iodine) are contained in milk, liver and egg yolks for copper, in fish scraps for iodine and most other foods contain the rest.

VITAMINS. Vitamin A is important to vision, bone growth and skin health. Deficiency may cause lack of appetite, poor growth, excessive shedding, lowered resistance to disease and infection etc. Severe deficiency can cause deafness in dogs. On the other hand, too much is harmful and can cause birth defects, anorexia, weight loss and bone problems.

Vitamin D deficiencies are most often found in large breeds. Deficiencies cause rickets in the young and softening of the bones in adults, and irregular teeth development or eruption. Sources of vitamin D are sunlight, irradiated yeast, fish liver oils and egg yolks. Too much vitamin D can cause anorexia, calcification, and other problems.

Vitamin E deficiency may involve reproductive and lactation problems. It may be involved in muscular dystrophy. Natural sources are corn oil, wheat germ oil, fish and egg yolk. It seems to be of some value topically in wound healing.

Vitamin K is involved in blood clotting. It is found in egg yolk, liver and alfalfa. Most dogs can synthesize enough in the intestines.

Thiamine deficiency causes anorexia, weight loss, dehydration, paralysis, and convulsions. Overheating during the processing of dog food destroys thiamine. It is also commonly destroyed if dry food is stored in a hot location, such as a feed store without adequate cooling facilities. Best natural sources are raw liver, wheat germ and brewer's yeast. High-carbohydrate diets (particularly bread and potatoes) increase the need for thiamine. Fats may decrease the need.

Riboflavin, niacin and pyridoxine are all B vitamins found in liver, wheat germ, leafy vegetables, yeast and milk. Riboflavin deficiency can cause dry scaly skin, muscular weakness, abnormal redness of hindlegs and chest due to capillary congestion, anemia, and sudden death. Niacin deficiency can lead to pellagra or black tongue disease with oral ulcers. Pyridoxine deficiency can also cause anemia.

Choline deficiency causes fatty liver. Best sources are liver, yeast and soybean oil.

Biotin deficiency causes posterior paralysis and seborrhea. Raw egg whites contain a substance that ties up biotin. A diet of all raw egg whites should not be fed. Natural sources are liver and yeast.

B-12 is important in blood formation. Dogs used in heavy work need a good supply. Dogs produce B-12 in their intestines and when given foods that have enough B-12, can function adequately. Large doses of antibiotics may stop this synthesis. Best sources are liver, milk, cheese, eggs and meat.

Vitamin C (ascorbic acid) deficiency may cause delayed wound healing and scurvy-type lesions of the mouth and gums, loose teeth, bloody diarrhea, and tender joints. Generally the bacteria in the gut produce sufficient C. However, intestinal problems can affect the amount produced.

The 7.5% protein in bitches' milk is equivalent to 30% dry dog food, but is probably all digestible. Dry dog food protein is only about 80% digestible unless it comes from a meat or fish source. A pup must consume twice as much cow's milk to get the protein of bitches' milk, but would then get three times as much lactose sugar which it has difficulty digesting. As a result, pups frequently have diarrhea on cow's milk. Non-fat dry milk is even worse for without the fat the percentage of lactose is even greater. (For more information on feeding the bitch, see chapter on The Bitch and Her Puppies.)

Table VII-3. Milk From The Lactating Bitch

	Bitch	Evaporated Milk	Cow
Fat	8.3%	6.6%	4.0%
Protein	7.5%	5.8%	3.5%
Lactose	3.7%	8.2%	4.9%
Calories	1.2	1.15	0.68

Weaning Puppies

It's a good idea to feed puppies a diet of 115 calories for each pound of their body weight three to four times a day. Begin to wean them at four to seven weeks of age. Seven to ten days should see the puppies no longer dependent on their mother. Often the dam will begin to wean the puppies on her own. During the weaning process, take the dam away during the day for gradually longer periods of time. Feed them three times a day. Puppies often gulp a lot of air when learning to eat solid foods. Slow them down by spreading out the food in a large pan. Chopped meat and small kibble may be better than finely ground meal because it passes through the intestines more slowly, causing fewer digestive problems.

Feeding Older Puppies

The first step in any puppy's feeding program is to weigh him. From birth through six months the breeder should weigh and record each pup's growth weekly.

The next step is to determine the diet to be fed. This depends, in a large measure, on the stage of growth the puppy has reached. Young puppies require twice as much energy per unit of body weight as an adult dog. But feeding the rapidly-growing puppy twice as much food of the adult variety is not the answer. The diet must include a protein with high net protein utilization value. This is because the puppy's digestive tract is immature and cannot fully digest and utilize the energy and nutrients which adult foods include. The total need for all nutrients is double for a puppy, and the nutrients must be in an easily digestible form.

When acquiring a puppy from a breeder be sure to find out the details of his feeding program. The breeder should provide you with the type of food the pup is used to, the feeding times and the amount of food to be fed. Whether you agree with the program or not, duplicate it for several days until the pup is accustomed to his new surroundings.

After the puppy is settled, don't hesitate to change food or feeding methods if there is a need to do so. Using the information above, use good judgment in selecting the commercial dog food best suited to his size and needs. Make the change in his diet gradual so as not to cause diarrhea. Dry food is the most popular because it is normally most convenient, feed efficient, and economical.

Be sure to choose a high quality dog food. Not only will it be better for the dog's health but it will also require less food to meet his nutritional needs. Don't be misled by how much the puppy eats, it's the performance of the food that counts. A lower quality food is also less digestible and will result in the puppy eating more to compensate; the increased food eaten will further reduce the digestibility of the food.

Don't try to save money by feeding maintenance, or low-quality foods. The pup can't possibly eat all he would need to meet his requirements for growth. The puppy will end up with a pot-bellied appearance, slower growth, poor muscle and bone development and less resistance to disease and parasites.

Regardless of the form of commercial dog food used, Donald R. Collins, DVM, author of *The Collins Guide To Dog Nutrition,* believes every growing puppy should have liver in his diet. Liver is a good source of most of the good things an animal needs. It can be fed chopped, raw, or slightly braised. To avoid giving the puppy diarrhea, feed small amounts at first and gradually increase to no more than 10% of his total diet.

Catering to a dog's nutritional needs is one thing; catering to his nutritional desires is yet another. Do not permit a puppy to dictate his food preferences. This reverses the positions of authority and can cause training problems as well. It could also create nutritional deficiencies.

The goal should be that by the time a pup has reached maturity, his digestive system should be capable of handling all the foods he will eat during his adult life. This program should help him to reach the average (as stipulated in the breed standard) height and weight. A great deal of time, effort, and money will—no doubt—be invested in this young prospective puppy. Many hopes and dreams may be fulfilled through him; help him to fulfill those aspirations by providing him with the best possible feeding program.

And when he reaches adulthood, continue feeding him a well-balanced nutritious diet. The payback is a healthy, handsome dog.

Material for the content of this chapter is drawn from three main sources: (1) "Nutrition and Feeding of Basenjis," by Russell V. Brown which appeared in the February 1987 issue of *The Basenji*; (2) "Feeding Your Puppy," by Ann Bierman which appeared in the March 1987 issue of *Golden Retriever Review*; and, (3) "Supplementation—May Be Hazardous to Your Pet's Health" by R.K. Mohrman published in the March/April 1980 issue of the *Great Dane Reporter*.

CHAPTER 26

Problems of Early Puppyhood

Breeding and raising puppies is a complex process. There are many factors that decide how puppies will turn out. Will they survive the embryonic stage only to fall victim to the myriad diseases of puppyhood? Often a puppy has no control over its own destiny. The health of the dam, the presence of parasites, the cleanliness of the environment and the quality of care his dam and breeders give to him, are all controlling factors in whether he survives. Whether or not a puppy develops along normal lines either before or after birth depends entirely on its environment and the hereditary characteristics and tendencies which have been handed down by its parents. Puppies which are fed inadequate, unbalanced diets not only fail to grow properly but also develop nutritional diseases and structural distortions such as anemia, rickets, etc. The diet provided his dam and that provided for the growing puppy constitutes part of his environment. If the diet is unsuitable, the puppy's environment is unfavorable for proper development.

Nursing

Bruce R. Wittels, DVM, writing in the January/February 1985 issue of the *Great Dane Reporter* states:

The ability to nurse is the most important factor in determining whether a newborn pup will survive the first few hours and days of life. Nursing ability depends upon the maturity of the litter, body temperature and adequate lung function. If a bitch is underfed or improperly nourished before and during pregnancy, the likelihood of premature whelping is greatly increased. This leads to underdevelopment of the lungs and therefore failure of the lungs to fully oxygenate the blood. This limited respiratory capacity causes a decreased nursing time due to more time needed for breathing. With a premature whelping there is a lack of subcutaneous fat on the newborn and as a result a decreased body temperature and chilling. Because of this, energy is expended to keep the body as warm as possible and less energy is available for nursing. Diminished nursing ability is directly caused by chilling with lack of energy secondary. Therefore, it is important not to let the litter become chilled no matter what the cause.

There are other diseases, cited later in this chapter, other than malnutrition of the bitch, that affect the nursing ability of the newly born.

It is very important that the pups suckle within the first few hours. The ingestion of nutrients gives them energy and strength since they are no longer being nourished by the placenta. Colostrum is only present in the mammary glands for four to six hours and nursing during this time provides maternal immunity to many viral and bacterial diseases. The puppy acquires some maternal immunity via the placenta during pregnancy, but the most important acquistion is by the ingestion of colostrum. If a pup isn't nursing, it must be placed on a nipple and encouraged to do so. It may be necessary to milk the bitch and force feed the pup. If all efforts are unsuccessful, put the pup on antibiotics, watch it closely, and keep it confined until it can be started on a series of adult vaccines.

Most people know that at six weeks of age their dogs need to be vaccinated, but apparently what isn't known is which vaccines are given. Almost all puppies seen in my practice that have previously been vaccinated have been given an adult vaccine at six weeks of age; i.e. distemper, hepatitis, leptospirosis, and parvovirus combination—this is not proper. If the bitch had previously been vaccinated, this vaccine has no beneficial effect and can do possible harm.

Colostrum contains many antibodies called immunoglobulins which function to destroy bacteria and viral infections to which a pup is exposed. These immunoglobulins last for approximately eight to ten weeks. If an adult vaccine is used at six weeks of age they act as foreign viruses and are destroyed by the antibodies of maternal immunity. This vaccine can be injurious to the animal if it is simultaneously being infected with the real disease entity. The specific immunoglobulins are then divided between destroying the real infection and the vaccine. If the viral strength is more than that of the antibodies, the body will succumb to the disease.

Many immunologists believe that six-week old dogs should be vaccinated with a human measles vaccine and a killed parvovirus vaccine. Human measles vaccine boosts the maternal immunity against canine distemper and does not challenge it. A killed parvovirus vaccine is used due to the lack of transmission of adequate antibodies from the bitch to properly protect the pups for more than six weeks. This vaccination will often help to stimulate the pups own immune system to produce antibodies against this potentially deadly virus.

Puppies should nurse for three to four weeks. During this nursing period the major emphasis is on nutrition of the mother, as well as all of the dietary needs of the litter which are derived from her. With a very large litter or if the dam is not producing enough milk, the diet should be supplemented with such milk replacements as Esbilac or Unilac. Generally, a pup should be gaining weight daily, at the rate of approximately one gram for each pound of body weight expected at maturity. However, attempts to over-supplement in order to reach this goal are highly inadvisable. The following table, abstracted from *Lab Report 2, #4 Neonatal Puppy Mortality* was prepared by the Cornell Research Laboratory, Veterinary Virus Research Institute, New York.

Weight Gain
Two-fold increase at 8–10 days
(1 gm. of expected adult weight/day)

Body Temperature
Week 1–2; 94–99°F
Week 2–4; 97–100°F

Water Requirements
2–3 oz./lb./day (newborn puppies)

Caloric Requirements
60–100 kcal/lb./day
(newborn puppies can become hypoglycemic if not fed every day)

Parasites

An unfavorable environment may seriously hinder normal development before birth as well as afterward. The prenatal environment provided for the growing embryo may be unsuitable because the mother has been improperly fed and cared for during pregnancy or because she is infested with worms. Even though nature will rob the mother to feed the unformed young, the puppies may be so lacking in vitality as the result of malnutrition that they are either born dead or die shortly after birth. Newborn puppies which are suffering from malnutrition are not necessarily skinny puppies. They may be well formed and appear to be healthy, but like adult dogs that have waxed fat from an unbalanced diet and lack of exercise, they may be anemic and so weak that they are unable to cope with the difficulties encountered during birth and unable to adjust themselves successfully to the new environment. Puppies which are born with worms acquired from their dam, may not show signs of illness until they are three or four weeks of age, when they may sicken and die very quickly. There are a number of worm infestations that a breeder needs to be concerned about. Table VII-4 (taken from Dr. Leon Whitney's *This is the Cocker Spaniel*, published by Practical Science Publishing Co.) illustrates the wide variety of internal parasites and the probability of infestation at any age by percent. People have misconceptions about internal parasites. Some think you can immunize dogs against them. Others apparently think that when parasites are removed that is the end of them. Yet others have the idea that when a dog reaches a year of age he is no longer susceptible to them. By studying the table you will see that there is no time in a dog's life when he is immune to parasites, but in certain cases—such as coccidiosis—he is more likely to be infected when he is quite young. Because information concerning the proper care of the bitch (see chapter on The Bitch and Her Puppies) during pregnancy and the prevention of worm infestations is readily avail-

Table VII-4. Estimated Probability of Intestinal Parasite Infestation at Any Age by Percent*

Age	Roundworms	Hookworms	Whipworms	Tapeworms Flea-Host	Tapeworms Rabbit-Host	Rivolta	Coccidiosis Bigemina	Coccidiosis Felis
0–3 weeks	40	20	0	3	0	0	0	8
4–11 weeks	50	20	5	9	1	9	1	7
12–23 weeks	42	20	10	10	1	6	1	5
24–51 weeks	27	20	25	14	1	3	2	3
1 year	17	20	28	14	3	2	3	3
2 years	16	20	30	14	5	2	1	2
3 years	15	20	30	14	4	2	1	1
4 years	14	20	30	14	4	2	1	1
5 years	13	20	30	14	3	2	0	1
6 years	12	20	30	14	2	2	0	1
7 years	11	20	30	14	1	1	0	0
8 years	10	20	30	14	0	1	0	0
9 years	9	20	30	14	0	1	0	0
10–15 years	8	20	30	14	0	1	0	0

*Based on a study of 4,000 fecal examinations of Connecticut dogs.

From This is the Cocker Spaniel, by Leon F. Whitney, DVM, Practical Science Publishing Co.

able today, malnutrition and parasites need not be major causes of puppy losses.

Injuries

Injuries recieved either before or after birth may result in the death of one or more puppies in a litter, in spite of the fact that every precaution may have been taken to prevent such injuries. In the case of a large litter (but even in a small or average size litter), the embryos may be crowded together too closely to allow for proper development, resulting in distortions or in the premature birth of small, weak puppies.

Carelessness on the part of a nervous or inexperienced bitch undoubtedly accounts for the loss of many puppies which are born alive and which appear to be strong and healthy at birth. Even the best of mothers may occasionally sit or lie on a puppy, crushing or smothering it.

Pre-Natal Problems

The bitch's endocrine system—which is responsible for the secretions of such important glands as the thyroid, pituitary, adrenal and reproductive glands—may fail to work properly during pregnancy because of disease or hereditary factors, resulting in the arrested development or malformation of the embryos or in the premature birth of the litter. Abnormal functioning of the endocrine system may also cause various mating and whelping difficulties, such as dystocia (painful or delayed delivery), and lack of an adequate milk supply, which may account for puppy losses. If an inadequate amount of endocrine secretions (hormones) is produced within the unborn puppy itself, its development may be temporarily or permanently stopped at any stage. If development is arrested in the early stages, the partly-formed embryo or embyros affected may be aborted or reabsorbed by the bitch, or they may lie dormant in a "petrified" state awaiting the termination of gestation. If development is arrested in latter stages, the embryo may be born alive but malformed.

Many so-called "freaks" are the result of arrested development during the embryonic stage, resulting in such malformations as harelip, cleft palate, cleft abdomen, cleft skull, etc. All of the malformations are the result of the parts of the embryo failing to unite properly during development. If this failure is complete, any part of the embryo may be disunited by a deep cleft which may affect one side of the body more than the other, or it may affect both sides equally. If the growth of the embryo is retarded in a very late stage of development, only a slight cleft or other malformation may mar its perfection.

An analysis of litter records done by the Roscoe B. Jackson Memorial Laboratory indicates a higher percentage of puppies are stillborn or die shortly after birth in the first litter than in the second, third, fourth, and fifth litters. In a study of 337 litters, the percentage of dead puppies in the first litter was 5.7 percent, while in the fourth litter the percentage was 2.0 percent and in the fifth litter 2.8 percent. Because the cause of death could not be determined accurately in most cases, it is assumed that inexperience on the part of the bitch in whelping and caring for her first litter is partly responsible for the higher death rate. After the fifth litter, however, the death rate increased considerably, the percentage of dead puppies in the sixth litter averaging 18.7 percent. However, the steady decrease in incidence of death until the fourth or fifth litters indicates intra-uterine conditions in older bitches are more likely to be unfavorable for the production of normal young.

Fading Puppies

Fading puppy syndrome is often confused with toxic milk syndrome. It is estimated that 28% of all puppies die in the first week after birth. Some of these puppies suffer from lethal congenital defects, maternal neglect or accidents, such as being crushed in a whelping box. A large proportion of them, however, die from what is defined as the "fading puppy syndrome." The syndrome is part of a specific disease entity but perhaps the true "fading puppy" is the individual who: (1) was born malnourished because its dam did not receive adequate nutrition during gestation; (2) is too weak to nurse effectively; (3) is not receiving an adequate supply of milk; (4) is in an environment that is not sufficiently warm; or, (5) a combination of these factors. Unless supplementary feeding is started within a few hours of birth, with frequent weight checks to monitor progress, and unless adequate heat is provided, these puppies become chilled, weak, and ultimately "fade" and die.

Newborn puppies differ physiologically from adult dogs in several important ways. It is necessary to understand these differences to realize why puppies succumb rapidly to stress and to appreciate the importance of proper environment and care. They have body temperatures of 94 to 97°F for the first two weeks of life as compared to the adult dog's normal temperature of 100 to 101.5°F. They do not have a shivering reflex until about six days of age and thus cannot maintain body heat. Their heart beats and respiratory rates are faster than the adult dog. Newborns must be kept in an environmental temperature of 85 to 90°F for the first week of life; the temperature is gradually decreased to 70°F by the time the puppies are weaning age. They should gain 1 to 1½ grams daily for each pound of anticipated adult weight and should double birth rate in eight to ten days.

Neonatal Septicemia

Neonatal septicemia affects puppies from one to four days of age. It is caused by a staphylococcus infection in the vaginal tract of the bitch, transmitted to the puppy at birth. An unclean environment should not be overlooked as a precipitating factor in the disease.

Infected puppies have swollen abdomens with bluish discoloration on the flanks. They cry, are hypothermic, dehydrated and refuse to nurse. Death occurs 12 to 18 hours after bloating and crying unless antibiotic treatment is started immediately. Supportive therapy (heat, glucose and water) as described under Puppy Septicemia also must be administered.

Prevention involves a pre-breeding veterinary examination with antibiotic therapy if necessary to counteract infection. Since an unsanitary environment is frequently involved in neonatal (and puppy) septicemia, kenneling should be clean and so should everything to which the newborn puppies are exposed. This includes your hands and the scissors used to cut the umbilical cords. The cords should be dipped in or swabbed with iodine.

Puppy Septicemia

Puppy septicemia is the leading cause of death by disease in infant puppies, occurring from four to forty days of age. It happens typically in vigorous puppies that were born normally and are efficient nursers. Illness is sudden. First one puppy starts to cry. It has abdominal distension, diarrhea and may have rapid respiration. Then it refuses to nurse, becomes dehydrated and loses weight rapidly. Death usually follows 18 hours after onset of symptoms. Another puppy becomes sick, then another and another. Septicemia can demolish most or all of a litter within five to six days.

It is caused by bacteria of the streptococcus, staphylococcus, escherichia or pseudomonas types and frequently is associated with a metritis or mastitis (inflamation of the womb or of the breasts) infection in the bitch. Metritis is a uterine infection that may be acute or chronic. In the acute phase, the bitch becomes ill soon after the litter is whelped; depressed with an abnormal vaginal discharge and a temperature which may rise to 104°F. Chronic metritis may not cause overt symptoms in the bitch and, in fact, may not be evidenced until she whelps stillborn puppies or puppies that succumb to infection shortly after birth. Mastitis is painful and fever producing for the bitch. It can transmit bacterial infection to the litter.

Sick puppies are chilled, have low blood sugar, and are dehydrated. Immediate concerns are to counteract these conditions. Otherwise, the puppies will die too quickly for further therapy to be effective. They must be taken from the bitch and the following actions taken:

For Chilling: Slow warming. The sick puppy's body temperature has usually fallen to 78 to 94°F. It must be placed in an environmental temperature—incubator, heat lamp or heat pad—of 85 to 90°F until the body temperature has risen to normal for the infant puppy. Circulation must be stimulated by frequently turning and massaging the puppy during the slow warming process. Only the surfaces of the puppy's body will be warmed if this is not done. Temperature of the newborn puppy can be taken with an infant's rectal thermometer. Hold the puppy up by the base of the tail and insert the thermometer one-half inch into the rectum. Enviromental temperature can be monitored with an inside thermometer on the floor of the whelping box or incubator. Relative humidity should be 55 to 60 percent; this can be accomplished by using a home humidifier in the room in which the whelping box is placed.

For Low Blood Sugar (Hypoglycemia): Glucose therapy. The sick puppy's blood sugar must be increased rapidly and the administration of glucose solution, which is absorbed directly into the stomach, is the best way of doing this. Give the puppy 5 to 15% glucose in water, orally, 1 to 2 cc. (milliliters) every half hour. As the puppy's condition improves, gradually increase the dosage to 4 to 6 cc. These puppies should not be given formula; it may not be absorbed and thus may cause intestinal blockage.

For Dehydration: Water, given orally. The glucose and water therapy described above should be sufficient. If the puppy's condition is extremely serious, the veterinarian may think it advisable to administer subcutaneous hydrating solutions.

Other therapy, recommended by the veterinarian, may be to give antibiotics in some cases. Gamma globulin serum is considered effective. The owner may also be asked to give the puppies commercial formula or a few drops of *very fresh* liver juice every few hours after they have started to rally; this is strength enhancing.

As was learned in a preceding chapter, prevention starts with a prebreeding veterinary examination of the bitch. Bacterial culture and sensitivity testing should be performed on specimens removed from the vagina. These tests should be mandatory when a bitch has a history of uterine infection, stillborn puppies or puppies that die soon after birth from bacterial infection. Appropriate antibiotic therapy should take place before breeding if the bitch tests positive. It may be advisable to have another course of antibiotics 48 hours before whelping and immediately after whelping. In no case should this be done haphazardly; antibiotics should be given only when necessary and under veterinary supervision.

Every effort should be made to have all the puppies take colostrum, the "first milk" produced by the bitch for 24 hours after whelping. This protects the puppy from disease for the first weeks of its life. Lack of colostrom seems to be among the precipitating factors of puppy septicemia.

The bitch should be in a state of nutritional good health, fed ample quantities of good-quality commercial dog food product recommended complete for gestation and lactation. A feeding alternative is a complete and balanced puppy food product. Its high caloric density and protein content are advantageous for the gestating or lactating bitch. Liver, one-half ounce per thirty pounds, is considered an excellent food supplement for the gestating bitch, contributing to the strength and vigor of the newborn litter.

Kenneling should be clean and well ventilated with appropriate temperature and humidity. Unsanitary quarters will predispose the litter to disease.

Canine Herpes Virus (Puppy Viremia)

This is another leading cause of death in young puppies, transmitted at whelping as puppies pass through the vagina of a recently infected bitch. Puppies can also be infected by littermates or infected adult dogs. The disease is usually fatal if contracted by puppies during the first three weeks of life. Older puppies with herpes virus usually have mild upper respiratory infections from which recovery is uneventful. Susceptibility of infant puppies is thought to be caused by their low body temperature. The canine herpes virus has been shown to multiply optimally at temperatures of 94 to 97°F, that of the neonatal puppy. It grows poorly at the body temperature of the adult dog.

Affected puppies have soft, green odorless bowel movements; this is the first symptom. They may vomit or retch, have shallow respiration which becomes gasping as the disease progresses, and they refuse to nurse. They cry pitifully and continuously.

Keeping puppies in a high environmental temperature for 24 hours is the only effective treatment; but even this is problematical. For three hours the temperature must be 100 degrees. The puppies need fluid to be given orally every 15 minutes, to prevent dehydration. Then the temperature can be reduced to 90° for the remainder of the 24-hour period. If the puppies survive, the chances are better than average that they will live. Treatment is not advised if a puppy already has started to cry; this indicates that hemorrhaging has started and survival is doubtful. If it should live, chronic kidney disease may develop during the first year of life.

In kennels where herpes virus is a recurrent problem, a preventive method is giving gamma globulin serum as an immunizing agent to neonatal puppies from dogs recovered from the disease. Since canine herpes virus is spread by direct contact with infected dogs, urine and other body secretions, overcrowding in kennels is a factor in disease transmission.

Toxic Milk Syndrome

Bacterial toxins in the bitch's milk, caused by incomplete emptying of the uterus, produce toxic effects in very young puppies, (up to two weeks of age). Sick puppies cry, bloat, have diarrhea and red swollen protruding rectums.

They must be taken from the bitch, placed in a warm environment and given 5 to 15% glucose in water orally until the bloating has subsided. The bitch should be treated with appropriate medication to cleanse the uterus and antibiotics to prevent infection. The puppies can be put back with her as soon as treatment has started. They should be given a simulated bitch's milk product during the interval between glucose and water therapy and being returned to the bitch.

Hemorrhagic Syndrome

Puppies have minimal production of a plasma protein called prothrombin during their first two or three days of life. Prothrombin is produced in the liver and, in conjunction with vitamin K_1, controls the clotting function of the blood. Without sufficient prothrombin, a hemorrhagic tendency can develop.

Affected puppies die within the first two or three days. They are lethargic, weak and decline rapidly in condition. Signs of hemorrhage may be lesions on the lips or tongue. Surviving puppies in the litter should receive vitamin K_1. Most complete and balanced dog foods have sufficient vitamin K for growth and maintenance of normal dogs.

Canine Parvovirus

Canine parvovirus has been recognized only since 1978 when epidemics were reported throughout the world. In 1979, the virus became a formidable disease in the United States. At this time, random studies revealed that between 20 and 50% of dogs tested had significantly high antibody titers suggestive of previous parvovirus infection. By the summer of 1980, new cases seemed to occur primarily among puppies under six months of age and in family pets that had not encountered the virus previously. Recent information indicates that while the over-all mortality of those dogs infected with canine parvovirus is less than 1%, the mortality among clinically-ill dogs may be as great as 10-50%. These figures vary greatly among certain populations, since the severity of the disease appears to be influenced by such factors as crowding, age, and coinciding parasitic, protozoan infections. The incidence of the disease can be expected to decline as more dogs become resistant to the virus following infection or vaccination.

Canine parvovirus manifests itself in two distinct forms: enteritis and myocarditis. This chapter will concern itself only with the myocarditis form since it principally attacks puppies.

The myocarditis form occurs only in puppies born to a female that has no antibodies to parvovirus (one that has not had either the infection or current vaccination) and becomes infected with the virus during the first few days after giving birth. Lesions develop slowly in the puppies' heart muscle and heart failure is apparent several weeks later. The mortality rates in affected litters usually exceed 50%. Fortunately, the prevalence of the myocardial form already seems to be decreasing. The decrease is due to the fact that many breeding bitches have been infected previously and thus have circulating antibodies which are transferred to the puppies through the placenta and in the colostrum. This maternal antibody protects the newborns during their first five weeks when they are the most susceptible to the myocardial form of parvovirus.

Parvoviruses are especially hard to inactivate because they are resistant to heat, detergents, and alcohol. They have been known to remain active in dog feces, the primary source of infection, for more than three months at room temperature. A dilute (1:30) bleach solution is recommended for disinfection, because it will inactivate the virus. Since sanitation alone is not adequate to completely halt the spread of parvovirus, vaccination is the most effective method for control.

Brucellosis

Brucella Canis is relatively newly found and just recently recognized. Infections frequently become chronic. It occurs explosively and spreads rapidly among dog populations. The all-prevailing nature of this disease under kennel conditions has been documented. One study found 86% of adult dogs became infected and 41 of 118 females aborted.

Although all breeds of dogs are susceptible and the disease is widespread in the U.S., reported incidence rates vary from one through six percent, depending upon the area samples (there seems to be a higher concentration in the south) and the type of diagnostic test employed.

Manifestations of B. Canis are similar to each of the other species of Brucella.

In the bitches:
1. Infected females may abort their litter without previous illness (typically in the final two weeks of gestation).
2. Pups born to infected mothers may be extremely weak; all or part of the litter may be still born.
3. Following an abortion there is usually a discharge from the vagina lasting for several weeks.
4. Early embryonic deaths with termination of the pregnancy may occur, suggesting to the owner that the bitch failed to conceive.

Once the disease has been established in the male, the organisms are primarily transmitted venerally.

Other Causes

When confronted with neonatal puppy deaths, the breeder also should consider the possibility of other infectious canine diseases: distemper, leptospirosis, canine infectious hepatitis and the "newest" disease coronavirus.

Most puppy deaths are preventible. With: (1) selection of sound breeding stock; (2) a healthy, well-nourished bitch; (3) clean kenneling; (4) adequate heat for the bitch and the litter; (5) careful supervision of puppies' early weight gains; and, (6) prompt veterinary assistance should puppies start to "fade," cry, or have any of the early symptoms of puppy diseases.

CHAPTER 27

Choosing the Best Puppies

Heredity and environment both play a major role in the development of a puppy. Understanding how a particular bloodline "works" can help a breeder immeasurably. By keeping careful records of each litter, a breeder should be able to more or less predict the outcome of each puppy in a given litter. And optimizing the puppies' environment should allow the puppies to reach their maximum growth potential.

Of course, no system is foolproof. Puppies which start off looking like real winners may end up as pet quality. Also, a puppy could seem like pet quality, be sold at a pet price, and end up succeeding in the show ring. It's impossible to be 100 percent absolute each and every time. But the information in this chapter should help reduce the number of bad judgment calls, and should help you—the breeder—develop puppies to their maximum potential and select the best show quality puppies in each litter.

Keeping Records

Keeping records of each litter provides the breeder with an invaluable tool. It allows the breeder to learn from the past, to predict the development of each puppy with a measure of confidence, and to relax a little during the "plaining out" and awkward phases (more about this later).

The more information available on past litters, the better. More information allows the breeder to predict more accurately the outcome of a particular puppy. It also makes apparent patterns of development peculiar to a given bloodline. For instance, the "plaining out" phase for bloodline X may start at three months and end at eight months. So if a puppy still looks "iffy" at seven months, the breeder need not worry too much. However, if he still has a case of the "uglies" at ten months, he's got to go.

Development is always easier to predict if the breeder is dealing within one family. When new bloodlines are added to the genetic maze, development and outcome will probably be different from earlier results. Even experienced breeders can expect unpredictable results and a few trying times when outcrossing.

This is not to say that results are always completely predictable even if the bloodline has not changed. Individual differences will always play a major role in the genetic makeup of puppies. No system, no matter how extensive and accurate, can guarantee results every time. But by keeping good records, a breeder should be able to stack the deck in his or her favor.

What kind of records? The measurements that are most useful are weight, height (floor to withers, floor to elbow, elbow to withers), and length (withers to tailset, point of shoulder to tailset.) The measurements should be taken at birth, two weeks, four weeks, and then every four weeks until maturity is reached. Notes on head development, heaviness of bone, and personality should also be recorded.

With enough "statistical" information the breeder should be able to answer the following types of questions with some accuracy:

1. At what age will this puppy attain ultimate size?
2. At what age will this puppy attain ultimate development?
3. Will ultimate size and development be reached at the same time?
4. Can ultimate size be predicted by size at birth?
5. Do puppies in bloodline X develop at a uniform rate or do they go through growth spurts?
6. When will the growth spurts most likely occur?
7. When is the "plaining out" period for this bloodline?
8. Will one part of the body develop sooner than another part?
9. If more than one bloodline is bred at the kennel, what are the differences between them?

Being able to answer questions such as these can help the breeder predict the development of each puppy and to select the best show quality puppies from the litter. **Caution**—*just because a puppy is the best in his litter does not automatically make him a show dog.*

Puppy Development

Puppies are so cute and cuddly when they are born, each one is a winner in his own way. One may have a promising head, another may have great markings and a wonderful disposition. Your personal favorite may be the shy, gentle one in the corner. One thing is certain; most of these puppies will go through the awkward "plaining out" stage. Slowly, their promising heads will turn into ski slopes which could rival Sun Valley. Their bodies will lose all signs of cuddliness as they take on an adolescent appearance becoming gangly "teenagers." But have patience! Most puppies emerge unscathed from this stage, and redisplay most of their original promise. **Caution**—*a poor puppy going into this phase will most likely emerge still a poor puppy.*

Not all puppies go through this phase. Some puppies are born beautiful and maintain beauty, balance, and proportion throughout their first year. These puppies, called "flyers," outshine their gangly siblings. These puppies are few and far between. In some cases their litter mates also become outstanding dogs. However, when one of these comes along, treasure it.

A good rule of thumb for beginning breeders is to pick the show quality puppies at eight weeks of age, before the onset of the "plaining out" phase. At this time they usually will reflect their adult potential more accurately than later during the awkward phase. More sophisticated breeders can draw from past experience to determine the appropriate timing for selecting show quality puppies from their bloodlines.

It is impossible to predict the exact timing of a puppy's awkward stage. It can start as early as eight weeks, but may not start until the puppy is three or four months old. Most puppies are out of the awkward stage by

The same tri-color bitch at 8 weeks and at 2 years old.

the time they are eight months old. Or, a puppy could come out of it at six or seven months. Generally, the timing is similar within the same bloodline. From past litters, a breeder could determine that progeny of bloodline X usually enter the awkward stage between three and seven months of age. Then, when the next litter is born, the breeder can expect the same general timing. This helps reduce the amount of anxiety felt by the breeder. He or she may mentally "lock the puppy away" until it is seven months old and then pull it out for reevaluation.

Dentition (the loss of baby teeth and subsequent replacement with adult teeth) and rapid growth rate are the two main causes of the awkward stage(s) in puppies. During this period, the head can "plain out," losing all previous chiseling and embellishment. Even the deepest stop can turn into a sloping muzzle.

Generally, the head will improve with maturity, regaining its former promise. If the head remains in balance during the "plaining out" period, if the muzzle retains its squareness, the puppy's head will probably turn out nicely. If, however, the skull becomes broader than the muzzle, or the head loses its original balance, the puppy may not grow into a top-quality show dog.

A very nice head on a Basenji bitch at 6 weeks, 2 years (above) and 12 years of age.

The rapid rate of growth during this time can cause many puppies to develop an awkward, uncoordinated body. To make matters worse, different parts of the body can develop at different times. One puppy's legs may develop before its chest, giving it an "up-on-leg," pipestem look. It may walk around on stilts for months before finally filling in. Another pup may develop his forechest early. This may cause him to look low-to-the-ground and "dumpy" until his legs catch up.

Usually the body parts even out by the time maturity is reached, but not always. Many dreams of best-in-shows have been shattered by a puppy whose forelegs just never caught up with his hindlegs. Try to take it all in stride; learn from experience which dogs to pin your hopes on. Depend on overall balance rather than a few great parts.

An extremely enlightening article appeared in the September 1987 *AKC Gazette* by Patricia Gail Burnham (whom we have quoted before) titled "Understanding Flexibility and Soundness." She points out:

> . . . dogs with lots of front reach have long, flexible tendons and ligaments which allow the leg to reach forward freely. The problem is that you cannot just have flexible tendons and ligaments in the shoulder. If a dog has them there, then he has them all over. And if they are excessively flexible, then the topline may get a little slack, and there may not be enough support in the rear quarters to prevent cow hocks. On the other hand, if a dog has very tight, inflexible tendons, he will indeed have a strong rear, but if the tendons are too short and inflexible then the dog may have a restricted or hackney front, and can also have an inflexible back.
>
> Since breeders want considerable front reach on dogs that also have strong, sound rears, it may help them if they realize that those qualities are opposed. If one breeds for unlimited front reach and the flexibility that allows it, then that quality is likely to be accompanied by a tendency toward cow hocks and slack toplines. If the choice is to breed for super strong rears and the short, tight tendons that support them, then the breeder is likely to have to excuse some very restricted fronts and inflexible backs. What is actually desired, of course, is a dog with enough flexibility to give it considerable front reach, while he still has enough inflexibility to support a strong rear. And while that is a lovely dog when it does appear, breeding for it is like breeding for a razor's edge between the two extremes.

Moderation and balance should be your choice at all times when picking the best puppies. Burnham goes on to say:

> So, how much flexibility and reach is desirable and how much is dangerous [leading to hip dysplasia]? . . . When, if a little is good then more is considered better, and soundness and even the dog's health can be sacrificed in pursuit of an extreme. The key is to know when enough is enough. If a moderate extended trot is attractive, then a more extreme one with even more reach and the feet flying out in front like they are only loosely connected to the body is not better. It is worse both genetically and orthopedically . . . The only solution that seems promising is to breed for the middle ground, between the extremes of excessive restriction and excessive flexibility.

That advice is sound when followed in considering the total dog you breed. In balance with the whole, each part appearing to be more than the sum of its parts.

Environment

A puppy's genetic potential is determined at conception. But beneficial environmental factors help the puppy reach that potential. Having a doting mother, avoiding illness, eating nutritious food in the right amount, and proper grooming and handling all help the puppy develop into a healthy, happy dog.

Not all good bitches make good mothers. If a bitch is lacking in maternal instinct, a lot of tender loving care may be required on the part of the breeder. You will need to pick the puppy up, fondle it gently in your lap and stroke and speak to it. This needs to be done at least twice a day. Nothing is as cute as a baby pup who needs to nuzzle up to a warm, comforting body. Do not handle the puppy roughly. Use two hands when picking it up and putting it back with its littermates. Gentleness is most important.

If a puppy gets off to a poor start, either through poor eating habits or illness, it will probably catch up with the rest of the pack eventually. It may continue growing after its littermates have reached maturity in order to make up for earlier lost time. Similarly, an older puppy which may have been set back through illness will usually end up being about the same size as its littermates. Sometimes a breeder will write these puppies off before they reach their full size. This can be a heart-breaking mistake.

Another mistake commonly made is to discard the too thin or too chubby puppy. If a puppy doesn't have enough meat on him, the breeder should seek to determine the reason for his lack of appetite. There may be something in his genetic makeup which does not allow him to properly utilize all his nutrients. On the other hand, sometimes a puppy will simply be a poor eater. If it's an ingrained part of his personality there may be nothing the breeder can do to help him fill out. Read the chapters on "The Bitch and Her Puppies" and "Nutrition for Puppies and Adults" for more information on this vexing matter.

Chubby puppies tend to look the most awkward during the "plaining out" phase. Their extra weight exaggerates faults. Before the breeder's final evaluation, this type of puppy should be put on a diet. Watch their weight closely, for extreme and prolonged obesity can lead to permanent structural defects.

The normal, healthy puppy will display a glossy coat. Proper grooming is necessary for good coat development. Left dirty and matted, the coat will never obtain its potential.

Even if all the above guidelines are followed, even if the puppy has the benefit of the most experienced breeder, it still needs that magic spark to be a winner. This elusive spark of personality adds life and spunk to an otherwise empty, albeit lovely, animal. Without it, the dog may never be able to handle itself with confidence in the ring. A winning dog is flashy and knows it. He prances into the ring and says "look at me, aren't I something!" And sure enough, he IS something. A duplicate of that dog, minus the personality, could become the all time reserve winner.

Personality can be developed to a degree. Gently—and I do mean gently—playing with a puppy can help the puppy see that human beings are okay. Never lunge at a puppy or hold it in an improper manner. Both hands supporting the puppy underneath at the chest and at the rear legs is the proper way. Never frighten it or be rough. Puppies, like human babies, thrive on love and tenderness. Providing that emotional food will help the puppy gain confidence, and hopefully that "spark" of personality.

When grading out the puppies at eight weeks, do not judge them only in a posed manner. First of all, it's possible to crank a puppy around to get it to look the way you think it should look. All you achieve when you do this is deceive yourself. Look for a neck blending correctly into the shoulder. Check for balance—balance—and balance! Check for strong rears without evidence of hocking in or out. Look at the distance between the withers and set-on of the tail. Being a trifle long here isn't too bad. On the other hand do not exult because the puppy is shorter than the standard requires. How will he get his front legs out of the way of his driving rear quarters? Do not seek extremes. Put them down on the ground. It's important to see how they handle their feet and the shifting of weight as they move about. Any puppy that appears well coordinated, is up on his toes and cuts and turns easily—that's the one to seriously consider. A posed dog does not give you the view that you need to fully evaluate the puppy. Down on the ground, on his own, the puppy that acts like he is king and goes all out, plus handling himself well, is the one to mark and keep an eye out for his future development.

With the information gleaned from this section on Becoming a Breeder, you should have the knowledge to breed good ones and to be a successful exhibitor. Now it's up to you to put into practice what you have learned. Good luck!

CHAPTER 28

Frozen and Extended Semen

American dogs have made their presence known throughout the world. Breeders in such far-away countries as Australia, Sweden, New Zealand, etc. have made remarkable strides in successfully introducing the breed to their countries. There is, however, a major problem in importation of high-quality breeding stock. Stringent quarantine rules make it extremely difficult and financially prohibitive to import quality stock. Now, at long last, there may be a solution to this problem. Artificial insemination has been approved by the AKC under certain controlled conditions for use in this country. However, shipping semen over long distances has proven to be a formidable task.

In October and November of 1986, Howard H. Furumoto, D.V.M., Ph.D. writing in *Ilio*, Hawaii's dog magazine, cast a new light on the problem. Dr. Furumoto writes:

Recent research on canine semen preservation and storage offers Hawaiian dog breeders a promising future *[as well as foreign countries and continents that maintain strict quarantine regulations such as the state of Hawaii requires]*. The technology and expertise are available today to overcome the hitherto insurmountable barriers of time, logistics, and statutory requirements when considering the importation of new bloodlines.

To properly understand and appreciate the significance of these advancements, a short review of the evolution of the two methods of semen preservation are in order.

When approval was granted by the American Kennel Club to legitimize registration of litters conceived by stored semen and artificial insemination, the way was opened for Hawaii's breeders *[and breeders of other countries]* to take advantage of the golden opportunity presented by the new technology. Here, at last, was an AKC-accredited program which provided the means to circumvent the quarantine requirements and to eliminate the expense, inconvenience, and stress [of] shipping animals to and from destination points. An added attraction for many breeders was the preservation of valuable bloodlines for posterity by the establishment of frozen semen banks.

The original work on frozen semen was done by Dr. Stephen Seager and co-workers at the University of Oregon under the auspices of the American Kennel Club. The widespread interest he created led to *[a collaboration with the University of Hawaii]*. The objective was to determine whether or not we could duplicate the results obtained by Dr. Seager and his co-workers with the additional variables of air shipping frozen semen and bitches in estrus cycle. Much to our disappointment the four bitches shipped to Hawaii and inseminated with frozen semen shipped from Oregon failed to become impregnated. Subsequently, other investigators have reported similar negative results.

Because of the unreliable results obtained from the insemination of stored semen, canine theriogenologists began searching for more productive methodologies. Two such programs came to my attention. *[One effort was led by]* Dr. Frances Smith who had obtained her Ph.D. from the University of Minnesota. Her dissertation was based on the successful development of a semen extender which prolongs the viability of spermatazoa for up to seven days after collection without freezing.

Dr. Smith is widely recognized by dog breeders throughout the continental United States for her work with top line-breeding stock of various breeds. In her experience she has been just as successful in obtaining pregnancies with the use of the newly formulated extended semen as with natural breeding.

The second source of information *[led me to]* Mr. George Govette of the Cryogenics Laboratories in Chester Spring, Pennsylvania. Mr. Govette has earned the reputation of being the foremost frozen semen specialist in the country, having successfully registered 44 litters out of the approximately 50 now-recognized by the AKC by this method. In addition, he has reported successful frozen semen usage in Japan.

Gleaning germane information from both sources, Dr. Furumoto wrote a second article in which he briefly described the methods employed in semen collection, extension, preservation, storage, and preparation for artificial insemination.

He then projected the long-term benefits and potential hazards of these new technologies as they relate to breed improvement.

Semen Collection

Semen is collected for a number of overlapping reasons—for qualitative and quantitative evaluation, for immediate insemination when natural breeding fails or cannot be used due to physical and psychological inhibitions, for extending the volume of semen, for semen preservation and storage and for legal reasons (quarantine restrictions).

To collect semen, it is generally helpful to excite the dog with the scent of a bitch in estrus. Ejaculation is usually performed by digital manipulation and the semen is collected in a graduated sterile collecting tube fitted to a funnel-shaped latex sleeve which is held around the penis.

Three distinct fractions are observed from the ejaculate. The scant first fraction is clear and is secreted by the glands of the urethral mucosa; the opaque second fraction is secreted by the testicles and contains spermatozoa; the third and most voluminous fraction is clear and is secreted by the prostate glands.

Qualitative and quantitative evaluations are made after the semen is collected. The volume and turbidity of the semen are noted. Microscopically, the sperm concentration, motility, ratio of live to dead sperm cells and the shape and size are evaluated. Fresh undiluted semen is used for immediate artificial insemination.

Semen Extenders and Semen Preservation

After semen evaluation, semen of good to excellent quality is selected for preservation by one of two basic methods: chilling or chilling and freezing. In both methods, a vehicle—or media for dilution and maintenance called "semen extenders"—is used.

A great deal of research has been done to determine which media serves as the best semen extender. Various combinations of sterlized skim milk, homogenized milk, egg yolk, glucose, sodium citrate, sodium bicarbonate, potassium chloride and other substances have been used. The tremendous success in conception rate obtained by Dr. Frances Smith is the direct result of her newly-developed and tested semen extender.

Fresh, undiluted semen maintains its viability for 24 to 48 hours. Beyond this period, the viability of the semen may be prolonged for approximately 4 more days by suspending it in special media known as semen extenders and chilling. The viability of spermatozoa may be continued over an indefinite period of years by freezing the semen after it is suspended in a suitable vehicle (semen extender). By a gradual chilling process spermatozoa are conditioned for freezing at –70°C. The extended semen suspension is then shaped into pellets by placing single drops into super-cooled styrofoam wells. Enough frozen pellets are placed in each vial to yield about 50 million spermatozoa. Each vial is properly identified and stored at –70°C in a liquid nitrogen tank.

An alternative method of preservation is to pipette the extended semen into straws, one end of which is presealed. When the straw is filled, the top end is sealed and the semen is conditioned for freezing as with the pelletized semen, frozen, and stored.

Preparation for Insemination

The reverse of cooling and freezing is carried out to prepare frozen semen for artificial insemination. A suitable number of pellets or straws are selected to yield 100 to 300 million spermatozoa and gradually thawed to ambient temperature. At this point, an evaluation of the thawed semen quality is made. If viability and motility are satisfactory the semen is introduced in the anterior vagina or cervix of the bitch. At least two inseminations usually 24 to 48 hours apart is recommended.

Long-Term Benefits of Extended and Frozen Semen

In the context of *[foreign countries with]* quarantine restrictions, the greatest advantage to be derived from the use of extended and frozen semen is the by-passing of the trans-oceanic shipment of stud dogs and their confinement in *[government]* quarantine facilities for a specified period of time (10 days beyond the last insemination date). Extended or frozen semen *[on the other hand]* may be shipped in special compact containers over long distances.

Another attraction of extended and frozen semen is the flexibility and convenience of synchronizing semen shipment with the optimal breeding period in the estrus cycle of a prospective bitch. This advantage is particularly applicable when long distance shipment of stud dogs and bitches is involved in conventional breeding programs.

Venereal diseases, particularly canine brucellosis and transmissible venereal tumor may be circumvented, simply by the process of screening out potential carriers in the collection process.

By far the most significant benefit to accrue from extended and frozen semen is the concentration of proven or select gene pools for the improvement of the breed to more rapidly attain that elusive goal known as the ideal breed standard. By extending and freezing semen many more bitches can be inseminated with "matching" semen which would complement the desirable qualities of the sire and dam.

Disadvantages of Extended and Frozen Semen

In addition to the purely technical difficulties of implementing an artificial insemination program which [uses] extended and frozen semen, the success rate among breeders [so far] has been very limited.

The greatest concern regarding frozen and extended semen is the potential for intensifying or replicating undesirable genetic traits. Just as much as the potential for breed improvement over a shorter period exists, there is also the danger of perpetuating undesirable heritable traits, i.e., juvenile cataracts, subvalvular aortic stenosis, hip dysplasia, etc. within an abbreviated time frame. Therefore, a great deal of selectivity and objectivity must be exercised in the utilization of preserved semen. Any abnormal offspring must be dealt with objectively and decisively and either euthanized or neutered so that the genetic defect will not become established within a given line or breed.

Another area of concern is the requirement for meticulous attention to details of proper identification and documentation. One only needs to refer to the AKC regulations on "Registration of Litters Produced Through Artificial Insemination Using Frozen Semen" to appreciate the complexity of the stringent requirements.

Conclusion

Notwithstanding the objectionable features of semen preservation and storage, the technical and scientific feasibility of their application to canine reproduction have been amply demonstrated. The acceptance of the program depends—to a large extent—on the interest and support of dog breeders and the professsional and technical competence of veterinarians to deliver the "goods" when the chips are down. Ultimately, the success of the program depends on the development of special interest and expertise in the handling of extended and frozen semen from collection to insemination.

Success breeds success. Nowhere is this truism more important than in the pioneering [use of these techniques.]

SECTION VIII
Appendices

- Appendix A
  To Find a Basenji
- Appendix B
  The Health of the Basenji

The puppy you purchase will be with you many years. Photo courtesy of Alex Lewin.

Appendix A
To Find A Basenji

Once you've decided the inquisitive Basenji is perfect for your home and you have proper facilities for keeping one safe, the next step is to find the right Basenji. Try to lead with your head rather than completely with your heart in your search for a companion who should be with you from 10 to 15 years! This is a major purchase not only in price but also in future peace of mind. Don't be in a hurry, do your homework, and ask the right questions.

The first step is to determine what you really want. Will this be strictly a pet to be spayed or neutered, do you want to raise a litter of pups, or are you interested in showing and breeding Basenjis? Be honest about your plans for the dog when contacting breeders. The more you can tell the breeder about what you want, the easier it will be for him to determine if he has the right Basenji for you. You will not be helping a breeder if you buy a top-quality bitch and then have it spayed. In fact, the show puppies probably won't look very different from the pet pups when you go to see them all together. If you are going to insist on a particular color or sex, have it in mind when you call the breeder. Remember that most Basenjis are born in the winter. Will you be willing to wait? Think about what age puppy or dog will be appropriate for you.

Most people contemplating getting a dog assume they want a young puppy. Yes, if you get a puppy that is about 8 weeks old, you will be the one to mold its personality as it grows. The mental development of the puppy between 8 and 12 weeks of age allows for an easy transfer from breeder to new home. The puppy is old enough to begin learning to be housetrained, to continue the socialization the breeder started, and begin to learn good behavior. The key words here are "begin" and "continue." Raising a baby puppy into a well-mannered and well-adjusted adult is time consuming. Young puppies locked up all day while the owners are away become bored. The result can be the development of chewing or howling habits. If you have a busy schedule, perhaps you should consider an older dog who is done with teething, already housetrained and well-socialized. If you are not strong physically, you may find that a young dog is too much for you to keep up with. A young untrained dog can pull badly on a leash or require a great deal of clean-up and pick-up. Earlier in this book we pointed out that the average Basenji is not mentally mature until he is about two years old. You may be able to eliminate much of the work by looking for an older Basenji. Older dogs can make the transfer to a new home and develop a deep affection for the new owner. The development of that special bond takes a little longer but will be just as deep. New owners of older dogs usually feel that the dog is comfortable with them within the first month. The dog becomes very content and adjusted after four to six months.

Mature or yearling Basenjis are usually available from two sources. Breeders often keep several puppies from their winter litters to watch them develop.

Some of these pups do not grow up as the breeder imagined and they may be for sale as older pups or perhaps at just over a year old. From time to time breeders also have young champions available to pet homes. These two- or three-year old champions are well-socialized, accustomed to travel and maintained in top condition for the dog shows. The breeder may find, however, that he has just too many dogs to properly take care of. In this case, the breeder realizes that a particular youngster would be better off in a home of his own. The personality of the older dog is evident and the breeder can tell you whether this is a quiet dog, or a sensitive dog, or an active, busy dog. My experience with placing these older dogs has been successful. The prospective new owner comes to our home to meet the dog in question. Then we can both see if the dog is responding well to the new family, if he likes everyone and is comfortable with them. If it seems like a good match, the dog goes home with the new family while I hold their check and the dog's papers. If there is any unsolvable problem, the dog comes back to me and the check is returned. If everything is still going well after a month, I cash the check and sign the ownership of the dog over to the new owner.

Older dogs also become available through humane societies, Basenji rescue groups, and occasionally are offered from the owner through newspaper advertisements. If you work through a Basenji rescue group, you will be dealing with concerned breeders who will give you straight answers and good advice. They want to see this dog settled into a permanent home. If you come across a Basenji at the humane society or through a previous owner, the dog will be equally in need of a new home, but the backup advice will not come from as experienced a source. If you consider such a pup, be sure to spend some time with the dog before committing yourself to him. You should be able to tell quite a bit about his temperament and activity level within an hour's visit. Do try to find out why the dog is not suitable in its present home. Sometimes you come across a dog with a bad temperament or a hyperactive nature who will not develop into a satisfactory pet for you. However, many times the dog is available because of an unavoidable transfer to smaller living quarters, the break up of a family or, perhaps, someone in the family has developed allergies to the dog. Sometimes you see a perfectly ordinary "naughty" Basenji who is simply mismatched with the family.

Finding A Breeder

There are Basenji breeders scattered across the country and there is probably one or more within a day's travel of your home. Some breeders advertise in general dog magazines such as *Dog World* or *Dog Fancy*. Sometimes they advertise in a local or nearby major newspaper when they have puppies available for sale. Local dog clubs or federations of dog clubs sometimes offer a breeder referral service which is advertised in the classified section of the newspaper or in the Yellow Pages section of your phone book. Many breeders advertise in the monthly magazine *The Basenji,* and the Basenji Club of America's quarterly magazine. *The Basenji's* address is 789 Linton Hill Road, Newtown, PA 18940. A few breeders advertise in the American Kennel Club's *Gazette.* If you write or call the AKC at 51 Madison Avenue, New York, NY 10010, they will give you this list. Additionally, you can request the address of the secretary of the Basenji Club of America. The secretary can send you a list of members in your area who may breed or who may be able to put you in touch with breeders.

Many localities have dog clubs which sponsor dog shows once or twice a year. Watch for announcements regarding upcoming events in your newspaper. The schedules are usually available about one week before the show. Perhaps you can ask your local newspaper to run a schedule of the upcoming judging. Breeders are often only at the show the few hours just before and after the time Basenjis are to be judged.

Avoid buying a Basenji puppy at a pet store or through any dealer in dogs. You will be buying blind if you obtain a pup through any dealer or shop. You have no idea about the quality of the parents, the temperament of the parents, or the way the pup was raised and handled during shipment. The incredibly poor conditions common in mass production of puppies for the pet store market would shock you.

Contacting Breeders

Write or call more than one Basenji breeder in your search. Explain what you expect from a Basenji, what type of dog you are looking for and let the breeder know if you have any special requests. Then listen to what the breeder has to say. If you like what you hear, make arrangements to visit the breeder either at his home or at a dog show in your area. If you can visit the breeder at home, you will gain a better insight into that breeder's dogs. Seeing just one or two dogs at a show doesn't compare with seeing the dogs at home. It is a good idea to arrange to meet the dogs and breeder long before the breeding and puppy season arrives.

Don't make the mistake of falling in love with the first cute puppy you see without realizing that this pup is going to grow up and probably be rather like its parents. One family called me this past year to ask for help in placing a pup they had purchased from a pet owner who had bred his bitch. After chatting a little, the man told me the pup was just eight months old and was biting and growling at the kids in the family. The pup had been about three-months old when purchased. Then he went on to say that perhaps their mistake had been to buy a pup even though while they were at the pet owner's home the pup's mother had walked right up and bitten his wife.

Do ask to see the area where the dogs are kept. It should be clean. The dogs should be friendly and appear healthy. Keep in mind that a normally friendly bitch may become protective of very young puppies. This is one reason to visit the breeder before the puppies are due to arrive.

Be sure you understand what inoculations the puppies will have and what health guarantee will be offered. You should have the right to return the dog for a full refund if your veterinarian finds it unhealthy within a specific number of days.

When you've decided which dogs you like and which breeder you feel most comfortable with, arrange to purchase an older dog or make arrangements to purchase a puppy from an upcoming litter.

If there are no breeders in your area of the country, you may have to make all these contacts through phone calls. Puppies can be shipped by air freight to a new owner if necessary. A puppy between 8- and 12-weeks of age can make a non-stop flight without temperament problems being created. Shipping pups between three- and six-months of age is not as successful. The trauma of the flight for a pup of this age may permanently affect its personality.

Appendix B
The Health of the Basenji
With the help of Russell Brown, Ph.D.

One of the first things that attracted us to Basenjis was their natural, sturdy, healthy appearance. Their moderate size, neither large nor small, does not predispose them to the type of stresses and odd bone problems typical of the giant and miniature breeds. Hip dysplasia is almost unheard of in this breed because of its size and structure, although one does hear of an occasional Basenji with "slipped stifles." The natural head with its moderate jaw has plenty of room for all the teeth, therefore, missing teeth are rarely a problem. The infected ears or skin folds often found in drop-eared dogs or heavily wrinkled dogs are non-existent as well. The short coat is easily maintained without the health problems associated with some of the heavier coated breeds.

Early breeders were able to bring several difficulties under control by selective breeding. The early dogs were often born with inguinal hernias, cleft palates and undershot bites. The frequency of these conditions has been vastly improved over the years.

The small pool of foundation stock has, however, brought us several health problems which still appear today. New breeders need to learn a bit about hemolytic anemia, Fanconi syndrome, malabsorption and eye disorders. These hereditary conditions found in Basenjis are also found in other breeds of dogs as well as in humans. Basenji breeders, often through breed clubs, have supported research on hereditary disorders in the breed resulting in great progress in the study of the disorders and the elimination of deleterious genes. The breed has an enviable record for elimination of health problems.

Hemolytic Anemia

In the 1960's, some Basenjis suffering from anemia were presented to the Veterinary Clinic at Colorado State University. This stimulated many studies. Tasker, Searcy, Ewing, Brown, and Miller were particularly interested in the nature of this anemia. Eventually it was determined that this was hemolytic anemia caused by an enzyme defect in the red blood cells. Hemolytic anemia is a hereditary type of anemia in which the red cells have a genetically controlled defective pyruvate kinase activity. This is not a curable anemia.

Red cells are formed in the bone marrow and released into the blood stream as needed. The red cells must have some form of energy to carry out their functions. This energy comes from the metabolizing of blood sugar (glucose) by a series of chemical reactions carried out within those red cells. One of the last, and most important, steps in creating energy is carried out by an enzyme called pyruvate kinase. If a dog does not have enough pyruvate kinase activity, there will not be enough energy within the red cells for them to carry out normal activities so the cells have inadequate energy and die off rather quickly.

When this occurs in the dog with hemolytic anemia, the bone marrow must replace the red cells more rapidly than normal due to the short life span of red cells. The bone marrow is not capable of sustaining this high production of mature red cells, so immature red cells are released into the blood. The bone marrow eventually wears out and stops producing red cells in sufficient quantities. The dog then dies.

There are several symptoms of hemolytic anemia. Having less red cells and hemoglobin, the normally pink tissues will be pale in affected dogs. Pale gums and toe nails can be easily spotted. Anemic puppies are more sensitive to cold and may shiver and huddle together when their littermates are romping around. Anemic puppies that do try to run with normal puppies may act dizzy or faint. Anemic puppies may sleep or rest more, and are described as having "golden" stools. Anemic puppies are not usually diagnosed until about 10-months of age. Some die before a year of age. Most die before two years of age.

If you have an older dog that becomes anemic, it is much more likely to be a non-hereditary type of anemia caused by poisonous substances, severe parasitic infestations, dietary deficiencies of iron or other vitamins, or auto-immune anemia. All these are considered non-hereditary types of anemia and can also be found in other breeds of dog. They are all treatable and dogs normally recover from them if they get prompt veterinary care.

Concerned breeders have almost completely controlled the problem of hereditary hemolytic anemia in Basenjis. There was a great deal of discussion about hemolytic anemia in the 1970's. Scientists developed a test for those dogs who carried the gene for "HA." Dr. Russell Brown worked out the genetics as a simple recessive trait. Most breeders generally understood the problem and tested their breeding stock for several generations. The heredi-tary anemia is now all but gone from the breed. However, the test for the defective gene is not all that simple and is subject to occasional errors. There is still a small chance that a dog carrying the defective gene may not have been tested or may have been tested as clear and used in breeding. It might be wise at this time (almost 20 years since the first flurry of testing), to again retest the basic Basenji breeding stock in order to guard against any carriers who may have slipped through the first testing. There really is no reason any Basenji should have to suffer from hereditary hemolytic anemia.

Malabsorption

This disease has more recently been named Immunoproliferative Small Intestinal Disease ("IPSID") and was previously called Diarrheal Syndrome. These names are sometimes used interchangeably in literature and references to this problem can be found under these various names in veterinary literature. There have been quite a few technical papers appearing in the *Journal of the American Veterinary Association* and the *American Journal of Veterinary Research*. The earliest articles appeared in 1976. The articles have been written by J.R. Easiey, E.B. Breitschwerdt and R. Ochoa.

The disease was first associated with diarrhea which is a typical symptom of IPSID. Edward Breitschwerdt, DVM, wrote that his preliminary studies suggest that, although the clinical signs of this disease entity relate primarily to intermittent anorexia (loss of appetite), chronic diarrhea, and weight loss, the disease appears to affect multiple organ systems including the skin, liver, endocrine system, immune system and gastrointestinal tract.

Dogs with IPSID often show signs of this condition over a period of several years. Most affected dogs have diarrhea along with periods of profound anorexia. However, some affected dogs have an excellent appetite but continue to lose weight. Despite the obvious illness of these dogs, they generally stay alert, active and playful. Most dogs with this disease have a decrease in serum proteins. The albumin content of the serum is especially likely to be low, while the gamma globulins are usually increased. When necropsied, the common finding in the affected dogs is lymphocytic plasmacytic enteritis. This simply means that the wall of the intestine contains many more lymphocytes and plasmacytes (a type of cell involved in immune reactions) than are normally present in that tissue. Changes in the stomach wall may also be found in the majority of the affected dogs.

One or more stresses, such as boarding, transport, vaccination, estrus, pregnancy, or major surgery are often documented before the development of diarrhea in some dogs. The disease syndrome, once established in an individual dog, may represent a self-perpetuating form of stress which contributes to the continuation of the clinical signs. The causes of this disease have not been established although some breeders suspect it to be caused by food allergies. The tendencies to these allergies may prove to be genetic.

Avoiding the disease in breeding stock will probably help establish a line of dogs without many problems with IPSID. Dogs with poor appetites, or good appetites but who do not maintain their weight at proper levels, dogs who come down with diarrhea when stressed or dogs who are particularly susceptible to upsets when their diets are varied should be avoided as breeding stock. Edward Breitschwerdt, North Carolina State University, Raleigh, continues to study this problem and has offered some advice on maintaining and controlling the symptoms in affected dogs. He writes, "It would appear that dietary manipulations, minimizing stress in the dog's environment and oral tylosin, metrometronidazole or trimethoprim plus sulfadiazine, represent the most beneficial forms of treatment currently available." In the past, living with a dog with this disease was like watching your friend starve to death. Affected dogs are being maintained in good health for much longer than they were 10 years ago. This is an encouraging development.

Eye Abnormalities

The most common eye problem in Basenjis is persistent pupillary membrane ("PPM"). It is also present in other breeds, as well as humans, and rarely develops into a debilitating problem.

As an embryo develops, the eye forms from an invagination, or the development of a pocket on each side of the head of the embryo. At one point it is like two teacups inset in the sides of the head. The pocket deepens and the rims of the cup come together until they meet forming the eye under a double layer of tissue. The iris then forms. The iris is the colored part of the eye and has a hole in the middle (the pupil) through which light will travel to the photosensitive rear part (the retina). Both the pupil and iris are under a membrane at this time. Before birth when the eyes are formed, they move with the development of the face to the front of the face with the membranes disappearing shortly before birth. Sometimes a part of the membrane remains and can be seen over the pupil. This is called a persistent pupillary membrane.

If something were to happen to the bitch during her pregnancy that slowed down the rate of fetal development, then some events which take place in the embryos might also be slowed down causing PPM strands to remain over the eyes. Such conditions that could occur would be poor nutrition, disease, parasitic infection, etc. We know that there are some genes that control or affect the rate of development. These genes could have something to do with PPM. Thus, PPM might be genetic or environmental or even a combination of both. Perhaps a bloodline has a tendency to PPM, but will not produce puppies with them unless the bitch (or embryos) are stressed at a certain time in embryonic development.

About 20% of the human population is born with some PPM, with about one in a thousand having some visual impairment as a result. This may mean that one out of every five Basenji owners has PPM (or had PPM, for the strands sometimes disappear after birth). Likewise, in Basenjis, visual impairment due to PPM is very rare but not unheard of. This is not a life-threatening problem in our breed; however, responsible breeders should be aware of the frequency of the problem in their own dogs and should watch that it does not develop into a serious problem in their line.

A less common eye-problem in dogs and occasionally in Basenjis is detached retina or progressive retinal atrophy ("PRA"). This is considerably more serious than PPM as the dog will go blind. The eye is normal until the dog is about four years of age. The earliest signs of the problem can sometimes be detected by an eye specialist at this age. Opthamologists suggest annual eye exams from the time the dog is four years old to keep track of this problem. Needless to say, when a problem does not show up until at least four years old, it is hard to deal with when breeding. Any four-year old dog may have had several litters and, should one of the parents develop detached retinas, the remaining pups would need to be religiously watched and the use of them in breeding should be carefully considered.

If you do have the misfortune of having one of the rare individuals who becomes blind later in life, your pet should still be able to get along with a little consideration on your part. You should, however, be sure that the breeder is informed so that he will be aware that the problem has developed in one of his dogs. This will be useful information for him in making future breeding decisions.

Fanconi Syndrome

Renal Tubular Dysfunction (Fanconi syndrome) was first reported in the Basenji in 1976, and has since drawn increasing interest from a number of veterinary researchers. This disease has been recognized as a clinical entity in human medicine since 1931. The Basenji has been studied more exhaustively than other breeds because of its unusually high incidence of the disease and the willingness of breeders to cooperate with researchers. Fanconi syndrome is believed to be transmitted as a result of a "late-acting recessive lethal gene."

It is the job of the kidney to filter body fluids, reclaiming amino acids, salts and various important chemicals and letting the wastes go into the urine. A dog with Fanconi syndrome has kidneys that do not function properly, so that nutrients that should be reclaimed are voided in the urine. The body thus loses vital substances needed for normal functions. There is also a loss of body fluids leading to dehydration. Without the reclaimed nutrients, there is a loss of body weight and muscle strength. The kidney eventually stops functioning well enough to maintain the animal and death quickly follows. There is no known cure.

Symptoms of Fanconi syndrome include polydipsia (frequent drinking), polyuria (frequent urination), dehydration, weight loss, poor hair coat, lack of energy, and osteomalacia (bone pain). These signs may begin to show up in a dog as young as three years but are more common between the ages of five and eight. If your veterinarian is not familiar with Fanconi syndrome, your dog may be misdiagnosed as having diabetes or another kidney problem. While not every dog with the above symptoms has Fanconi syndrome, you should be sure that your veterinarian is aware of the syndrome existing in Basenjis if you present him with a dog exhibiting these symptoms.

When some or all of the above symptoms are noted, your veterinarian should perform urine tests to evaluate kidney function. The presence of sugar (glucose) in the urine and a larger than normal percentage of water (hyposthenuria) will lead to further clinical laboratory tests. A blood glucose test is then performed for comparison with the amount of glucose found in the urine. If the blood glucose is found to be within normal levels, Fanconi syndrome becomes a strong suspect as the cause for the illness. More sophisticated urine testing is then necessary to see if normal reabsorption is failing to occur in the proximal renal tubule of the kidney.

While there is no cure for Fanconi syndrome, Dr. Steve Gonto has developed a Management Protocol. Dr. Gonto has helped many Basenjis affected with Fanconi syndrome lead normal lives by careful use of blood tests and dietary supplements. He has been collecting data on a large number of affected dogs and planned to submit an article in 1994 for publication in a veterinary journal. If your veterinarian is not familiar with this protocol, contact the Basenji Club of America (the address can be obtained from the American Kennel Club) and ask about details and how you can contact Dr. Gonto. Act quickly if you notice any symptoms in your Basenji because the sooner the syndrome is caught and the supplementation starts, the better chance your dog has.

At this time, even breeding to untested healthy, older dogs will not guarantee freedom from Fanconi syndrome because those old dogs could be carriers of the syndrome. It will be fortunate for the breed when we can recognize carriers and remove them from the breeding pool.

Research is currently being done at two universities to find DNA markers for Fanconi carriers. All ethical Basenji breeders are looking forward to the day when this devastating syndrome can be brought under control. Research is also being carried out to find the DNA markers for Progressive Retinal Atrophy (PRA). Within five to 10 years, we should see some significant improvement in these areas.

Thyroid

The thyroid of the Basenji functions a bit differently than other breeds. Generally, the Basenji has a more active thyroid than other breeds and they use up the hormones produced by the thyroid much more rapidly than other breeds. This is not an illness or a disease, rather just a fact about the Basenji breed that should be borne in mind. Through the years, I have seen a few Basenjis who have underactive thyroids. They are lethargic and apt to be overweight. They can become very (uncomfortably) overweight as the years go by. It is really a shame because the problem can be easily controlled by regular thyroid pills which bring their hormone level up to the Basenji normal.

Conversely, one also sometimes sees thin, hyperactive Basenjis who have problems with their skin and coat. These problems can also be controlled. If your Basenji is showing symptoms which could be related to thyroid output, be sure your veterinarian is aware of the differences between Basenjis and other breeds in relation to thyroid function. Two reported studies may be useful: one by Nunez and associates, *American Journal of Physiology*, 218: 1337–1341, 1970, and another by Nunez and colleagues, *American Journal of Anatomy*, 133:463–483, 1972.

SECTION IX
Bibliography & Index

- *Bibliography*
- *Index*

Bibliography

Books About Basenjis

Basenji Champions 1937–1977, Stringer, Jayne Wilson and Ford, Elspet M., Eds., England, 1978.

Basenji Champions 1945–1981, Staff of Jan Lindzy Freund, Calif., Camino E.E. & B. Co., 1982.

Basenji Champions 1982–1986, Compiled by Jan Bruner, Calif., Camino E.E. & B. Co., 1988.

Basenji Club of America Year Book 1965, Shirley Chambers, Ed., Basenji Club of America, USA, private, 1966.

Bickering, Jr., B. and Brach, R.J., *The Barkless Dog*, A Handbook for the Basenji Owner, New York, Exposition Press, 1962.

Cardew, Mirrie St. Erme, *A Basenji For Me*, England, Midland Counties Pub., 1st ed. 1979, 2nd ed. 1986.

Cole, Robert W., *The Basenji Illustrated*, An Illustrated Explanation Based on the Basenji Standard, Canada, private, 1978.

Cole, Robert W., *The Basenji Stacked and Moving*, Illustrated Explanation of the Breed Standard, Canada, Cole Book Imprint, 1987.

Evergreen Basenji Club, *Basenji Owners Manual*, Washington, private, 1st ed. and 2nd revised ed. ·

Green, Evelyn M., *Your Basenji*, Virginia, Denlinger's Publishers, Ltd., 1976.

Johnson, Forrest Bryant, *Basenji—Dog from the Past*, USA, private, 1st ed. 1971 and 2nd revised ed. 1978.

Kenworthy, Mary Lou, *So You Want To Course Your Basenji*, Georgia, private, 1989.

Scott, John Paul and Fuller, John L., *Genetics and the Social Behavior of the Dog*, Chicago, Univ. of Chicago Press, 1965—Basenjis are part of a study on behavior.

Shafer, Jack and Mankey, Bob, *How to Raise and Train a Basenji*, New Jersey, T.F.N. Publications, Inc., 1966.

Steele, Marie E. and Field, Barbara A., *At Home with Basenjis*, California, private, 1967. Revised and reissued by the Basenji Club of Southeastern Wisconsin, 1988.

Thackrah, Ron, *Why A Basenji*, England.

The Years of the American Basenji, Russell, Melody and Coe, Susan, Eds., USA, private, 1980 with yearly supplements.

Tudor-Williams, Veronica, *Basenjis, The Barkless Dogs*, England, 1st ed. James Heap, 1946, London; revised 2nd ed. Watmoughs, Ltd., 1954; reprinted 1966; and England, revised 3rd ed. David Charles, Ltd., 1976.

Tudor-Williams, Veronica, *Fula, Basenji From the Jungle*, England, Veronica Tudor-Williams, 1988.

Basenjis in Fiction

Chad, England, Reindeer Books—Child's book.

Coe, Jon and Susan, *Curly Tales and Other Basenji Nonsense*, Washington, private, 1975—Basenji stories.

Nason, K.D., *The Dog with a Bad Name*, London, Country Life, Ltd., 1936—Set in Africa about a Sealyham with a Basenji friend.

Rybot, Doris, *A Donkey and a Dandelion*, London, Hutchinson, 1966—The Dandelion is the Basenji, Fuyambio of the Congo.

Street, James, *Goodbye, My Lady*, Chicago, People's Book Club, 1941 (originally appeared in "Saturday Evening Post") and Phila., Lippincott, 1954—Classic child and dog story.

Street, James, *Weep No More My Lady*, "Saturday Evening Post," Dec. 6, 1941.

Suyin, Han, *A Many Splendored Thing*, Boston, Little, Brown, 1952—James and Flora Manton patterned after Mr. and Mrs. Anderson (Glenairley Basenjis) with Basenji based on Lotus of the Congo.

Vavra, Robert, *Anna and Dula*, New York, Harcourt, Brace and World, 1966, and London, Collins, 1966.

Vavra, Robert, *Canis Basenji*, USA, Basenji Club of America, 1958.

Wylie, Jill, *Call-of-the-Marsh*, Bulawayo, Books of Rhodesia, 1979—Story of life with a clever Basenji.

Books which mention Basenjis as seen in Africa

Allan, Doug, *Facing Danger in the Last Wilderness*. New York, Rolton House, Inc., 1962.

Bellotti, Felice, *Fabulous Congo*. translated from Italian by Mervyn Savill, London, Andrew Dakers, Ltd., 1954.

Denis, Michaela, *Leopard in My Lap*, New York, Julian Messner, Inc., 1955.

Epstein, Hellmut, *The Origin of the Domestic Animals of Africa*. New York, Africana Pub. Corp., 1971.

Fiennes, Richard and Alice, *The Natural History of the Dog*, London, Weidenfield & Nicolson, 1968, and USA, Natural History Press, 1970.

Hallet, Jean-Pierre, *Congo Kitabu*. New York, Random House, 4th printing 1966.

Hubbard, Clifford L.B., *"Observer's" Book of Dogs*. London & New York, F. Warne & Co., 1945 and 2nd ed. 1946.

Kenney, Lona B., *Mboka, The Way of Life in a Congo Village*. New York, Crown Publishers, 1972.

Leighton, Robert, *The New Book of the Dog*. London, Paris, Toronto, New York and Melbourne, Cassell & Co., 1907.

Myers, Rev. J.B., *The Congo for Christ*. Fleming H. Reveill Co., 2nd ed., approximately 1895.

Nolen, Barbara, Ed., *Africa is People. New York, E.P. Dutton & Co., 1967.*

Sanderson, Ivan T. with Loth, David, Ivan Sanderson's Book of Great Jungles. New York, Simon & Schuster, 1965.

Schebesta, Paul, *Among Congo Pygmies*. London, Hutchinson Co., 1933 and New York, AMS Press, 1977—*Bambuti, die Zwenge vom Kongo*, translated by G. Griffin.

Schebesta, Paul, *My Pygmy and Negro Hosts*. London, Hutchinson Co., 1936, and New York, AMS Press, 1978—*Vollblutneger und Halbzwerge*, translated by G. Griffin.

Schbesta, Paul, *Revisiting My Pygmy Hosts*. London, Hutchinson Co., 1936.

Simpson, Hilton, *Land and Peoples of the Kasai*, approximately 1907.

Schweinfurth, Dr., *Im Herzen von Afrika*, 1918. Leipzig.

Tabouis, G.R., *Private Life of Tutankhamen*. New York, R.M. McBride & Co., 1929—translated by M.R. Dobie.

Vlahos, Olivia, *African Beginnings*. New York, The Viking Press, 1967.

Canine Periodicals

Allen, Michael, Ed., *American Cocker Magazine*, numerous articles from several issues.

Ardnt, T.K., "Breeders Forum." *Akita World*, December 1985.

Asseltyne Claire, "Form Follows Function." *The Great Dane Reporter*, May–June, July–Aug., Sept.–Oct. 1980.

Bierman, Ann, "Feeding Your Puppy." *The Golden Retriever Review*, March 1987.

Brown, Russell V., "Nutrition and Feeding of the Basenji." *The Basenji*, Feb. 1987.

Burnham, Patricia Gail, "Breeding, Litter Size and Gender." *American Cocker Review*, 1981.

Donnely, Mary, "Caesarian Section . . . The Home Care." *Min Pin Monthly*, March 1987.

Furumoto, Howard H., "Frozen and Extended Semen." *The ILIO*, Hawaii's Dog News, Oct. & Nov. 1986.

Grossman, Alvin, "The Basis of Heredity." *American Kennel Club Gazette*, April 1980.

Hane, Curtis B., "Training Your Dog, A Consumers Guide." *The Great Dane Reporter*, March–April 1987.

Mohrman, R.K., "Supplementation—May Be Hazardous To Your Pet's Health." *The Great Dane Reporter*, March–April 1980.

Schaeffer, Ruth C., "The View From Here, A Breeder's Report On Collecting Frozen Sperm." *American Kennel Club Gazette*, November 1982.

Wittels, Bruce R., "Nutrition of Newly Born and Growing Individuals." *The Great Dane Reporter*, Jan./Feb. 1985.

Canine Books

Benjamin, Carol L., *Mother Knows Best, The Natural Way to Train Your Dog*. New York: Howell Book House, 253 pgs., 1987.

Burnham, Patricia G., *Play Training Your Dog*. New York: St. Martin's Press, 1980.

Burns, Marsh A. & Fraser, Margaret N., *The Genetics of the Dog*. Farnham Royal Eng.: Commonwealth Agricultural Bureau, 1952.

Collins, Donald R., D.V.M., *The Collins Guide to Dog Nutrition*. New York: Howell Book House, Inc., 1973.

Evans, Job M., *The Evans Guide For Counseling Dog Owners*. New York: Howell Book House, Inc., 1985.

Fox, Michael W., *Understanding Your Dog*. New York: Coward, McCann & Geoghegan, 1972.

Gaines Dog Research Center, *Training The Hunting Dog*. General Foods Corporation, 15 pgs, 1973.

Holst, Phyllis A., *Canine Reproduction—A Breeder's Guide*. Loveland, Colorado: Alpine Publications, 1985.

Hutt, Fredrick B., *Genetics For Dog Breeders*. San Francisco: W.H. Freeman & Co., 245 pgs, 1979.

Little, C.C., *The Inheritance of Coat Color In Dogs*. New York: Howell Book House, Inc., 194 pgs, 1973.

McAuliffe, Sharon & McAuliffe, Kathleen, *Life for Sale*. New York: Coward, McCann & Geoghegan, 243 pgs, 1981.

Sabella, Frank & Kalstone, Shirlee, *The Art of Handling Show Dogs*. Hollywood: B & E Publications, 140 pgs, 1980.

Smith, Anthony, *The Human Pedigree*. Philadelphia: J.B. Lippincott Company, 308 pgs, 1975.

Whitney, Leon F., D.V.M., *How to Breed Dogs*. New York: Orange Judd Company, 1947.

Winge, Dr. Ojvind, *Inheritance in Dogs*. Comstock Publishing Company, Ithaca, New York: 1950.

Index

00190   3239